Nationalism
and the Jewish Ethic

Nationalism
and the Jewish Ethic

BASIC WRITINGS OF

Ahad Ha'am

EDITED AND INTRODUCED BY HANS KOHN

SCHOCKEN BOOKS

New York

ACKNOWLEDGMENTS

Grateful acknowledgment is made to the following publishers for permission to reprint selections from the works listed:

Routledge & Kegan Paul Ltd: *Ten Essays on Zionism and Judaism* by Achad Ha-am, translated by Leon Simon.

Jewish Publication Society of America: *Selected Essays by Ahad Ha-'am*, translated by Leon Simon. Copyright 1912 by the publisher.

East and West Library: Ahad Ha-am, *Essays, Letters, Memoirs*, translated and edited by Leon Simon.

Library of Congress Catalog Card No. 62-17177

CONTENTS

Introduction by Hans Kohn

I

II

INTRODUCTION

The intellectual ferment which prevailed among the Jews of Eastern Europe towards the close of the nineteenth century, and which led to the growth of modern Jewish nationalism and, eventually, of the Zionist movement, produced many notable figures. Among these, Asher Ginzberg (1856-1927), who wrote under the pen name of Ahad Ha'am, "one of the people," occupies a place of special prominence. Of all his many contemporaries who joined the great debate over the meaning and future course of Jewish history, none was as widely and eagerly read in his lifetime, nor has any continued to enjoy as lasting and permanent an influence. Always highly individualistic in his thinking, Ahad Ha'am was nevertheless a seeker after a meaningful compromise between past and present, after a middle way between extremes. In him two traditions met and mingled: the Hasidic heritage of his father's home, and the critical rationalism of the Haskalah, or Jewish Enlightenment.

Ahad Ha'am's father belonged to the Hasidim of Sadagura, one of the many Hasidic sects which sprang up prolifically in the period following the founding of that movement in the middle of the eighteenth century. By the middle of the nineteenth century, however, Hasidism—whose origins lay in a pietistic reaction to excessive rabbinic legalism, and in a fresh affirmation of spontaneous religious emotion and communal solidarity —had lost much of its initial impetus; a process of

7

coagulation had set in, and in many instances an attitude of rigid fundamentalism. Early in his life Ahad Ha'am rebelled against these obscurantist tendencies. But it was from the Hasidim that he inherited the consuming intensity of his Jewish feeling. He always insisted on speaking of "Hibath Zion," the Love of Zion, instead of "Zionism," and his life was entirely dedicated to the nationalist ideal, to the practical exclusion of all other interests. Although a professed agnostic from his youth on, he retained to the very end his deep respect for the religious past, and was severely critical of those "emancipated" Jews who scoffed at Orthodoxy, and failed to appreciate the rich complexity of Jewish tradition.

Through the Haskalah Ahad Ha'am entered into the heritage of the modern West. His intellectual honesty and self-discipline, his sober and responsible realism, his meticulous attention to fact and form alike, and his contempt for rhetoric and demagogy associate him more closely with men like John Stuart Mill or Thomas Masaryk than with such a visionary nationalist as Mazzini. He also shared with Masaryk a religious concern with ethics rooted in the history of a people, quite apart from any orthodox faith. In the first sixty-five years of his life Masaryk was thoroughly unpopular among his fellow Czechs because of his emphasis on the moral and spiritual aspects of the Czech national revival, and the political moderation imposed by his sense of the possible. Similarly, despite his popularity as an essayist, Ahad Ha'am never commanded any large personal following. Yet, in his feelings he was profoundly in tune with the Jewish masses and their millenary nationalist

hopes; while he was able to view them critically and
with a dispassionate objectivity guided by universal
values, his emotions often shaped his ultimate outlook.

II

The conditions of his upbringing made Ahad Ha'am
a fervent and dedicated Jewish nationalist. He was
born in 1856 in the small town of Skvire, in the prov-
ince of Kiev, "one of the most benighted spots in the
Hasidic districts of Russia," as he later wrote in his
memoirs. His early education was devoted entirely to
traditional Jewish studies, without the slightest intru-
sion of any Russian or otherwise alien element. As a
student he was not even allowed to look at the letters
of the Russian alphabet, still less to learn Russian.
"The reason was," he wrote in his memoirs, "that my
mother's father had with his own ears heard one of
the great Tsaddikim [holy men] say that the sight of
a foreign letter made the eyes unclean." Only at the
age of twenty did he begin, almost surreptitiously, to
teach himself Russian and German in earnest. This
learning opened to him a new world with which he
longed for contact, living then, as he wrote, "in a
lonely village surrounded by towns in which there
were no books and no teachers." Not until he was
thirty could Ahad Ha'am leave the village—"the
prison in which I had spent eighteen of the best years
of my life, and which had eaten me up alive"—to
settle with his family in Odessa, then the center of
Jewish cultural life in Russia.

The life of the Jewish masses in the smaller towns
and villages in Ahad Ha'am's youth hardly permitted

any knowledge of Russian life or any identification with Russia. A feeling of indelible hostility prevailed between Israel and all other peoples, their governments and officials, a distrust and at the same time a contempt for the alien state within the borders of which they lived, and for their "fellow-citizens" who were "goyim"—gentiles—to them. Remembering as an old man the days of his youth, Ahad Ha'am told the story of how a visiting government official suggested to his father that the young lad be sent to a secular Russian high school. "My father did not tell us what his answer had been: but he ended his story thus, 'Now go and explain a thing like this to a goy!' From the expression on the faces of those at the table it was evident that they needed no explanation: with them it was simple and obvious, and it was only the goy whose brain could not take it in."[1]

At the time Ahad Ha'am moved to Odessa the hopes for liberal reform held by the small Russian progressive movement, and the similar, even smaller group of secularly educated Jews, had broken down. In 1881 Alexander II fell victim to the revolutionary movement; the brief era of hesitant reforms which he had started came to an end. His successor, Alexander III, pursued a policy of unmitigated reaction, characterized by the suppression not only of revolutionary

[1] See Ahad Ha'am, *Essays, Letters, Memoirs*, ed. by Leon Simon (Oxford, East and West Library, 1946), p. 338. This volume contains most valuable excerpts from Ahad Ha'am's memoirs and letters, which are an important contribution both to a knowledge of Russian Jewish life in the second half of the nineteenth century and to an understanding of Ahad Ha'am's unique personality. Equally valuable is the long introduction by Leon Simon, who has the great merit of having made much of Ahad Ha'am's work accessible to English readers. Cf. his *Ten Essays on Zionism and Judaism* (London, Routledge, 1922) and *Selected Essays* (Philadelphia, Jewish Publication Society, 1912).

elements but of all non-Russian and non-Orthodox
minorities. This new era was inaugurated with a great
wave of pogroms which swept through many cities
and towns of southern and southwestern Russia from
April to June, 1881. The widespread violence and
looting impressed upon many Russian Jews the de-
sirability of emigration. Masses of them left for the
United States and Western Europe, but a small number, the "Lovers of Zion" as they called themselves
(Hoveve Zion), turned hopefully to the Holy Land.
Odessa became the center of a movement for the re-
settlement of Jews in Palestine and the first pioneers
to settle there were supported by the Odessa Committee for Palestine Colonization. The president of the
Committee was Dr. Leo Pinsker (1831-1891), who in
1882 had published a pamphlet called *Autoemanzipa-
tion,* which advocated the establishment of a Jewish
state as the only remedy for anti-semitism.

Ahad Ha'am participated actively in this early
Zionist movement. In 1889, at the urging of the editor
of the Hebrew weekly *Hamelitz,* he wrote his first
article, *Lo Zeh Haderekh* ("The Wrong Way"), in
which he criticized the new colonization program for
its illusions and for paying insufficient attention to the
cultivation of an elite body of pioneers. Thus, he
"accidentally" became a Hebrew writer, "a thing he
had never thought of till then." Though he published
much in later years, he never became a professional
author. Unlike other Hebrew writers, who also wrote
in Yiddish or in Russian, Ahad Ha'am confined himself to Hebrew, and dealt exclusively with the concerns
and survival of the Jewish people. For him, as for
Mazzini, nationality was "sacred," and he considered

the Hebrew language alone fit to express the dignity and majesty of Jewish national life. But he never submitted to the pressure of Jewish public opinion, "that despotic queen to whom I have never owed allegiance." To maintain his independence of mind and thought, he remained a merchant.

Twice in the following years, in 1891 and again in 1893, he visited Palestine and published his impressions in a series of articles which he called "The Truth From Palestine." Like his first article these two reports aroused violent opposition because they shattered many of the illusions with which the Lovers of Zion viewed the colonization work and its accomplishments. In 1894 he collected his published essays in a volume entitled *Al Parashat D'rakhim* ("At The Crossroads"). Three more volumes were to follow in later years.[2]

In 1896 Ahad Ha'am became the founding editor of the Hebrew monthly *Hashiloah*. With it a new epoch began in modern Hebrew literature, which was then struggling to free itself from the provinciality of thought and cumbersomeness of expression which were its inheritance from former ages. Ahad Ha'am wished to create a Hebrew periodical equal to the best in Europe. The task laid a heavy burden on him, and his letters of the period are full of bitter complaints about the state of Hebrew letters and the mind of

[2] A new edition of the four volumes was published with an important new preface after World War I (Berlin, Jüdischer Verlag, 1921). In his last years Ahad Ha'am edited and published his letters in six volumes (*Iggeroth Ahad Ha'am*, Jerusalem, Jabneh, 1923-25). In 1931 some additional letters and his memoirs were published by the Bet Ahad Ha'am in Tel Aviv, and a one-volume edition of his collected works was published there by Dvir in 1946.

Hebrew writers at that time. Through the high standards which he exacted, however, and through his dedication to his work, he became the master of a new generation of younger writers who soon transformed Hebrew literature and rendered the Hebrew language an instrument capable of registering the demands and nuances of modern life.

III

The publication of *Hashiloah* was made possible financially by a rich Jewish tea merchant of Moscow, Kalonymos Wisstozky. The name of the monthly, however, was chosen independently by Ahad Ha'am, who wished to recall "the waters of Shiloah that go softly" (Isaiah, VIII, 6), whose slow sureness the prophet contrasted with Israel's blind trust in power and speed. Not only in this title, but in every word he wrote, Ahad Ha'am accepted as his own the prophetic tradition which opposed war and violence. Most of his writings can be regarded as an ethical commentary on the problems of Jewish history, past and contemporary. His role was generally that of a dissenter in the name of conscience and morality, but he also insisted on a cool and impartial judgment of realities, even if these were to conflict with deeply cherished dreams and wishes. Slow evolution and not rapid revolution, quality not quantity, a careful realism rather than an illusory messianism, were what he stressed for his own work and for the solution of the Jewish problem.

As editor of *Hashiloah* Ahad Ha'am did not wish the monthly to be a party organ but rather an open

forum which, far removed from any partisan or pre-
determined solution, would seek a deeper understanding of, and an unprejudiced approach to, Jewish
problems. He insisted upon a strict respect for meticulous standards of literary form and genuine expression, which were then rather the exception among
Hebrew writers.

Under his editorship *Hashiloah* rose to a position of
prominence in the Jewish intellectual community, but
its circulation failed to live up to advance expectations,
and Ahad Ha'am steadfastly refused to popularize the
magazine's content in the hope of gaining a wider
public. Faced with a mounting financial deficit and
under constant pressure from his fellow directors, Ahad
Ha'am reluctantly resigned the editorial chair at the
end of 1902 and joined the business firm of Wissotzky,
at first in Odessa and after 1907 as its branch manager
in London.[3]

In the years of Ahad Ha'am's association with
Hashiloah momentous events occurred in the history
of Zionism. Theodor Herzl, an "assimilated" Viennese
journalist, wrote his famous pamphlet *The Jewish State*.
Due largely to his indefatigable efforts, his impressive
personality and his qualities of leadership, the first
World Zionist Congress met in Basle in 1897. Ahad
Ha'am attended the Congress and was perhaps the
only one among the Lovers of Zion to voice angry dis-
appointment with a movement which he felt to be
"completely unrealistic and fundamentally un-Jewish in
spirit." His sharp campaign against Herzl's "political"

---

[3] *Hashiloah* continued, under the editorship of Dr. Joseph Klausner,
later a professor of modern Hebrew literature at the University of
Jerusalem, until 1927.

Zionism made him most unpopular at that time, even among his close friends in Russian Jewry. "My relations with the Zionists get worse and worse," he wrote on July 3, 1898 from Odessa to his friend Dr. S. Bernfeld. "I know that in present conditions whatever I say is a waste of breath; and if I were still a private individual, I should not go on preaching to deaf ears. But as the editor of a paper I am under obligation to express my views; and as I cannot be silent and do not wish to lie I am compelled to say what I believe to be true. The result is that I get into trouble on all sides."

In deed as well as in word Ahad Ha'am always strove to maintain the full integrity of his position. When he was invited in 1906, at the age of fifty, to head an institution of higher Jewish learning in the United States which was then about to be opened, he declined the proposition, although it promised to fulfill "the highest ideal of my early years." The letter which he wrote on April 30, 1906, from Odessa to New York reveals not only his modesty but also his fierce desire for independence. "You know that the thing I value above all else is my independence of mind and thought. I have suffered a great deal in my time, and have had many reverses; but no matter what my position, I have always succeeded in maintaining my independence, and I have never said or done the smallest thing against my conviction. And now you come to me with a suggestion which, I am afraid, is not consistent with my independence. The projected institution will of course be governed by a Board, and it will also be subject, like all communal institutions, to what is called public opinion—that despotic queen to whom I have never owed allegiance. Can I become her liege at my time of life? And if I do not, can I hold the position?"

IV

Ahad Ha'am's disagreement with political Zionism was not based upon the fact of his not being a Jewish nationalist. On the contrary, he was in that respect more extreme than most Western Jews. He could not understand how it was possible for people of Jewish descent or faith to become, by their cultural roots, their free decision, and their political loyalty, Americans or Italians. It was Ahad Ha'am's belief that the national allegiance of a man of Jewish ancestry was inescapably determined by his historical inheritance; as such he could live fully and freely only as a member of a Jewish nation, for all assimilation was a form of "inner slavery and spiritual degradation" which could not lead to "a life of dignity and freedom." In this respect he never departed from the outlook of the traditional environment in which he was raised. Judaism to him was a sociological continuum, and it was this which guaranteed the survival of the "national spirit." In many ways Ahad Ha'am was under the influence of English empirical and positivist thinkers such as Locke, Hume and Mill; the German metaphysicians like Hegel "did not appeal to him." Nevertheless his concept of the national spirit was Hegelian, a metaphysical abstraction expressing itself in the concrete life of the nation which was regarded as a supra-individual organism. Not God but the organic factor was the beginning and foundation, the content and goal of Jewish life. "In my view our religion is national," Ahad Ha'am wrote to Dr. Judah L. Magnes, an American Rabbi and Zionist, in 1910, "—that is to say, it is a product of our national spirit—but the reverse is not true." Being at one and the same time an agnostic humanist and a fervent believer in the chosenness of the Jewish people and its innate moral superiority, Ahad Ha-Am could base his faith only upon an enlightened and informed ethnocentrism.[4]

Ahad Ha'am demanded the survival of the Jewish people with every fiber of his being, but as an ethical thinker and a realist, he considered survival desirable and even practicable only if the Jews lived in the prophetic tradition and did not surrender their own unique identity. The majority of Zionists were in agreement with Ahad Ha'am's position that the Jewish religion and Judaism were not the gift of Divine revelation but the creation of the *Volksgeist,* the national spirit; like the pan-Germans and the pan-Slavs, under whose influence many of their attitudes developed, they regarded the attachment to a homeland and rootedness in a specific soil as the almost mystical basis for spiritual creativity. But Ahad Ha'am at the same time rejected any devaluation of the prophetic message, which seemed to him the distinctive trait in the Jewish spiritual heritage: peoplehood was not an end in itself.

"The main point, upon which everything depends, is not how much we do but how we do it," he wrote in "The Truth From Palestine," the report on his first

---

[4] See the discussion of this point in Arthur Hertzberg, *The Zionist Idea* (Garden City, N.Y., Doubleday, 1959), pp. 51-72.

visit in 1891 to the land of his hopes. The Jews had survived, while all other ancient nations perished, because the prophets had taught them not to seek glory in the attainment of material power and political dominion. Merely to create a small state based upon publicly sponsored immigration and diplomatic favors would add no glorious chapter to Jewish history, but would undermine the historical basis of Jewish existence. In his criticism of the colonization movement Ahad Ha'am spoke not only as an idealist, but as a practical statesman who understood what others wishfully forgot, the geographic position and the population problem of Palestine.

Therein he disagreed with the political Zionists. Their program seemed to him based upon an overestimation of power and quantity, of numbers and speed, so characteristic of the era of nationalistic conflict in which he lived. By seeking to promote emigration to Palestine as the only feasible way of escaping anti-semitism and winning a measure of political and economic betterment, Ahad Ha'am felt that the political Zionists were mistakenly appealing to the motives of individual or collective self-interest. Ahad Ha'am was not concerned with Palestine as a means of helping redistribute the Jewish population of the world, but rather as a means of rescuing Judaism and its eternal message. "Ahad Ha'am was occasionally willing to imagine that Zionism would perhaps create, and should even strive to create, a Jewish settlement in Palestine of considerable size, but . . . this was, for him, not a matter of essence." [1] Neither did he con-

---

[5] See Arthur Hertzberg, *op. cit.*, p. 62.

ceive the attainment of Jewish sovereignty to be the be-all-and-end-all of the Zionist ideal. Like all self-demanding men he was modest as regards the goal and exacting about the means. Whatever the fate of Ahad Ha'am's political thought, he will remain of importance by virtue of his "insistence on the overriding character of moral action. In Judaism the moral requirement is supreme. The great sin today is the 'politicization' of our Judaism; the great need, the 'Judaization' of our politics." [6]

Late nineteenth-century Jewish nationalism contained many factions and subdivisions, but essentially there were two main schools of thought. The political Zionists, on the one hand, regarded anti-semitism as something permanent and ubiquitous, too powerful to allow of any Jewish future in the Diaspora. These followers of Leo Pinsker and Theodor Herzl demanded a "normalization" of Jewish life in a sovereign nation-state as the only possible solution for the Jewish problem. On the other hand, two Eastern European Jews, Nathan Birnbaum (1864-1937) and Simon Dubnow (1860-1941) believed that two thousand years of existence could not be effaced and that the "abnormal" life of Diaspora Jewry might represent a higher form of historical development than territorial nationalism. These so-called "Diaspora nationalists" looked forward

[6] See the lecture by Leon Roth, F.B.A., who was Ahad Ha'am Professor of Philosophy at the Hebrew University of Jerusalem and its Rector from 1940 to 1943, "Back to, forward from, Ahad Ha-Am?" in *Addresses given at the Thirteenth Conference of Anglo-Jewish Preachers,* London, May 1960, pp. 35-47.

to the evolution of autonomous, Yiddish-speaking communities throughout those areas of Eastern Europe heavily populated by Jews, but rejected the idea of a restoration within the boundaries of a national homeland. Ahad Ha'am took his position between these two camps. He was convinced of the permanency of the Diaspora, but he believed in the need of a center in Palestine which would rekindle the creative spirit of Judaism. Such a center could not solve the economic or political afflictions of the great majority of Jews, for the small country of Palestine could never gather, as the prayer book demands, all the scattered exiles from the four corners of the earth. Even orthodox tradition itself held that this could happen only in the days of the Messiah when all human and social problems would come to be resolved in a regenerated mankind. Ahad Ha'am firmly believed that to confound messianic hopes and political potentialities could lead only to moral and physical disaster.

The creation of such a center in Palestine, Ahad Ha'am felt, would be a necessity for Judaism even if there were no anti-semitism. In the villages and cities of Palestine, Jews would live in the spirit of the Jewish prophetic tradition, and this would exercise a revitalizing effect upon the Diaspora. For that reason Ahad Ha'am referred to the Land of Israel as a spiritual center, "a refuge not for all Jews who need peace and bread," as he wrote in 1907, "but for the spirit of the people, for the distinctive cultural form, the result of a historical development of thousands of years which is still strong enough to live and develop naturally in the future if only the fetters of the Diaspora are removed."

V

Like all nationalists who trust in the continuity of national identity throughout the ages, Ahad Ha'am was hopefully convinced that the center in Palestine would revive the ancient spirit of his people. In this faith he resembled Fichte, Mazzini and Dostoevsky as well as many of his fellow-Zionists. It was, however, because he saw continuity and value in the whole of the Jewish past, and not just in the more remote part of it, that he sharply disagreed with certain militant younger Zionists like Micah Joseph Berdichevsky or Joseph Hayyim Brenner, who looked forward to a complete break with the patterns of Diaspora life and to the emergence in Palestine of a radically new type of Jew. Ahad Ha'am did not, as they did, look down upon the two-thousand years of Jewish exile as a sorry exhibition of weakness and self-abasement, nor did he share their intense preoccupation with the Diaspora Jew's estrangement from nature and the natural life, which to them was the central tragedy of Jewish national existence. For Ahad Ha'am, Berdichevsky's impassioned cry—"We are the last Jews—or we are the first of a new nation" — could only be interpreted as an attempted flight from the realities of Jewish history. His disapproval of such thinking, as well as of political Zionism, was expressed in the fear that Jews would be driven to imitate alien habits to prove that they were no different from any other people. "It may suffice to mention the saddening incident which happened recently in Vienna," he wrote in 1897, "when Zionist students went out to spread the Zionist gospel, in the German fashion, with fists and sticks. And the

Zionist organ [Herzl's weekly *Die Welt,* then published
in Vienna] viewed this action sympathetically and for
all its caution could not hide its pleasure about the
valor of the Zionist fist."

Ahad Ha'am was convinced that "long ago, in the
days of the Prophets, we Jews learned to despise
physical force and to respect only spiritual power."
Therefore he turned against the "young men" who
wished to "cure" the Jews by emancipating their
physical life from its subservience to the limiting force
of the spirit. It seemed incredible to him that the Jews,
who had been taught by prophets and sages to base
their life and survival on the conviction that they had
to bear the yoke of the most exacting ethical duties,
could suddenly turn their backs on the mission with
which they had been entrusted. In his essay "The
Transvaluation of Values," a critique of Berdichevski's
intellectual flirtation with Nietzscheism, Ahad Ha-Am
argued that Nietzsche's idea of self-transcendence was
nothing new to Judaism—the only difference being that
whereas Nietzsche glorified the physical Superman,
the Jew had exalted the moral Supernation. But "actually we are not superior to other nations even in the
sphere of morality. We have been unable to fulfil our
mission in exile, because we could not make our lives a
true expression of our own character, independent of
the opinion or the will of others."

Ahad Ha'am did not belittle the flesh or the body,
but he believed, as he wrote in his essay "Flesh and
Spirit," that in Judaism the spiritual element penetrates
into the very heart of physical existence, "till its
cleansing and purifying influence makes the physical
life itself, in its very detail, a part of the spiritual life.

This union, so far from degrading the spirit, exalts the
flesh, which is irradiated by the sanctity of the spirit;
and through their joint life, each closely linked with
and completing the other, man achieves the true purpose of his being." Similarly, the Prophets insisted
that national life could derive meaning and purpose
only from the spirit, though they accepted the existence
of the state as the embodiment of the spiritual life.
They demanded that the end should not be subordinated to the means, that the body should not ascend
over the spirit. In their succession, the Pharisees,
opposing the Zealots, cared for the state only as an
instrument of the national spirit. For it they abandoned Jerusalem upon the destruction of the Temple
and went to Yabneh,[7] to found there the great rab-
binical academy whose scholars were to prescribe the
future norms of Jewish existence. Thus, despite his
formal skepticism, Ahad Ha'am felt himself to be the
representative of a religious outlook which he wished
to see preserved.

VI

It was from the point of view of national ethics that
Ahad Ha'am tried to prove the difference, and to
him the superiority, of Jewish ethics as compared with
Christian. According to him, the basis of morality in
Christianity was subjective altruism; in Judaism, objective justice. Jewish morality demanded that men
"feel even the slightest deviation from justice instan-

[7] See Hans Kohn, *The Idea of Nationalism,* (New York, Macmillan
Paperbacks, 1961) pp. 36-47.

taneously, and with the certainty of intuition. Personal
and group considerations will not affect them in the
slightest degree; the instinct will judge every action
with absolute impartiality, ignoring all human relations, and making no difference between the self and
the other," between one's own group and an alien
group. Justice demands that man should rise above his
emotional inclinations and utilitarian considerations,
for himself as well as for his group. Judaism furnishes
the principle which can help man to avoid weighting
the scales to suit his or his group's ends; in Hillel's
words: "Do not unto your neighbor what you would
not have him do unto you." Ahad Ha'am believed that
such a principle is needed above all to keep within
bounds that national egoism which he rightly regarded
as a greater danger to mankind than individual egoism.
It is natural, then, that he should have been among the
first of the Lovers of Zion to perceive the lasting importance, for the enduring fulfilment of Zionist hopes,
of the Arab people in Palestine.

Many Zionists regarded the land of their distant
forefathers and of their prayers as an empty land, waiting for the return of the dispersed descendants, as if
history had stood still for two thousand years. As
early as 1891, in his "The Truth From Palestine,"
Ahad Ha'am had pointed out that, except for waste-
lands or stony hills, it was difficult to find untilled soil
in Palestine. "We think that the Arabs are all savages
who live like animals and do not understand what is
happening around them. This is, however, a great
error." He warned then that the settlers must under
no circumstances arouse resentment among the natives
and must meet them in the friendly spirit of respect.

"Yet what do our brethren do in Palestine?" he asked in 1891. "Just the very opposite! Serfs they were in the lands of the Diaspora and suddenly they find themselves in unrestricted freedom and this change has awakened in them an inclination to despotism. They treat the Arabs with hostility and cruelty, deprive them of their rights, offend them without cause and even boast of these deeds; and nobody among us opposes this despicable and dangerous inclination."

His awareness of this attitude made him recognize as early as 1907 the great dangers of the approaching age with its violence, impatience and arrogance, an age in which so many enthusiasts became convinced that they knew the way to national and social "redemption." He wrote at the time a short essay with the characteristic subtitle, "In the Footsteps of the Messiah, Impudence Will Grow." These impudent men of ideology, whether Social-Democrats, Bundists or Zionists, appeared to him happy. "But how hard is life in such an age for one who is not of their group and who cannot go with closed eyes in the footsteps of this or that Messiah; for one who does not hear the voice announcing redemption (geul̕ah), neither for the immediate nor for the more distant future, neither for his generation nor for the time when his grandchildren will be buried; one for whom truth and knowledge and reason remain mighty gods standing above all the camps and judging them impartially, and are not servants of a Messiah to herald him as his standard-bearers and trumpeters."

Militancy of any sort made him uncomfortable. Thus, on at least two occasions, he found himself opposing actions taken by the Palestinian Jewish community with whose ultimate goal he could hardly have been unsympathetic. The first such occasion was the boycott of Arab labor proclaimed in 1913, which was designed to safeguard the then precarious status of the Jewish worker and to protect him against cheap Arab competition. The second, which occurred in 1914, was the boycott of the German Hilfsverein schools by the Hebrew teachers' union, which demanded the elimination of all languages other than Hebrew from the Palestinian school system. "If I were in Palestine, I would fight this loathsome practice with all my might," wrote this foremost lover and master of the Hebrew language on May 19, 1914. "I do not care if they call me reactionary, or even traitor, what was ugly in my eyes thirty years ago remains ugly now."

In the sobriety of his moral realism Ahad Ha'am remained intensely conscious that national life and culture could be securely built only on firm and humane foundations. To the very end he tried to live up to his own standards. A famous letter which he wrote to the Hebrew daily, *Haaretz,* in the early autumn of 1922, expressed his reaction to the report that in retaliation for attacks on Jews, some young Jews had killed an Arab boy. "Jews and blood—are there two greater opposites than these? With these words I concluded one of my first essays many, many years ago; and I was certain at that time that this was a truth which no Jew could doubt. And now, what can we say, and how can we speak if there is truth in this report? God, is this the end? Is this the goal for which our ancestors longed and for which they suffered all those tribulations? Is this the dream of the return to Zion which our people dreamt for thousands of years: that we should come to Zion and pollute its soil with the spilling of innocent blood?

"I concluded, also many years ago, another article, feeling confident that the people will not give up its prophets as a price for the state ... But there is growing today in it a tendency to sacrifice, on the altar of the 'revival,' its prophets, the great moral principles for which our people lived and suffered and for which alone it thought it worthwhile to labor to become a people again in the land of its fathers. For without these— God in Heaven, what are we, and what is the future of our life in this country. . . . ? Is it only to add another little Levantine people in one of the corners of the Orient to compete with the Levantines who are there already in those corrupt moral habits—the thirst for blood, revenge and strife—which make up the content of their lives? If this be the Messiah, let him come and let me not see him." [8]

VII

In 1907 Ahad Ha'am moved to London. Although he was a great admirer of English ways and thought, he did not feel happy there. The London Jewish community with its comparative lifelessness and lack of intellectual stimulation was a far cry from the Odessa he had known, and his entire fourteen years in London

[8] This letter was first published in *Haaretz* and then in the collection of letters arranged by Ahad Ha'am in his last years, *Iggeroth* (see footnote 2) vol. VI, p. 205 f. It was also reprinted on p. 462 of Ahad Ha'am's collected works (1946). Prof. Roth, *loc. cit.,* p. 37, regards the letter as "all important for Ahad Ha'am's memory. Without it his life is a fraud. For his life which was his work meant sincerity of feeling . . . coupled with complete honesty of judgment and expression." Prof. Roth's translation of the letter is reprinted with his permission.

were spent in voluntary semi-isolation. In 1911 he attended the tenth Zionist Congress in Basle, and for the fifth time he visited Palestine. In his report from Palestine, published after the visit, he noted with satisfaction that Zionism seemed on the road toward the spiritual center which he had always envisaged. Many of the drawbacks in the colonization program which he had noted in the course of his previous visits were now rectified and, despite the obstacles which remained to be overcome, he felt that "the instinct of self-preservation" was succeeding in doing what no amount of theorizing could ever have done. "Ask no questions! In our present state of spiritual disorganization we have no idea of the measure of our national strength, nor of what it will be able to achieve when all its elements are united round a single center, and quickened by a single strong and healthy spirit . . . Enough for us to know the things revealed, the things that are to be done by us and our children in a future that is near."

Throughout the First World War, whose militaristic cant and barbarism upset him deeply, Ahad Ha'am lived in London. He was one of the closest advisers of Chaim Weizmann in the negotiations for the Balfour Declaration, and he welcomed and helped to bring about this promise of support for the foundation of a Jewish national home in Palestine. However, in an introduction written in 1920 for a new edition of his *Al Parashat D'rakhim*, he objected to what seemed to him wide-spread misconceptions concerning the true intentions of the British promise, which were not, he felt, simply to turn Palestine into a purely Jewish state. Ahad Ha'am further pointed out that the

Balfour Declaration had already aroused considerable fear among the Arabs, and unless the Jews trod very carefully in all their endeavours, mutual antagonism could only increase. Under these circumstances he favored a bi-national Palestinian state. That both his predictions should have come true is a somber but impressive reminder of his political acumen.

In 1922 Ahad Ha'am moved to Palestine, to that Eretz Israel which he had frequently visited since 1891, more than thirty years before, and on which all his thoughts, emotions and hopes had centered. There he settled in Tel Aviv, the first and at that time only modern Jewish city. In recognition of his services he was presented with a house, not far from the busy street which bore his name. There he lived, together with his wife, until his death.

His last years in Palestine were ironically among the unhappiest of his life. Suffering from ill-health, from enforced inactivity and an inability to work, he derived little enjoyment from his surroundings, even though Jewish Palestine at the time was going through a period of unprecedented prosperity and expansion. "What can I tell you about my wretched self?" he wrote to his old friend Simon Dubnow, little more than a year after his arrival. "I am broken, shattered, utterly and incurably depressed . . . And all this in Palestine which has been my dream for years and years. And in the midst of all these blessings, I long for—London!"

As long as his dwindling energies did not fail him completely, he continued to do what he could. He allowed himself to be elected to the Municipal Council of Tel Aviv and took particular interest in the plans for the new Hebrew University, which was formally dedicated in 1925. Most important of all, however, was the editing of his own letters, which appeared in six volumes published at intervals between 1923 and 1925. Although his personal reticence is only slightly less marked in these than in the essays, they nevertheless throw great light on both Ahad Ha'am himself, and on the Zionist and Jewish milieus in which he moved and thought.

Ahad Ha'am's seventieth birthday, which came in July, 1926, was a jubilee celebrated by his admirers throughout the world. Less than six months later, on January 2, 1927, he died in his sleep, having told his secretary upon retiring that he knew he would not get up again. He was buried the same day in the Old Cemetery of Tel Aviv.

VIII

Thirty-five years after his death Ahad Ha-Am's position in the world of Jewish thought is still something of an anomaly. In Western Europe and America, except for small Hebrew-reading, Zionist-oriented circles, his name is practically unknown—and this despite the fact that he has been extensively translated into English, German, Russian, and several other European languages. In Israel the situation is, of course, different. But there too, although Ahad Ha'am's essays are considered to be classics of Hebrew prose and are standard reading matter for every schoolboy, he can hardly be said to be held in official favor. His early record of opposition to political Zionism;

his repeated criticisms of what he considered to be the highhandedness of Palestinian Jewry in its struggle to attain self-sufficiency and self-determination; his lukewarmness on the issue of Jewish sovereignty; none of these has endeared him to the architects of Jewish Statehood, nor to those members of the literary establishment who share their views.

Yet, as was bound to happen, there is today both in Israel and the countries of the Diaspora a growing appreciation of Ahad Ha'am's importance. History, which has proved him wrong in some respects, has also been his greatest corroborator. The very fact that he refused to conceive of Statehood as an end in itself lent him the perspective to look beyond the vexatious political and ideological entanglements of the moment, and to concentrate on what he realized would be the more enduring problems of Jewish national identity. Thus, to take an outstanding example, Ahad Ha'am saw more clearly than any of his contemporaries the difficulties that would arise in the future course of Israel-Diaspora relations. Classical Zionism had always held that between immigration to the Land of Israel on the one hand, and assimilation on the other, the liquidation of the Diaspora would be accomplished. That great masses of Jews should, after the creation of a State of Israel, wish to retain their Jewish identity and communal institutions, yet show no inclination to return to the restored homeland, was for classical Zionist theory an inconceivable historical contradiction, and a shock from which it has never recovered. In both Israel and the Diaspora the need to re-define this puzzling relationship, to insure that it neither becomes narrowly political nor degenerates into a vague sentimental attachment, has become increasingly pressing. As a result, leaders on either side have found themselves resorting more and more to an outlook strikingly similar to Ahad Ha'am's concept of Israel as a "spiritual center" and of a Diaspora Jewry which though flourishing and creative in its own right may draw continual cultural sustenance from the presence of the Jewish State. Ahad Ha'am's type of compromise may someday be reached between the Diaspora's desire to be a free and equal partner in the making of modern Judaism, and a Zionist Israel's claim to historical and religious uniqueness.

Above all, however, it was Ahad Ha'am's most probing insight, as well as his widest divergence from the bulk of Zionist thought, that neither Zionism nor any other "ism" could ever "solve" the Jewish problem, for the very reason that Judaism itself is intrinsically problematical; that is to say, it demands from its adherents an understanding of history, of nationality, and perhaps even of life, which knows no parallel and is thus by its very definition "abnormal." Nowhere has this been more strikingly illustrated in recent years than in Israel itself, where a generation of European-born Zionist educators, having made it their proud policy to "normalize" the lives of Israeli-born youth, have proved so successful that their "normalized" products no longer feel any particular affinity with the Jewish or Zionist past. The enormous amount of discussion that has lately taken place in Israel over how to instill in Israeli youth a *toda'ah yehudit,* a "Jewish consciousness," reflects a major reappraisal of Zionist philosophy which Ahad Ha'am felt was necessary even in his own day. Inherent in this growing concern is a return to Ahad Ha'am's belief that only by re-affirming the historic link between Jewish present and Jewish past, between Diaspora Jew and Israeli Jew, can the Jewish people as a whole survive and prosper.

Ahad Ha'am believed that he was living at a time when Judaism was, as the title of his first volume of collected essays implied, "at the crossroads." Distasteful as assimilation was to him, the vulgarized, distorted Judaism whose emergence he feared seemed no less so. Yet, Ahad Ha'am was too aware of the dilemma of modern Jewish history to pretend to possess any clear-cut answer. His preponderant pessimism, which undoubtedly sprang from roots deep within his personality, was an honest reaction to what he saw going on all around him. What he was willing to offer, both to his times and our own, was the faith that the Jewish people had not yet played out its historic role, that "If this nation could have become another, it would long since have found many ways to its salvation. . . . But the *national* Ego, the eternal Ego of the Jewish people, is another matter; and they err who think it possible to lead this also along the path of their own choice. The path of the national Ego is already marked and laid out by its essential character, and that character has its foundation in the Past, and its completion in the Future."

HANS KOHN

New York, January 1962.

THE WRONG WAY*

(1889)

I

For many centuries the Jewish people, sunk in poverty and degradation, has been sustained by faith and hope in the divine mercy. The present generation has seen the birth of a new and far-reaching idea, which promises to bring down our faith and hope from heaven, and transform both into living and active forces, making our land the goal of hope, and our people the anchor of faith.

Historic ideas of this kind spring forth suddenly, as though of their own accord, when the time is ripe. They at once establish their sway over the minds which respond to them, and from these they spread abroad and make their way through the world—as a spark first sets fire to the most inflammable material, and then spreads to the framework of the building. It was in this way that our idea came to birth, without our being able to say who discovered it, and won adherents among those who halted half-way : among those, that is, whose faith had weakened, and who had no longer the patience to wait for miracles, but who, on the other hand, were still attached to their people by bonds which had not lost their strength, and had not yet abandoned belief in its right to exist as a single people. These first " nationalists " raised the banner of the new idea, and went out to fight

*With minor abridgment   34

its battle full of confidence. The sincerity of their own conviction gradually awoke conviction in others, and daily fresh recruits joined them from Left and Right : so that one might have expected them in a short time to be numbered by tens of thousands.

But meanwhile the movement underwent a fundamental change. The idea took practical shape in the work of Palestinian colonisation. This unlooked-for development surprised friends and foes alike. The friends of the idea raised a shout of victory, and cried in exultation : Is not this a thing unheard-of, that an idea so young has strength to force its way into the world of action ? Does not this prove clearly that we were not mere dreamers ? The foes of the movement, on their side, who had hitherto despised it and mocked it, as an idle fancy of dreamers and visionaries, now began grudgingly to admit that after all it showed signs of life and was worthy of attention.

From that time dates a new period in the history of the idea ; and if we glance at the whole course of its development from that time to the present, we shall find once again matter for surprise. Whereas previously the idea grew ever stronger and stronger and spread more and more widely among all sections of the people, while its sponsors looked to the future with exultation and high hopes, now, after its victory, it has ceased to win new adherents, and even its old adherents seem to lose their energy, and ask for nothing more than the well-being of the few poor colonies[1] already in existence, which are what remains of all their pleasant visions of an earlier day. But even this modest demand remains unfulfilled ; the land is full of intrigues and quarrels and pettiness—

[1] [i.e., Jewish agricultural settlements in Palestine.]

all for the sake and for the glory of the great idea—which give them no peace and endless worry ; and who knows what will be the end of it all?

If, as a philosopher has said, it is melancholy to witness the death from old age of a religion which brought comfort to men in the past, how much more sad is it when an idea full of youthful vigour—the hope of the passing generation and the salvation of that which is coming—stumbles and falls at the outset of its career ! Add to this that the idea in question is one which we see exercising so profound an influence over many peoples, and surely we are bound to ask ourselves the old question : Why are we so different from any other race or nation ? Or are those of our people really right, who say that we have ceased to be a nation and are held together only by the bond of religion ? But, after all, those who take that view can speak only for themselves. It is true that between them and us there is no longer any bond except that of a common religion and the hatred which our enemies have for us ; but we ourselves, who feel our Jewish nationality in our own hearts, very properly deride anybody who tries to argue out of existence something of which we have an intuitive conviction. If this is so, why has not the idea of the national rebirth succeeded in taking root even among ourselves and in making that progress for which we hoped?

The idea which we are here discussing is not new in the sense of setting up a new object of endeavour ; but the methods which it suggests for the attainment of its object demand a great expenditure of effort, and it cannot prove the adequacy of its methods so conclusively as to compel reason to assent to the truth of its judgments. What it needs, therefore, is to make of the devotion and the desire which are felt for its ideal an instrument for the strengthening of faith and the sharpening of resolution. Now the devotion of the individual to the well-being of the community, which is the ideal here in question, is a sentiment to which we Jews are no strangers. But if we would estimate aright its capacity to produce the faith and the resolution that are needed for the realisation of our idea, we must first of all study the vicissitudes through which it has passed, and examine its present condition.

All the laws and ordinances, all the blessings and curses of the Law of Moses have but one unvarying object : the well-being of the nation as a whole in the land of its inheritance. The happiness of the individual is not regarded. The individual Israelite is treated as standing to the people of Israel in the relation of a single limb to the whole body : the actions of the individual have their reward in the good of the community. One long chain unites all the generations, from Abraham, Isaac, and Jacob to the end of time ; the covenant which God made with the Patriarchs he keeps with their descendants, and if the fathers eat sour grapes, the teeth of the children will be set on edge. For the people is one people throughout all its generations, and the individuals who come and go in each generation are but as those minute parts of the living body which change every day, without affecting in any degree the character of that organic unity which is the whole body.

It is difficult to say definitely whether at any period our people as a whole really entertained the sentiment of national loyalty in this high degree, or whether it was only a moral ideal cherished by the most important section of the people. But at any rate it is clear that after the destruction of the first Temple, when the nation's star had almost set, and its well-being was so nearly shattered

that even its best sons despaired, and when the elders
of Israel sat before Ezekiel and said : " We will be as
the heathen, as the families of the countries," and " Our
bones are dried, and our hope is lost "—-it is clear that
at that time our people began to be more concerned
about the fate of the righteous individual who perishes
despite his righteousness. From that time date the
familiar speculations about the relation between goodness
and happiness which we find in Ezekiel, in Ecclesiastes,
and in many of the Psalms (and in Job some would add,
holding that book also to have been written in this
period) ; and many men, not satisfied by any of the
solutions which were propounded, came to the conclusion that " it is vain to serve God," and that " to
serve the Master without expectation of reward " is a
fruitless proceeding. It would seem that then, and not
till then, when the well-being of the community could
no longer inspire enthusiasm and idealism, did our
people suddenly remember the individual, remember
that besides the life of the body corporate the individual
has a life peculiarly his own, and that in this life of
his own he wants pleasure and happiness, and demands
a personal reward for his personal righteousness.

The effect of this discovery on the Jewish thought of
that epoch is found in such pronouncements as this :
" The present life is like an entrance-hall to the future
life." The happiness which the individual desires will
become his when he enters the banqueting-hall, if only
he qualifies for it by his conduct in the ante-room. The
national ideal having ceased to satisfy, the religious
ordinances are endowed instead with a meaning and a
purpose for the individual, as the spirit of the age
demands, and are put outside the domain of the national
sentiment. Despite this change, the national sentiment

continued for a long time to live on and to play its part in the *political* life of the people : witness the whole history of the long period which ended with the wars of Titus and Hadrian. But since on the political side there was a continuous decline, the religious life grew correspondingly stronger, and concurrently the individualist element in the individual members of the nation prevailed more and more over the nationalist element, and drove it ultimately from its last stronghold—the hope for a future redemption. That hope, the heartfelt yearning of a nation seeking in a distant future what the present could not give, ceased in time to satisfy people in its original form, which looked forward to a Messianic Age "differing from the life of to-day in nothing except the emancipation of Israel from servitude." For living men and women no longer found any comfort for themselves in the abundance of good which was to come to their nation in the latter end of days, when they would be dead and gone. Each individual demanded his own private and personal share of the expected general happiness. And religion went so far as to satisfy even this demand, by laying less emphasis on the redemption than on the resurrection of the dead.

Thus the national ideal was completely changed. No longer is patriotism a pure, unselfish devotion ; no longer is the common good the highest of all aims, overriding the personal aims of each individual. On the contrary : henceforward the *summum bonum* is for each individual his personal well-being, in time or in eternity, and the individual cares about the common good only in so far as he himself participates in it. To realise how complete the change of attitude became in course of time, we need only recall the surprise expressed by the Tannaim[1] because the Pentateuch speaks of "the land which the Lord swore to your ancestors to give *to them*." In fact, the land was given not to them, but only to their descendants, and so the Tannaim find in this passage an allusion to the resurrection of the dead (*Sifré*).[1] This shows that in their time that deep-rooted consciousness of the union of all ages in the body corporate of the people, which pervades the whole of the Pentateuch, had become so weak that they could not understand the words "to them" except as referring to the actual individuals to whom they were addressed.

Subsequent events—the terrible oppressions and frequent migrations, which intensified immeasurably the personal anxiety of every Jew for his own safety and that of his family—contributed still further to the enfeebling of the already weakened national sentiment, and to the concentration of interest primarily in the life of the family, secondarily in that of the congregation (in which the individual finds satisfaction for his needs). The national life of the people as a whole practically ceased to matter to the individual. Even those Jews who are still capable of feeling occasionally an impulse to work for the nation cannot as a rule so far transcend their individualism as to subordinate their own love of self and their own ambition, or their immediate family or communal interests, to the requirements of the nation. The demon of egoism—individual or congregational— haunts us in all that we do for our people, and suppresses

---

[1] [The Jewish teachers of the period (roughly) from 200 B.C. to 200 C.E. They were responsible for the Mishnah—the first Code of Jewish Law after the Pentateuch—and for the earliest commentaries on the Bible or parts of it, one of which is called *Sifré*. —*Tr*.]

the rare manifestations of national feeling, being the
stronger of the two.

This, then, was the state of feeling to which we had
to appeal, by means of which we had to create the
invincible faith and the indomitable will that are needed
for a great, constructive national effort.

What ought we to have done?

It follows from what has been said above that we ought
to have made it our first object to bring about a *revival*—
to inspire men with a deeper attachment to the national
life, and a more ardent desire for the national well-being.
By these means we should have aroused the necessary
determination, and we should have obtained devoted
adherents. No doubt such work is very difficult and
takes a long time, not one year or one decade; and, I
repeat, it is not to be accomplished by speeches alone,
but demands the employment of all means by which
men's hearts can be won. Hence it is probable—in fact
almost certain—that if we had chosen this method we
should not yet have had time to produce concrete results
in Palestine itself: lacking the resources necessary to
do things well, we should have been too prudent to do
things badly. But, on the other side, we should have
made strenuous endeavours to train up Jews who would
work for their people. We should have striven gradually to extend the empire of our ideal in Jewry, till at
last it could find genuine, whole-hearted devotees, with
all the qualities needed to enable them to work for its
practical realisation.

But such was not the policy of the first champions of
our ideal. As Jews, they had a spice of individualism
in their nationalism, and were not capable of planting
a tree so that others might eat its fruit after they them-

selves were dead and gone. Not satisfied with working among the people to train up those who would ultimately work in the land, they wanted to see with their own eyes the actual work in the land and its results. When, therefore, they found that their first rallying-cry, in which they based their appeal on the general good, did not at once rouse the national determination to take up Palestinian work, they summoned to their aid—like our teachers of old—the individualistic motive, and rested their appeal on economic want, which is always sure of sympathy. To this end they began to publish favourable reports, and to make optimistic calculations, which plainly showed that so many dunams[1] of land, so many head of cattle and so much equipment, costing so-and-so much, were sufficient in Palestine to keep a whole family in comfort and affluence : so that anybody who wanted to do well and had the necessary capital should betake him to the goodly land, where he and his family would prosper, while the nation too would benefit. An appeal on these lines did really induce some people to go to Palestine in order to win comfort and affluence ; whereat the promoters of the idea were mightily pleased, and did not examine very closely what kind of people the emigrants to Palestine were, and why they went. But these people, most of whom were by no means prepared to submit cheerfully to discomfort for the sake of a national ideal, found when they reached Palestine that they had been taken in by imaginative reports and estimates ; and they set up—and are still keeping up— a loud and bitter outcry, seeking to gain their individual ends by all means in their power, and regardless of any distinction between what is legitimate and what is not,

---

[1] [A Turkish measure=about ¼ acre.]

or of the fair name of the ideal which they dishonour. The details of the story are public property.

What wonder, then, that so great an ideal, presented in so unworthy a form, can no longer gain adherents; that a national building founded on the expectation of profit and self-interest falls to ruins when it becomes generally known that the expectation has not been realised, and self-interest bids men keep away?

This, then, is the wrong way. Certainly, seeing that these ruins are already there, we are not at liberty to neglect the task of mending and improving so far as we can. But at the same time we must remember that it is not on these that we must base our hope of ultimate success. The heart of the people—that is the foundation on which the land will be regenerated. And the people is broken into fragments.

So let us return to the road on which we started when our idea first arose. Instead of adding yet more ruins, let us endeavour to give the idea itself strong roots and to strengthen and deepen its hold on the Jewish people, not by force, but by the spirit. Then we shall in time have the possibility of doing actual work.

" I shall see it, but not now : I shall behold it, but not nigh."

SLAVERY IN FREEDOM [1]

(1891)

The opponents of the Hoveve Zion in the Russian Jewish press think that they have need of no more formidable weapons than those which they used to employ when they fought the battle of "culture" against the "obscurantists." That is to say, instead of examining our views and proving us in the wrong by arguments based on reason and facts, they think that they can put us out of court by an array of distinguished names; they think that they can frighten us by pointing out how widely we differ from the Jewish thinkers of Western Europe. They forget that their new opponents include many who are no strangers to Western culture, and who are therefore quite aware that even professors sometimes sin against the light, that even members of Academies have been known to cling to obsolete beliefs.

Thus, these opponents of ours try to make us see, for our own good, to what a pitch of spiritual exaltation our people have risen in France, where even anti-Semitism has not made them "narrow." Anti-Semit-

[1] This essay, published in Ha-Meliz (1892), was a reply to an article entitled "Eternal Ideals," which had appeared in the Russian Voschod, from the pen of a prominent Jewish writer. The Voschod was a Russian Jewish monthly, since defunct. It will be observed that this essay was written many years before the Dreyfus case, which was the first practical revelation of French anti-Semitism.

ism! To the French Jews, with their "breadth of view," it is as though it did not exist: they go securely and calmly on their way towards those "eternal ideals" which their predecessors, the Jewish scholars of the last generation, set before them. But we, the small of soul, we have lost the way and turned back. Such, at least, is the opinion of our opponents: and for evidence they bring an array of distinguished names, in the face of which who so bold as to doubt that they are right?

And yet I for one am bold enough to doubt the "calmness" of the Jews of France in the face of anti-Semitism; to doubt even their "spiritual exaltation," and the value of those "eternal ideals" which they pursue. And, indeed, I find ground for these doubts in the very words of those "distinguished" people who are held up to us *in terrorem*.

Four years ago, at a meeting of the Société des Études Juives in Paris, Theodore Reinach, the secretary of the society, drew the attention of his hearers to the danger which threatened the Jews in France through the growth of anti-Semitism. "Ah!" he cried, "anti-Semitism, which was thought dead in this *beautiful France* of ours, is trying to raise its head. A single pamphleteer [1] beat his drum, and now he is surprised at his wonderful success. The success—*so I would fain believe*—is only temporary; but for all that it is a bad sign." M. Reinach thinks, all the same, that there is no smoke without fire, that there must be a grain of truth in the charges of the anti-Semites. "Being, as we are, the smallest religious sect; being, as we are, strangers newly arrived in the French

[1] [Drumont.]

household, we are especially subject to jealousy and criticism." Even our abilities and our successes in every field are no protection for us. On the contrary, "it is just these that inflame jealousy." There is, therefore, but one remedy for us. We must be very circumspect in all our actions, so as not to give an opening to our enemies. "Our merchants must all be honest, our rich men all unassuming and charitable, our scholars all modest, our writers all disinterested patriots." Then, naturally, such angels will please even the French.[1]

It is unnecessary to say that this excellent advice of M. Reinach has never been followed, and never will be. Since then things have not become better, but the reverse. Instead of the "single pamphleteer" we find now many pamphleteers, none of whom need grumble, for "beautiful France" listens to them with keen pleasure, takes their words to heart, and is roused to increased jealousy and more inflamed hatred every day. Our brethren in France endeavor, indeed, to believe, with M. Reinach, that "this success is only temporary." But there are not many who feel, like him, and not all those who so feel proclaim it as he did, that this belief is without foundation, but is only what "they *would fain* believe," or, rather, what they *must* believe, if they are not willing to give up in despair the struggle of a hundred years. And yet, if you listen carefully to their quavering voices, when all their talk is of belief and hope, you will hear the stifled sigh, and the voice of a secret doubt, which would make

[1] Comp. Actes et conférences de la société des études juives, 1887, p. cxxxii.

themselves heard, but that they are forced back and buried under a heap of high-sounding phrases.

I have before me as I write a new French book, in which the writers whom I mentioned at the outset have found the beautiful ideas to which I have referred, a book called *La Gerbe*.[1] It was issued last year by the publisher of the Archives Israélites, to commemorate the fiftieth anniversary of that publication. Had such a jubilee volume been published twenty years ago, it would undoubtedly have recounted with paeans of triumph all the victories of the "Frenchmen of the Jewish persuasion" during these fifty years. It would have described exultantly their success, their advance in every sphere of life, their present happiness and honored estate, their bright hopes for the future. But in fact it appears now, and not twenty years ago; and what is it that we hear? Without offence to its authors and admirers be it spoken: we hear cries of defeat, not paeans of triumph. It is in vain that we look for any sign of genuine rejoicing, of such "exaltation of spirit" as would be proper to this jubilee festival. Through the whole book, from beginning to end, there runs an undercurrent of grief, a dark thread of lamentation.

First of all let us hear the editor himself, the central figure of the celebration, give his account of the achievements of his publication. "In the year 1840," he tells us, "fifty years after the promulgation of the principles of 1789, the Jews possessed rights on paper; but in practice their rights were non-existent." And then he asks in a parenthesis, "Do they exist fully even in

---

[1] La Gerbe: études, souvenirs, etc., Paris, 1890.

1890?" After this question, which calls for no answer, he goes on to recount his battles against prejudice, and tells how he has tried unceasingly to spread the great principle of "social assimilation (*la fusion sociale*) with all its corollaries." What he says amounts to this, that even the second jubilee after the principles of '89 has not brought the desired happiness; that hatred of the Jews has revived even in France, despite the principles of '89, and despite all the battles against prejudice and all efforts to promote assimilation. And so—our respected editor promises to continue to fight and strive.

There follow a large number of articles, almost all written by distinguished men, and almost all, whatever their subject, working round as it were automatically to the question of anti-Semitism. Is not this a sure indication that this accursed question fills their whole horizon, so that they cannot turn their attention from it even for a moment, but it must needs force itself to the front, of whatever subject they may treat?

The writers in *La Gerbe* are certainly men of parts and distinction, and it is not for such men as these to turn back in fright at the sight of the enemy—still less to let others see that they are afraid. They know how to control themselves and make a show of looking at all these things from above; they know how to comfort themselves and their readers with pleasant hopes and fair promises, which read sometimes like little prophecies. One of the writers promises us on his word that this is the last battle between the Jews and their enemies, and it will end in complete victory for us, to be followed by real peace for all time. The great Revolution of '89 is always on their tongues. They refer again and again to the "rights of man" (*les droits de l'homme*), or, as some put it, "the new Ten Commandments" which that Revolution promulgated; and each time they express the hope—a hope which is also a sort of prayer—that the French people will not forever forget those great days, that the French people will not, *cannot* turn back, that the French people is still, as of old, the great, the enlightened, the glorious, the mighty people, and so forth, and so forth.

Whether these prophecies will be fulfilled or not is a question with which we are not here concerned. But in the meantime it requires no very penetrating vision to discern from them, and from the pages of *La Gerbe* generally, the true spiritual condition of the French Jews at the present time. There is here none of that "exaltation" which some would fain discover, but the exact opposite. Their condition may be justly defined as *spiritual slavery under the veil of outward freedom*. In reality they accepted this slavery a hundred years ago, together with their "rights"; but it is only in these evil days that it stands revealed in all its glory.

The writers of *La Gerbe* try, for instance, to prove to us and to our enemies that the fortunes of the Jews in every country are inextricably bound up with those of its other inhabitants, or even with those of humanity as a whole; that the troubles of the Jews in any particular country are not, therefore, peculiar to them, but are shared by all the other inhabitants, or even by humanity as a whole; and that for this reason . . . . but the conclusion is self-evident. One writer, wishing to reassure the *rich* Jews of France, whose apprehensions have been aroused by the anti-Semitic movement, tells them this very pleasing story. In 1840, during the February Revolution, a rumor got abroad in a certain Alsatian city that the revolutionaries intended to attack and loot the houses of the rich Jews. The Jews were very much perturbed, and hastened to seek the protection of the commander of the garrison which was permanently quartered in the city. He, however, refused to protect them, unless the National Guard would assist him. To the commander of the National Guard, therefore, they addressed themselves, only to be met with contemptuous jeers from men who did not see any harm in the looting of a few Jewish houses. So the Jews returned home in fear and trembling. But on the following day it became known that the revolutionaries had designs on all men of property, without distinction of creed, and were going to include the houses of rich Christians in their round of visits. At once both the permanent garrison and the National Guard appeared in the streets, and "the Jewish question was settled"—so our narrator concludes, with a smile of satisfaction: adding that he thinks it necessary "to expatiate on the *lofty moral* of this story." In truth, *we* can find a lofty moral in this story, from our own point of view. But shall we really find the "moral" which our narrator wishes to draw? At any rate, his moral is not exactly "lofty."

This trick of exciting sympathy with the Jews on the ground that it will benefit other people is very familiar to us here also. Our Russian Jewish writers, from the time of Orshansky to the present day, are never weary of seeking arguments to prove that the

Jews are a milch cow, which must be treated gently for the sake of its milk. Naturally, our French *savants* do not condescend to use this ugly metaphor. They wrap up the idea in a nice "ideal" form. But when all is said, the idea is the same there as here; and a terrible idea it is, sufficient in itself to show how far even Western Jews are from being free men at heart. Picture the situation to yourself. Surrounded by armed bandits, I cry out "Help! Help! Danger!" Is not every man bound to hasten to my help? Is it not a fearful, an indelible disgrace, that I am forced to prove first of all that my danger affects other people, affects the whole human race? As though my blood were not good enough, unless it be mingled with the blood of others! As though the human race were something apart, in which I have no share, and not simply a collective name for its individual members, of whom I am one!

This slavery becomes more and more apparent, when the writers in *La Gerbe* come to deal with the internal affairs of Judaism. Valiantly they champion the cause of our religion against its rivals, knowing as they do that this is permitted in France, where neither the Government nor the people cares very much about such discussions. But when they have to disclose the *national* connection between the Jews of France and other Jews, or between them and their ancestral land, a connection in which it is possible to find something inconsistent to a certain extent with the extreme and zealot patriotism which is in vogue in France, then we discover once more their moral slavery—a spiritual yoke which throttles them, and reduces them to a condition of undisguised embarrassment.

One of the contributors, the distinguished philosopher Adolphe Franck, expresses the opinion that every Jew, *without distinction of nationality*, who enjoys the fruits of emancipation in any country, is bound to be grateful, first and foremost, to the Frenchmen of the Revolution, and must therefore regard France as his *first* fatherland, the *second* being his actual birthplace. And here our philosopher finds it his duty suddenly to add: "Jerusalem is [for the Jew] nothing more than the birthplace of his memories and his faith. He may give it a place in his religious service; but he himself belongs to the land of his birth." This way of regarding Jerusalem is a very trite commonplace, which our Western thinkers grind out again and again in various forms. Not long ago another philosopher, a German Jew, published a new volume, which contains a *scientific* article on the Book of Lamentations. Now, a scientific article has no concern with questions of practical conduct; and yet the author finds it necessary to touch in conclusion on the practical question, whether at the present day we have a right to read this book in our synagogues. He answers in the affirmative, on the ground that the Christians too read it in their churches three days before Easter. "If we are asked, 'What is Zion to you, and what are you to Zion?' we reply calmly, 'Zion is the innermost kernel of the inner consciousness of modern nations.' " [1] This answer is not perhaps so clear as it might be, even in the original; but the writer's object is perfectly clear. We have, therefore, no right to be angry if our French philosopher also adopts this view. But

[1] Steinthal, Zu Bibel und Religionsphilosophie (Berlin, 1890), p. 33.

when we read the whole article in *La Gerbe,* and find
the author concluding that the Jews have a special
"mission," which they received *in Jerusalem,* which
they have not yet completely fulfilled, and for the
sake of which they live, and *must live* till they do fulfil
it completely, then we shall have a serious question
to put. The duty of gratitude, we argue, is so important in our author's view, that he would have
every Jew put France before the country of his birth—
France, which was nothing more than the cause of our
obtaining external rights, which we might have obtained without her, if only we had deserted our "mission." That being so, does it not follow *a fortiori* that
Jerusalem, which gave us this very "mission," the
cause and object of our life, has a claim on our gratitude
prior even to that of France? Even so great a philosopher as our author could not, I think, find a logical
flaw in this argument: and yet he could write as he
has done. Is not this moral slavery?

Another thinker—a man who bears all the troubles
of French Jewry on his shoulders, and is withal an
active participator in work for the good of the Jews
as a whole—recounts the good services rendered by
the journal which is celebrating its jubilee; and one
of them is this, that it has helped to strengthen the
bond between the Jews in France and those in other
countries. But as he wrote these words, the recollec-
tion of "beautiful France," and of the anti-Semitism
which prevails there, must have crossed his mind; for
he pauses to justify the slip of the pen by which he, a
Frenchman, could welcome a strengthening of the bond
between the Jewish community in France and Jewish
communities elsewhere. He tries to show that though

the French Jews are well known for the thoroughness of their patriotism and their devotion to their country, yet it is no breach of duty on their part to sympathize with their brother Jews, who are still subject to disabilities in other countries, or to rejoice with those of them whose position improves. For my part, I have sufficient confidence in this distinguished man, and in his whole-hearted devotion to *his people,* the Jews, to believe that, even if it were proved to him beyond all doubt that French patriotism is inconsistent with affection for his flesh and blood in other countries, he would still feel that affection for them secretly, in the depths of his being; that even if all the Jews were blessed with full emancipation, and there were no longer any room for "sympathy" with these and "rejoicing" with those, he would still desire to maintain permanently his connection with the whole body, and to take part in all their interests. But if this be so, what are all these excuses, what is this constraint which he pleads, if not moral slavery?

But this *moral* slavery is only half the price which Western Jews have paid for their emancipation. Beneath the cloak of their political freedom there lies another, perhaps a harder, form of slavery—*intellectual* slavery; and this, too, has left its mark on the book which we are considering.

Having agreed, for the sake of emancipation, to deny the existence of the Jews as a people, and regard Judaism simply and solely as a religion, Western Jews have thereby pledged themselves and their posterity to guard with the utmost care the religious unity of Israel. But emancipation demanded certain practical changes in religious matters; and not everybody could make this sacrifice. Hence people "of the Jewish persuasion" have split into various sects; the unity of the religion, on its practical side, has vanished. There remains, then, no other bond than that of religion on its theoretical side—that is to say, certain abstract beliefs which are held by all Jews. This bond, apart from the inherent weakness which it has in common with every spiritual conception that is not crystallized into practice, has grown still weaker of recent years, and is becoming more and more feeble every day. Scientific development has shaken the foundations of every faith, and the Jewish faith has not escaped: so much so that even the editor of *La Gerbe* confesses, with a sigh, that "the scientific heresy which bears the name of Darwin" is gaining ground, and it is only from a feeling of *noblesse oblige* that he still continues to combat it. What, then, are those Jews to do who have nothing left but this theoretical religion, which is itself losing its hold on them? Are they to give up Judaism altogether, and become completely assimilated to their surroundings? A few of them have done this: but why should they not all adopt the same course? Why do most of them feel that they cannot? Where is the chain to which they can point as that which holds them fast to Judaism, and does not allow them to be free? Is it the instinctive national feeling which they have inherited, which is independent of religious beliefs or practices? Away with the suggestion! Did they not give up this feeling a hundred years ago, in exchange for emancipation? Yet the fact remains that it is not in their power to uproot this feeling. Try as they will to conceal it, seek as they will for subterfuges to deceive the world and themselves, it lives none the less; resent it as they will, it is a force at the centre of their being. But this answer, though it satisfies us, does not satisfy them. They have publicly renounced their Jewish nationality, and they cannot go back on their words; they cannot confess that they have sold that which was not theirs to sell. But this being so, how can they justify their obstinate clinging to the name of Jew—a name which brings them neither honor nor profit—for the sake of certain theoretical beliefs which they no longer hold, or which, if they do really and sincerely maintain them, they might equally hold without this special name, as every non-Jewish Deist has done?

For a long time this question has been constantly troubling the Jewish thinkers of Western Europe; and it is this question which drove them, in the last generation, to propound that new, strange gospel to which they cling so tenaciously to this very day—I mean that famous gospel of "the mission of Israel among the nations." This theory is based on an antiquated idea, which is at variance with all the principles of modern science: as though every nation had been created from the first for some particular purpose, and so had a "mission" which it must fulfil, living on against its will until its Heaven-sent task is done. Thus, for example, the Greeks were created to polish and perfect external beauty; the Romans to exalt and extol physical force.[1] On this hypothesis, it is not difficult to find an answer to our own question—an answer not inconsistent, on the one hand, with emancipation, and, on the other hand, with the unity of Judaism. The

---

[1] Munk, Palestine (Paris, 1845), p. 99.

answer is this: Israel as a *people* is dead; but the
Jewish Church still lives, and must live, because the
mission of Israel is not completely fulfilled, so long as
absolute monotheism, with all its consequences, has
not conquered the whole world. Till that victory is
achieved, Israel must live in spite of itself, must bear
and suffer and fight: to this end it was created—"to
know God and to bring others to that knowledge." [1]
If, then, we wish really to fulfil our function, is it not
our duty to be God's apostles, to consecrate all our
strength to the diffusion of that knowledge for the sake
of which we live?

"Heaven forbid!" answer our "missionists"—and
their attitude needs no explanation—"it is not for us
to hasten on the end. God has entrusted the truth to
our keeping; but he has not imposed on us the task
of spreading the truth." [2]

How, then, shall we arrive ultimately at the fulfilment of our mission?

Munk answers thus: "Our mission advances cease-
lessly towards its fulfilment *through the progress of religious ideas.*" [3] And since our Scriptures are, according to the "missionists," the foundation and cause of
this progress, they give us the credit of it, as though
we ourselves were doing our duty on behalf of religious progress. It is for this reason, and for this
reason alone, that we must remain loyal to our standard
until the very end.

In itself, therefore, our mission is an easy and a
comfortable one. At least there is nothing disgraceful

[1] Munk, ibid.; La Gerbe, p. 7.
[2] La Gerbe, p. 12.
[3] Ibid. p. 7.

in being the teachers of the whole world, in regarding
the whole human race, to the end of time, as pupils
who slake their thirst at the fountain of our inspiration: more especially when this honorable task of ours
involves no labor or worry on our part. We are like
the Israelites at the Red Sea: the progress which
emanates from the Scriptures is to fight for our mission,
while we look on and rejoice. Now, this would be very
well indeed, if the pupils on their side were amenable
and docile, and paid the proper respect to their teacher.
But in fact they are impertinent fellows, these pupils.
They kick their teacher: they heap curses on him:
they are forever besmirching his name, until his life
becomes a positive burden to him. And so we are left
face to face with the same question. We are no longer
doing anything useful towards the fulfilment of our
mission: the Scriptures, and consequently religious
progress, are independent of us, and will do their
work without us: we are nothing but a monument on
the path of religious progress, which marches on to
its consummation without our assistance. Why, then,
this life of trouble? The Greeks, who were created,
according to this theory, for the sake of beauty, produced all those beautiful works of art, wrote all those
beautiful books; and then, when there was nothing
more for them to do, although their mission was not
completely fulfilled, and although during all the centuries which separated them from the Renaissance their
beauty lay hidden from the world—then history removed them from the stage, and left the rest to that
progress which proceeded automatically from the Greek
legacy of works of art and books. Why, then, should
not history allow *us* to make our exit? We have

done all that we could for our mission: we have produced the Scriptures. Further there is nothing for us to do: why, then, must we live?

One of our "missionist" thinkers, a learned preacher, deals with this question in an article entitled, "Why Do We Remain Jews?", and tries to answer the question from another side. We remain faithful to Judaism, he thinks, because there is no other religion for which we could change it. Every other religion contains something which we cannot accept. "Natural religion" would, indeed, be sufficient for us. But if we think of accepting natural religion, we must first know what are its principles. Let us, then, look for them in books which set out to expound them, for instance, in Simon's *Natural Religion*. We find that this religion has three fundamental principles: creation, revelation, and reward and punishment. At once we remember that as much as five hundred years ago Rabbi Joseph Albo, author of the *Principles,* based Judaism on three dogmas very much like these. Judaism, therefore, *is* natural religion, and there is no need to change.

Now I might ask this preacher how he would answer those Jews (and there are many of them nowadays) for whom the religion of Simon and his school is an antiquated philosophy, very far from being "natural," and who still desire to remain Jews, without knowing why they so desire. But I will not ask him this question: for as a preacher he is only concerned with philosophers who are also believers. And there is another question which I might put to him. Does he really and honestly believe that there is no difference between Simon's "Revelation of the Godhead" and Albo's "Law from Heaven"? But this also I will not

ask, because I know that it has always been the habit
of religious philosophy—a habit long since recognized
and sanctioned—to twist texts for the purpose of reconciling contradictions.   The criticism that I do offer—
and it is one which deserves our preacher's attention
—I will put in the form of the following dilemma.
If Judaism includes, in addition to those principles
mentioned above, certain things which have no parallel
in natural religion, then the question confronts us
again: Why should we not change the one for the
other?   But if there is no real difference except that of
name, then, indeed, the question becomes more insis-
tent: Why not accept a change of name, if by means of
this purely external change we can win freedom from
all our sufferings?   It is not the name that is of importance to our mission, but the power to fulfil it: that
is, the power to spread the knowledge of the Godhead
in the Jewish sense: and our power to do this will
surely increase out of all proportion if we substitute
the name of "natural religion" for that of "Jewish religion."   But in that case it is not merely permissible,
it is *obligatory* on us to take this step, for the sake of
that mission for which we were created.

It is perhaps superfluous to deal at length with this
theory, which, indeed, it is difficult, in our day, to
treat seriously.   We are forced, despite ourselves, into
a smile, a smile of bitter irony, when we see distinguished men, who might have shown their sorely tried
people real light on its hard and thorny path, wasting
their time with such pleasant sophistries as these; trying to believe, and to persuade others, that a whole
people can have maintained its existence, and borne a
heavy burden of religious observance and an iron

yoke of persecutions, torments, and curses for thousands of years, all for the purpose of teaching the world a certain philosophy, which is already expounded in whole libraries of books, in every conceivable language and every conceivable style, from which who will may learn without any assistance from us: and especially at the present time, when the number of those who wish to learn grows less every day, nay, when we ourselves are every day forgetting our own teaching.

It is, indeed, surprising that such a thinker as Munk, and even the older thinkers of our own day, could and still can believe in the mission of Israel in the sense explained above. But we shall be less surprised if we remember that Munk wrote in the "forties," and that the older contributors to *La Gerbe* are for the most part children of that earlier generation which educated them—children of an age in which the idea of a "final cause" was intelligible and current as a scientific theory. It is, however, a stranger phenomenon, and more difficult to explain, that the same position should be adopted by thinkers and writers of the present generation. These men, who know and admit that "the scientific heresy which bears the name of Darwin" is gaining ground, that is to say, that the world is accepting gradually a scientific theory which does not admit the existence of purpose or end even where it seems most obvious—how can these men still cling to a doctrine which demands belief in the missions of nations generally, in the mission of Israel in particular, and, above all, in such a wonderful mission as this? There can be but one answer. They are *compelled* to do so, because they can find no other way of reconciling Judaism with emancipation. In the first place, Israel has no right to be anything but a Church consecrated to Heaven; in the second place, this heavenly bond has become too weak; and in the third place—and this is the important thing—they *feel,* in spite of it all, that Jews they are, and Jews they want to be. And so, in order to conceal the contradiction between these "truths," they are forced to take refuge in this antiquated theory. On all other questions of conduct or of scholarship they belong to their own generation; but on the Jewish question they cannot move from the position which their fathers took up fifty years ago. As though these fifty years had brought no change of idea and outlook into the world!

Thus this intellectual slavery also is a result of political freedom. If not for this freedom, emancipated Jews would not deny the existence of the Jewish nation; they would not have to climb up to Heaven, on an old and rickety ladder, to seek there what they might have found on earth. It might be maintained, indeed, that even then there would have been thinkers who inclined to look for some "mission" for their people, or, to speak more accurately, for some spiritual *aim* suited to its spiritual characteristics. But then they might have found a different aim—not, perhaps, a finer one, but still one that would have gained acceptance more readily, one more in accordance with the ideas of modern times and with the truths of logic and of history. For instance, they might have argued thus: Here has our people been wandering over the face of the earth for some two thousand years, in the course of which we do not find that it has ever consciously invented any new thing of importance, has

ever beaten out any new highway on the tract of life.
Its part has been always that of the huckster; it has
peddled about all kinds of goods, material and spiritual,
of other people's making. All the good work which
the Jews did for the world's culture in the Middle
Ages was at bottom nothing but huckstering and ped-
dling: they picked up learning in the East, and gave
it to the West. "Yes" replies Munk, in extenuation,
"because the mission of Israel does not lie in making
new discoveries."[1] Well, so let it be! But now that
we see that Israel was fitted to be, and in fact has
been, a huckster of culture, surely common sense will
tell us that this is the occupation for Israel to follow
now, if some spiritual aim is wanted. Now, therefore,
that we have acquired culture in the West, let us
return and carry it to the East. And, if we are so
very fond of teaching, it is surely better for us to go
where there is a more evident lack of teachers, and
where it is easier to find attentive pupils.

But the truth is that if Western Jews were not slaves
to their emancipation, it would never have entered
their heads to consecrate their people to spiritual missions or aims before it had fulfilled that physical,
natural "mission" which belongs to every organism—
before it had created for itself conditions suitable to
its character, in which it could develop its latent
powers and aptitudes, its own particular form of life,
in a normal manner, and in obedience to the demands
of its nature. Then, and only then, after all this had
been achieved—then and only then, we may well believe, its development might lead it in course of time

---

[1] Dictionnaire des sciences philosophiques, iii, article "Juifs."

to some field of work in which it would be specially fitted to act as teacher, and thus contribute once again to the general good of humanity, in a way suited to the spirit of the modern world. And if *then* philosophers tell us that in this field of work lies the "mission" of our people, for which it was created, I shall not, indeed, be able to subscribe to their view; but I shall not quarrel with them on a mere question of names.

But alas! I shall doubtless be dead and buried before then. To-day, while I am still alive, I try mayhap to give my weary eyes a rest from the scene of ignorance, of degradation, of unutterable poverty that confronts me here in Russia, and find comfort by looking yonder across the border, where there are Jewish professors, Jewish members of Academies, Jewish officers in the army, Jewish civil servants; and when I see there, behind the glory and the grandeur of it all, a twofold spiritual slavery—moral slavery and intellectual slavery—and ask myself: Do I envy these fellow-Jews of mine their emancipation?—I answer, in all truth and sincerity: No! a thousand times No! The privileges are not worth the price! I may not be emancipated; but at least I have not sold my soul for emancipation. I at least can proclaim from the housetops that my kith and kin are dear to me wherever they are, without being constrained to find forced and unsatisfactory excuses. I at least can remember Jerusalem at other times than those of "divine service": I can mourn for its loss, in public or in private, without being asked what Zion is to me, or I to Zion. I at least have no need to exalt my people to Heaven, to trumpet its superiority above all other nations, in order

to find a justification for its existence. I at least know "why I remain a Jew"—or, rather, I can find no meaning in such a question, any more than if I were asked why I remain my father's son. I at least can speak my mind concerning the beliefs and the opinions which I have inherited from my ancestors, without fearing to snap the bond that unites me to my people. I can even adopt that "scientific heresy which bears the name of Darwin," without any danger to my Judaism. In a word, I am my own, and my opinions and feelings are my own. I have no reason for concealing or denying them, for deceiving others or myself. And this spiritual freedom—scoff who will!—I would not exchange or barter for all the emancipation in the world.

THE JEWISH STATE AND THE JEWISH PROBLEM

(1897[1])

Some months have passed since the Zionist Congress, but its echoes are still heard in daily life and in the press. In daily life the echoes take the form of meetings small and big, local and central. Since the delegates returned home, they have been gathering the public together and recounting over and over again the wonders that they saw enacted before their eyes. The wretched, hungry public listens and waxes enthusiastic and hopes for salvation : for can " they "—the Jews of the West—fail to carry out anything that they plan ? Heads grow hot and hearts beat fast ; and many " communal workers " whose one care in life had been for years—until last August— the Palestinian settlement, and who would have given the whole world for a penny donation in aid of Palestine workmen or the Jaffa School, have now quite lost their bearings, and ask one another : " What's the good of this sort of work ? The Messiah is near at hand, and we busy ourselves with trifles ! The time has come for great deeds : great men, men of the West, march before us in the van."—There has been a revolution in their world, and to emphasise it they give a new name to the cause : it is no longer " Love of Zion " (*Chibbath Zion*), but " Zionism " (*Zioniyuth*). Nay, the more careful among them, determined to leave no loop-hole for error, even keep the European form of the name

[1] [One of a series of three essays on " Political Zionism." —*Tr.*]

("Zionismus")—thus announcing to all and sundry that they are not talking about anything so antiquated as *Chibbath Zion,* but about a new, up-to-date movement, which comes, like its name, from the West, where people do not use Hebrew.

In the press all these meetings, with their addresses, motions and resolutions, appear over again in the guise of articles—articles written in a vein of enthusiasm and triumph. The meeting was magnificent, every speaker was a Demosthenes, the resolutions were carried by acclamation, all those present were swept off their feet and shouted with one voice : "We will do and obey !"— in a word, everything was delightful, entrancing, perfect. And the Congress itself still produces a literature of its own. Pamphlets specially devoted to its praises appear in several languages ; Jewish and non-Jewish papers still occasionally publish articles and notes about it ; and, needless to say, the "Zionist" organ[1] itself endeavours to maintain the impression which the Congress made, and not to allow it to fade too rapidly from the public memory. It searches the press of every nation and every land, and wherever it finds a favourable mention of the Congress, even in some insignificant journal published in the language of one of the smaller European national-ities, it immediately gives a summary of the article, with much jubilation. Only one small nation's language has thus far not been honoured with such attention, though its journals too have lavished praise on the Congress : I mean Hebrew.

In short, the universal note is one of rejoicing ; and it is therefore small wonder that in the midst of this general harmony my little Note on the Congress sounded

[1] [*Die Welt,* the German organ founded by Herzl.]

discordant and aroused the most violent displeasure in many quarters. I knew from the start that I should not be forgiven for saying such things at such a time, and I had steeled myself to hear with equanimity the clatter of high-sounding phrases and obscure innuendoes—of which our writers are so prolific—and hold my peace. But when I was attacked by M. L. Lilienblum,[1] a writer whose habit it is not to write *àpropos des bottes* for the sake of displaying his style, I became convinced that this time I had really relied too much on the old adage : *Verbum sapienti satis*. It is not pleasant to swim against the stream ; and when one does something without enjoyment, purely as a duty, one does not put more than the necessary minimum of work into the task. Hence in the note referred to I allowed myself to be extremely brief, relying on my readers to fill in the gaps out of their own knowledge, by connecting what I wrote with earlier expressions of my views, which were already familiar to them. I see now that I made a mistake, and left room for the ascription to me of ideas and opinions which are utterly remote from my true intention. Consequently I have now to perform the hard and ungrateful task of writing a commentary on myself, and expressing my views on the matter in hand with greater explicitness.

Nordau's address on the general condition of the Jews was a sort of introduction to the business of the Congress. It exposed in incisive language the sore troubles, material or moral, which beset the Jews the world over. In Eastern countries their trouble is material : they have

---

[1] [The first Secretary of the *Chovevé Zion*, and an opponent of the " spiritual " ideas of Achad Ha-Am. —*Tr.*]

a constant struggle to satisfy the most elementary physical needs, to win a crust of bread and a breath of air—things which are denied them because they are Jews. In the West, in lands of emancipation, their material condition is not particularly bad, but the moral trouble is serious. They want to take full advantage of their rights, and cannot ; they long to become attached to the people of the country, and to take part in its social life, and they are kept at arm's length ; they strive after love and brotherhood, and are met by looks of hatred and contempt on all sides ; conscious that they are not inferior to their neighbours in any kind of ability or virtue, they have it continually thrown in their teeth that they are an inferior type, and are not fit to rise to the same level as the Aryans. And more to the same effect.

Well—what then ?

Nordau himself did not touch on this question : it was outside the scope of his address. But the whole Congress was the answer. Beginning as it did with Nordau's address, the Congress meant this : that in order to escape from all these troubles it is necessary to establish a Jewish State.

Let us imagine, then, that the consent of Turkey and the other Powers has already been obtained, and the State is established—and, if you will, established *völkerrechtlich,* with the full sanction of international law, as the more extreme members of the Congress desire. Does this bring, or bring near, the end of the material trouble ? No doubt, every poor Jew will be at perfect liberty to go to his State and to seek his living there, without any artificial hindrances in the shape of restrictive laws or anything of that kind. But liberty to *seek* a livelihood is not enough : he must be able to *find*

what he seeks. There are natural laws which fetter
man's freedom of action much more than artificial laws.
Modern economic life is so complex, and the development of any single one of its departments depends on so
many conditions, that no nation, not even the strongest
and richest, could in a short time create in any country
new sources of livelihood sufficient for many millions
of human beings. The single country is no longer an
economic unit : the whole world is one great market, in
which every State has to struggle hard for its place.
Hence only a fantasy bordering on madness can believe
that so soon as the Jewish State is established millions
of Jews will flock to it, and the land will afford them
adequate sustenance. Think of the labour and the
money that had to be sunk in Palestine over a long
period of years before one new branch of production—
vine-growing—could be established there ! And even
to-day, after all the work that has been done, we cannot
yet say that Palestinian wine has found the openings that
it needs in the world market, although its quantity is
still small. But if in 1891 Palestine had been a Jewish
State, and all the dozens of Colonies that were then
going to be established for the cultivation of the vine had
in fact been established, Palestinian wine would be to-day
as common as water, and would fetch no price at all.
Using the analogy of this small example, we can see
how difficult it will be to start new branches of production in Palestine, and to find openings for its products
in the world market. But if the Jews are to flock to
their State in large numbers, all at once, we may
prophesy with perfect certainty that home competition
in every branch of production (and home competition
will be inevitable because the amount of labour available

will increase more quickly than the demand for it) will
prevent any one branch from developing as it should.
And then the Jews will turn and leave their State, flying
from the most deadly of all enemies—an enemy not to be
kept off even by the magic word *völkerrechtlich* : from
hunger.

True, agriculture in its elementary form does not
depend to any great extent on the world market, and
at any rate it will provide those engaged in it with food,
if not with plenty. But if the Jewish State sets out to
save all those Jews who are in the grip of the material
problems, or most of them, by turning them into agriculturists in Palestine, then it must first find the necessary capital. At Basle, no doubt, one heard naïve and
confident references to a "National Fund" of ten
million pounds sterling. But even if we silence reason,
and give the rein to fancy so far as to believe that we can
obtain a Fund of those dimensions in a short time, we
are still no further. Those very speeches that we heard
at Basle about the economic condition of the Jews in
various countries showed beyond a doubt that our
national wealth is very small, and most of our people
are below the poverty-line. From this any man of sense,
though he be no great mathematician, can readily
calculate that ten million pounds are a mere nothing
compared with the sum necessary for the emigration of
the Jews and their settlement in Palestine on an agricultural basis. Even if all the rich Jews suddenly became
ardent "Zionists," and every one of them gave half his
wealth to the cause, the whole would still not make up
the thousands of millions that would be needed for the
purpose.

There is no doubt, then, that even when the Jewish

State is established the Jews will be able to settle in it only little by little, the determining factors being the resources of the people themselves and the degree of economic development reached by the country. Meanwhile the natural increase of population will continue, both among those who settle in the country and among those who remain outside it, with the inevitable result that on the one hand Palestine will have less and less room for new immigrants, and on the other hand the number of those remaining outside Palestine will not diminish very much, in spite of the continual emigration. In his opening speech at the Congress, Dr. Herzl, wishing to demonstrate the superiority of his State idea over the method of Palestinian colonisation adopted hitherto, calculated that by the latter method it would take nine hundred years before all the Jews could be settled in their land. The members of the Congress applauded this as a conclusive argument. But it was a cheap victory. The Jewish State itself, do what it will, cannot make a more favourable calculation.

Truth is bitter, but with all its bitterness it is better than illusion. We must confess to ourselves that the "ingathering of the exiles" is unattainable by natural means. We may, by natural means, establish a Jewish State one day, and the Jews may increase and multiply in it until the country will hold no more : but even then the greater part of the people will remain scattered in strange lands. "To gather our scattered ones from the four corners of the earth" (in the words of the Prayer Book) is impossible. Only religion, with its belief in a miraculous redemption, can promise that consummation.

But if this is so, if the Jewish State too means not an

"ingathering of the exiles," but the settlement of a small part of our people in Palestine, then how will it solve the material problem of the Jewish masses in the lands of the Diaspora?

Or do the champions of the State idea think, perhaps, that, being masters in our own country, we shall be able by diplomatic means to get the various governments to relieve the material sufferings of our scattered fellow-Jews? That is, it seems to me, Dr. Herzl's latest theory. In his new pamphlet (*Der Baseler Kongress*) we no longer find any calculation of the number of years that it will take for the Jews to enter their country. Instead, he tells us in so many words (p. 9) that if the land becomes the *national* property of the Jewish people, even though no individual Jew owns privately a single square yard of it, then the Jewish problem will be solved for ever. These words (unless we exclude the material aspect of the Jewish problem) can be understood only in the way suggested above. But this hope seems to me so fantastic that I see no need to waste words in demolishing it. We have seen often enough, even in the case of nations more in favour than Jews are with powerful Governments, how little diplomacy can do in matters of this kind, if it is not backed by a large armed force. Nay, it is conceivable that in the days of the Jewish State, when economic conditions in this or that country are such as to induce a Government to protect its people against Jewish competition by restrictive legislation, that Government will find it easier then than it is now to find an excuse for such action, for it will be able to plead that if the Jews are not happy where they are, they can go to their own State.

The material problem, then, will not be ended by the foundation of a Jewish State, nor, generally speaking, does it lie in our power to end it (though it could be eased more or less even now by various means, such as the encouragement of agriculture and handicrafts among Jews in all countries) ; and whether we found a State or not, this particular problem will always turn at bottom on the economic condition of each country and the degree of civilisation attained by each people.

Thus we are driven to the conclusion that the only true basis of Zionism is to be found in the other problem, the moral one.

But the moral problem appears in two forms, one in the West and one in the East ; and this fact explains the fundamental difference between Western " Zionism " and Eastern *Chibbath Zion*. Nordau dealt only with the Western problem, apparently knowing nothing about the Eastern ; and the Congress as a whole concentrated on the first, and paid little attention to the second.

The Western Jew, after leaving the Ghetto and seeking to attach himself to the people of the country in which he lives, is unhappy because his hope of an open-armed welcome is disappointed. He returns reluctantly to his own people, and tries to find within the Jewish community that life for which he yearns—but in vain. Communal life and communal problems no longer satisfy him. He has already grown accustomed to a broader social and political life ; and on the intellectual side Jewish cultural work has no attraction, because Jewish culture has played no part in his education from childhood, and is a closed book to him. So in his trouble he turns to the land of his ancestors, and pictures to himself how good it would be if a Jewish State were re-established there—a State arranged and organised exactly after the pattern of other States. Then he could live a full, complete life among his own people, and find at home all that he now sees outside, dangled before his eyes, but out of reach. Of course, not all the Jews will be able to take wing and go to their State ; but the very existence of the Jewish State will raise the prestige of those who remain in exile, and their fellow citizens will no more despise them and keep them at arm's length, as though they were ignoble slaves, dependent entirely on the hospitality of others. As he contemplates this fascinating vision, it suddenly dawns on his inner consciousness that even now, before the Jewish State is established, the mere idea of it gives him almost complete relief. He has an opportunity for organised work, for political excitement ; he finds a suitable field of activity without having to become subservient to non-Jews ; and he feels that thanks to this ideal he stands once more spiritually erect, and has regained human dignity, without overmuch trouble and without external aid. So he devotes himself to the ideal with all the ardour of which he is capable ; he gives rein to his fancy, and lets it soar as it will, up above reality and the limitations of human power. For it is not the attainment of the ideal that he needs : its pursuit alone is sufficient to cure him of his moral sickness, which is the consciousness of inferiority ; and the higher and more distant the ideal, the greater its power of exaltation.

This is the basis of Western Zionism and the secret of its attraction. But Eastern *Chibbath Zion* has a different origin and development. Originally, like " Zionism," it was political ; but being a result of material evils, it could not rest satisfied with an " activity" consisting only of outbursts of feeling and fine phrases. These things may satisfy the heart, but not the stomach. So *Chibbath Zion* began at once to express itself in concrete activities—in the establishment of colonies in Palestine. This practical work soon clipped the wings of fancy, and made it clear that *Chibbath Zion* could not lessen the material evil by one iota. One might have thought, then, that when this fact became patent the *Chovevé Zion* would give up their activity, and cease wasting time and energy on work which brought them no nearer their goal. But, no : they remained true to their flag, and went on working with the old enthusiasm, though most of them did not understand even in their own minds why they did so. They felt instinctively that so they must do ; but as they did not clearly appreciate the nature of this feeling, the things that they did were not always rightly directed towards that object which in reality was drawing them on without their knowledge.

For at the very time when the material tragedy in the East was at its height, the heart of the Eastern Jew was still oppressed by another tragedy—the moral one ; and when the *Chovevé Zion* began to work for the solution of the material problem, the national instinct of the people felt that just in such work could it find the remedy for its moral trouble. Hence the people took up this work and would not abandon it even after it had become obvious that the material trouble could not be cured in this way. The Eastern form of the moral trouble is absolutely different from the Western. In the West it is the problem of the Jews, in the East the problem of Judaism. The one weighs on the individual, the other on the nation. The one is felt by Jews who have had a European education, the other by Jews whose education has been Jewish. The one is a product of anti-Semitism, and is dependent on anti-Semitism for its existence ; the other is a natural product of a real link with a culture of thousands of years, which will retain its hold even if the troubles of the Jews all over the world come to an end, together with anti-Semitism, and all the Jews in every land have comfortable positions, are on the best possible terms with their neighbours, and are allowed by them to take part in every sphere of social and political life on terms of absolute equality.

It is not only Jews who have come out of the Ghetto : Judaism has come out, too. For Jews the exodus is confined to certain countries, and is due to toleration ; but Judaism has come out (or is coming out) of its own accord wherever it has come into contact with modern culture. This contact with modern culture overturns the defences of Judaism from within, so that Judaism can no longer remain isolated and live a life apart. The spirit of our people strives for development : it wants to absorb those elements of general culture which reach it from outside, to digest them and to make them a part of itself, as it has done before at different periods of its history. But the conditions of its life in exile are not suitable. In our time culture wears in each country the garb of the national spirit, and the stranger who would woo her must sink his individuality and become absorbed in the dominant spirit. For this reason Judaism in exile cannot develop its individuality in its own way. When it leaves the Ghetto walls it is in danger of losing its essential being or—at best—its national unity : it is in danger of being split up into as many kinds of Judaism, each with a different character and life, as there are countries of the Jewish dispersion.[1]

[1] See my essay *Imitation and Assimilation*. [Selected essays by Achad Ha-Am, pp. 107-124. —*Tr.*]

And now Judaism finds that it can no longer tolerate
the *galuth*[1] form which it had to take on, in obedience to
its will-to-live, when it was exiled from its own country,
and that if it loses that form its life is in danger. So
it seeks to return to its historic centre, in order to live
there a life of natural development, to bring its powers
into play in every department of human culture, to
develop and perfect those national possessions which it
has acquired up to now, and thus to contribute to the
common stock of humanity, in the future as in the past,
a great national culture, the fruit of the unhampered
activity of a people living according to its own spirit.
For this purpose Judaism needs at present but little. It
needs not an independent State, but only the creation
in its native land of conditions favourable to its development : a good-sized settlement of Jews working *without
hindrance*[2] in every branch of culture, from agriculture
and handicrafts to science and literature. This Jewish
settlement, which will be a gradual growth, will become
in course of time the centre of the nation, wherein its
spirit will find pure expression and develop in all its
aspects up to the highest degree of perfection of which
it is capable. Then from this centre the spirit of
Judaism will go forth to the great circumference, to all
the communities of the Diaspora, and will breathe new

---

[1] [*Galuth*—" exile "—is the word commonly used by Jews to denote
the condition of the Jewish people so long as it is not in its own land,
Palestine. —*Tr.*]

[2] The " political " Zionists generally think and say that they were
the first to lay it down as a principle that the colonisation of
Palestine by secret and surreptitious means, without organisation and
in defiance of the ruling Power, is of no value and ought to be
abandoned. They do not know that this truth was discovered by
others first, and that years ago the *Chibbath Zion* of Judaism
demanded that everything should be done openly, with proper
organisation and with the consent of the Turkish Government.

life into them and preserve their unity ; and when our national culture in Palestine has attained that level, we may be confident that it will produce men in the country who will be able, on a favourable opportunity, to establish a State which will be a *Jewish* State, and not merely a State of Jews.

This *Chibbath Zion,* which takes thought for the preservation of Judaism at a time when Jewry suffers so much, is something odd and unintelligible to the " political " Zionists of the West, just as the demand of R. Jochanan ben Zakkai for Jabneh was strange and unintelligible to the corresponding people of that time.[1] And so political Zionism cannot satisfy those Jews who care for Judaism : its growth seems to them to be fraught with danger to the object of their own aspiration.

The secret of our people's persistence is—as I have tried to show elsewhere[2]—that at a very early period the Prophets taught it to respect only spiritual power, and not to worship material power. For this reason the clash with enemies stronger than itself never brought the Jewish nation, as it did the other nations of antiquity, to the point of self-effacement. So long as we are faithful to this principle, our existence has a secure basis : for in spiritual power we are not inferior to other nations, and we have no reason to efface ourselves. But a political ideal *which does not rest on the national culture* is apt to seduce us from our loyalty to spiritual

---

[1] [After the fall of Jerusalem in 70 C.E., Titus asked Rabbi Jochanan, one of the leading Jews of the time, what he wanted. The reply was, " Give me Jabneh and its scholars." The Rabbi understood—though the Roman conqueror did not—that in the conditions then existing a centre of Jewish learning would do more to preserve Israel than political institutions. —*Tr.*]

[2] In *Imitation and Assimilation.*

greatness, and to beget in us a tendency to find the path of glory in the attainment of material power and political dominion, thus breaking the thread that unites us with the past, and undermining our historical basis. Needless to say, if the political ideal is not attained, it will have disastrous consequences, because we shall have lost the old basis without finding a new one. But even if it is attained under present conditions, when we are a scattered people not only in the physical but also in the spiritual sense—even then Judaism will be in great danger. Almost all our great men, those, that is, whose education and social position fit them to be at the head of a Jewish State, are spiritually far removed from Judaism, and have no true conception of its nature and its value. Such men, however loyal to their State and devoted to its interests, will necessarily regard those interests as bound up with the foreign culture which they themselves have imbibed ; and they will endeavour, by moral persuasion or even by force, to implant that culture in the Jewish State, so that in the end the Jewish State will be a State of Germans or Frenchmen of the Jewish race. We have even now a small example of this process in Palestine.[1] And history teaches us that in the days of the Herodian house Palestine was indeed a Jewish State, but the national culture was despised and persecuted, and the ruling house did everything in its power to implant Roman culture in the country, and frittered away the national resources in the building of heathen temples and amphitheatres and so forth. Such

[1] [The reference here is to the schools of the *Alliance Israélite Universelle*, which were French in spirit. Many years after this essay was written, in 1913, the Germanising tendencies of the schools maintained by the *Hilfsverein der deutschen Juden* in Palestine led to an acute conflict between that body and the Zionists. —*Tr.*]

a Jewish State would spell death and utter degradation
for our people.   We should never achieve sufficient
political power to deserve respect, while we should miss
the living moral force within.   The puny State, being
" tossed about like a ball between its powerful neighbours, and maintaining its existence only by diplomatic
shifts and continual truckling to the favoured of fortune,"
would not be able to give us a feeling of national glory ;
and the national culture, in which we might have sought
and found our glory, would not have been implanted in
our State and would not be the principle of its life.   So
we should really be then—much more than we are now—
" a small and insignificant nation," enslaved *in spirit* to
" the favoured of fortune," turning an envious and
covetous eye on the armed force of our " powerful
neighbours " ; and our existence as a sovereign State
would not add a glorious chapter to our national history.
Were it not better for " an ancient people which was
once a beacon to the world " to disappear than to end
by reaching such a goal as this ?[1]   Mr. Lilienblum
reminds me that there are in our time small States, like
Switzerland, which are safeguarded against interference
by the other nations, and have no need of " continual
truckling."   But a comparison between Palestine
and small countries like Switzerland overlooks the
geographical position of Palestine and its religious
importance for all nations. These two facts will make
it quite impossible for its " powerful neighbours " (by
which expression, of course, I did not mean, as Mr.
Lilienblum interprets, " the Druses and the Persians ")

---

[1] The phrases in inverted commas are taken from my note on the
Congress. As my critics have misinterpreted them, I have taken
this opportunity of explaining their true meaning.

to leave it alone altogether; and when it has become a Jewish State they will all still keep an eye on it, and each Power will try to influence its policy in a direction favourable to itself, just as we see happening in the case of other weak states (like Turkey) in which the great European nations have " interests."

In a word : *Chibbath Zion,* no less than " Zionism," wants a Jewish State and believes in the possibility of the establishment of a Jewish State in the future. But while " Zionism " looks to the Jewish State to provide a remedy for poverty, complete tranquillity and national glory, *Chibbath Zion* knows that our State will not give us all these things until " universal Righteousness is enthroned and holds sway over nations and States " : and it looks to a Jewish State to provide only a " secure refuge " for Judaism and a cultural bond of unity for our nation. " Zionism," therefore, begins its work with political propaganda ; *Chibbath Zion* begins with national culture, because only through the national culture and for its sake can a Jewish State be established in such a way as to correspond with the will and the needs of the Jewish people.

Dr. Herzl, it is true, said in the speech mentioned above that " Zionism " demands the return to Judaism before the return to the Jewish State. But these nice-sounding words are so much at variance with his deeds that we are forced to the unpleasant conclusion that they are nothing but a well-turned phrase.

It is very difficult for me to deal with individual actions, on which one cannot touch without reflecting on individual men. For this reason I contented myself, in my note on the Congress, with general allusions, which, I believed, would be readily intelligible to those who were versed in the subject, and especially to Congress delegates. But some of my opponents have turned this scrupulousness to use against me by pretending not to understand at all. They ask, with affected simplicity, what fault I have to find with the Congress, and they have even the assurance to deny publicly facts which are common knowledge. These tactics constrain me here, against my will, to raise the artistic veil which they have cast over the whole proceedings, and to mention some details which throw light on the character of this movement and the mental attitude of its adherents.

If it were really the aim of " Zionism " to bring the people back to Judaism—to make it not merely a nation in the political sense, but a nation living according to its own spirit—then the Congress would not have postponed questions of national culture—of language and literature, of education and the diffusion of Jewish knowledge—to the very last moment, after the end of all the debates on *rechtlich* and *völkerrechtlich*, on the election of X. as a member of the Committee, on the imaginary millions, and so forth. When all those present were tired out, and welcomed the setting sun on the last day as a sign of the approaching end, a short time was allowed for a discourse by one of the members on all those important questions, which are in reality the most vital and essential questions. Naturally, the discourse, however good, had to be hurried and shortened ; there was no time for discussion of details ; a suggestion was made from the platform that all these problems should be handed over to a Commission consisting of certain writers, who were named ; and the whole assembly agreed simply for the sake of finishing the business and getting away.

But there is no need to ascertain the attitude of the Congress by inference, because it was stated quite explicitly in one of the official speeches—a speech which appeared on the agenda as " An Exposition of the basis of Zionism," and was submitted to Dr. Herzl before it was read to the Congress. In this speech we were told plainly that the Western Jews were nearer than those of the East to the goal of Zionism, because they had already done half the work : they had annihilated the Jewish culture of the Ghetto, and were thus emancipated from the yoke of the past. This speech, too, was received with prolonged applause, and the Congress passed a motion ordering it to be published as a pamphlet for distribution among Jews.

In one of the numbers of the Zionist organ *Die Welt* there appeared a good allegorical description of those Jews who remained in the National German party in Austria even after it had united with the anti-Semites. The allegory is of an old lady whose lover deserts her for another, and who, after trying without success to bring him back by all the arts which used to win him, begins to display affection for his new love, hoping that he may take pity on her for her magnanimity.

I have a shrewd suspicion that this allegory can equally well be applied, with a slight change, to its inventors themselves. There is an old lady who, despairing utterly of regaining her lover by entreaties, submission and humility, suddenly decks herself out in splendour and begins to treat him with hatred and contempt. Her object is still to influence him. She wants him at least to respect her in his heart of hearts, if he can no longer love her. Whoever reads *Die Welt* attentively and critically will not be able to avoid the impression that

the Western "Zionists" always have their eyes fixed
on the non-Jewish world, and that they, like the
assimilated Jews, are aiming simply at finding favour in
the eyes of the nations : only that whereas the others
want love, the "Zionists" want respect. They are
enormously pleased when a Gentile says openly that the
" Zionists " deserve respect, when a journal prints some
reference to the "Zionists" without making a joke of
them, and so forth. Nay, at the last sitting of the Congress
the President found it necessary publicly to tender special
thanks to the three Gentiles who had honoured the
meeting by taking part in it, although they were all
three silent members, and there is no sign of their having
done anything. If I wished to go into small details, I
could show from various incidents that in their general
conduct and procedure these "Zionists" do not try to
get close to Jewish culture and imbibe its spirit, but that,
on the contrary, they endeavour to imitate, as Jews, the
conduct and procedure of the Germans, even where they
are most foreign to the Jewish spirit, as a means of
showing that Jews, too, can live and act like all other
nations. It may suffice to mention the unpleasant incident at Vienna recently, when the young "Zionists"
went out to spread the gospel of "Zionism" with sticks
and fisticuffs, in German fashion. And the Zionist organ
regarded this incident sympathetically, and, for all its
carefulness, could not conceal its satisfaction at the
success of the Zionist fist.

The whole Congress, too, was designed rather as a
demonstration to the world than as a means of making
it clear to ourselves what we want and what we can do.
The founders of the movement wanted to show the outside world that they had behind them a united and

unanimous Jewish people. It must be admitted that from beginning to end they pursued this object with clear consciousness and determination. In those countries where Jews are preoccupied with material troubles, and are not likely on the whole to get enthusiastic about a political ideal for the distant future, a special emissary went about, before the Congress, spreading favourable reports, from which it might be concluded that both the consent of Turkey and the necessary millions were nearly within our reach, and that nothing was lacking except a national representative body to negotiate with all parties on behalf of the Jewish people : for which reason it was necessary to send many delegates to the Congress, and also to send in petitions with thousands of signatures, and then the Committee to be chosen by the Congress would be the body which was required.[1] On the other hand, they were careful not to announce clearly in advance that Herzl's Zionism, and that only, would be the basis of the Congress, that that basis would be above criticism, and no delegate to the Congress would have the right to question it. The Order of Proceedings, which was sent out with the invitation to the Congress, said merely in general terms that anybody could be a delegate "who expresses his agreement with the *general* programme of Zionism," without explaining what the general programme was or where it could be found. Thus there met at Basle men utterly at variance with one another in their views and aspirations. They thought in their simplicity that everybody whose gaze was turned Zion-

[1] The fact mentioned is familiar to many *Chovevé Zion* in all the towns which the emissary visited with a letter from the headquarters of the movement. In my Note I only alluded to it briefly, and I am sorry that the denials of my opponents have compelled me here to refer to it again more fully.

wards, though he did not see eye to eye with Herzl, had done his duty to the general programme and had a right to be a member of the Congress and to express his views before it. But the heads of the Congress tried with all their might to prevent any difference of opinion on fundamental questions from coming to the surface, and used every "parliamentary" device to avoid giving opportunity for discussion and elucidation of such questions. The question of the programme actually came up at one of the preliminary meetings held before the Congress itself (a *Vorkonferenz*); and some of the delegates from Vienna pointed to the statement on the Order of Proceedings, and tried to prove from it that that question could not properly be raised, since all the delegates had accepted the general programme of Zionism, and there was no Zionism but that of Vienna, and *Die Welt* was its prophet. But many of those present would not agree, and a Commission had to be appointed to draw up a programme. This Commission skilfully contrived a programme capable of a dozen interpretations, to suit all tastes; and this programme was put before Congress with a request that it should be accepted as it stood, without any discussion. But one delegate refused to submit, and his action led to a long debate on a single word. This debate showed, to the consternation of many people, that there were several kind of " Zionists," and the cloak of unanimity was in danger of being publicly rent asunder; but the leaders quickly and skilfully patched up the rent, before it had got very far. Dr. Herzl, in his new pamphlet, uses this to prove what great importance Zionists attached to this single word (*völkerrechtlich*). But in truth similar " dangerous " debates might have been raised on many other words.

For many delegates quite failed to notice the wide gulf between the various views on points of principle, and a discussion on any such point was calculated to open people's eyes and to shatter the whole structure to atoms. But such discussions were not raised, because even the few who saw clearly and understood the position shrank from the risk of " wrecking." And so the object was attained; the illusion of unanimity was preserved till the last; the outside world saw a united people demanding a State; and those who were inside returned home full of enthusiasm, but no whit the clearer as to their ideas or the relation of one idea to another.

Yet, after all, I confess that Western " Zionism " is very good and useful for those Western Jews who have long since almost forgotten Judaism, and have no link with their people except a vague sentiment which they themselves do not understand. The establishment of a Jewish State by their agency is at present but a distant vision; but the idea of a State induces them meanwhile to devote their energies to the service of their people, lifts them out of the mire of assimilation, and strengthens their Jewish national consciousness. Possibly, when they find out that it will be a long time before we have police-men and watchmen of our own, many of them may leave us altogether; but even then our loss through this move-ment will not be greater than our gain, because undoubtedly there will be among them men of larger heart, who, in course of time, will be moved to get to the bottom of the matter and to understand their people and its spirit : and these men will arrive of themselves at that genuine *Chibbath Zion* which is in harmony with our national spirit. But in the East, the home of refuge of Judaism and the birthplace of Jewish *Chibbath Zion,* this " political " tendency can bring us only harm. Its attractive force is at the same time a force repellent to the moral ideal which has till now been the inspiration of Eastern Jewry. Those who now abandon that ideal in exchange for the political idea will never return again, not even when the excitement dies down and the State is not established : for rarely in history do we find a movement retracing its steps before it has tried to go on and on, and finally lost its way. When, therefore, I see what chaos this movement has brought into the camp of the Eastern *Chovevé Zion*—when I see men who till recently seemed to know what they wanted and how to get it, now suddenly deserting the flag which but yesterday they held sacred, and bowing the knee to an idea which has no roots in their being, simply because it comes from the West : when I see all this, and remember how many paroxysms of sudden and evanescent enthusiasm we have already experienced, then I really feel the heavy hand of despair beginning to lay hold on me.

It was under the stress of that feeling that I wrote my Note on the Congress, a few days after its conclusion. The impression was all very fresh in my mind, and my grief was acute ; and I let slip some hard expressions, which I now regret, because it is not my habit to use such expressions. But as regards the actual question at issue I have nothing to withdraw. What has happened since then has not convinced me that I was wrong : on the contrary, it has strengthened my conviction that though I wrote in anger, I did not write in error.

PINSKER AND POLITICAL ZIONISM

*(To the memory of Dr. Pinsker, on the tenth anniversary
of his death)*

(1902)

The 21st of December last (1901) was the tenth
anniversary of the death of Dr. Leo Pinsker.

A decade is a long time in our days, when everything
keeps changing with extraordinary rapidity ; when events
come pell-mell, pushing and jostling one another, with a
new sensation every day ; when men rise and fall one
after the other, famous to-day and forgotten to-morrow,
rising to the top in an hour, and going under in
the next ; when the tumult of to-day is so loud that men
have no time to pause and look calmly back on
yesterday.

Pinsker is one of those men of yesterday, whom the
men of to-day have already had time to forget.   He
died ten years ago, and in these ten years things have
changed, and we with them.   New birds have come and
brought new songs.   They pipe in a loud and strident
chorus, in the din of which who shall remember the
forlorn lay of a lonely songster whom earth knows no
more ?

In his day Pinsker was head of the *Chovevé Zion,* and
he worked hard for Palestinian colonisation.   But in the
interval *Chibbath Zion* itself has given place to Zionism.

90

Petty colonisation, the result of the "infiltration" policy, which absorbed the time and energy of Pinsker and the *Chovevé Zion* of yesterday, is to-day a source of merriment even for the merest tyro in Zionism. Everybody knows that Herzl has enlarged the narrow horizon of his predecessors by basing the Zionist ideal on a broader foundation—on politics and diplomacy, on the Bank and the Charter.

Twenty years ago Pinsker wrote a small pamphlet of thirty-six pages, called *Auto-Emancipation*. In its day this pamphlet made a certain stir and evoked some response. But who pays attention now to a little pamphlet that dates from before the new dispensation? Have we not now the *Judenstaat,* and Reports of four Congresses, full of debates and speeches, as well as a heap of pamphlets and leaflets in every language, explaining and expounding Zionism in every aspect and every detail?

Yes—Pinsker was a great man in his day; he was one of the "precursors" of Zionism—so much even the new Zionists admit. And when they have occasion to recount the history of the Zionist idea to non-Zionists, they begin, in the most approved scientific manner, with the "embryonic" period. Here they commend in one breath all the worthy men who came before the birth of Zionism and prepared the way for it, not forgetting Pinsker and other leaders of the *Chovevé Zion* who were contemporary with him. But all this is for them simply by way of introduction to the main theme, which enters with the year 1896—the year when Herzl revealed himself in his pamphlet *Der Judenstaat*. Here they draw a line, as who should say, "Thus far the embryonic period of Zionism, the period of its preparation for birth. Now behold Zionism itself in all its glory and magnificence."

How is it, then, that many people have now suddenly remembered that Pinsker died ten years ago, on the 21st of December; and that in so many places there have been prayers recited for the peace of his soul, and memorial addresses delivered in his honour, on this sad anniversary? Truth to tell, it is only because the work of the "petty colonisation" movement still maintains its existence, and there is still a Society which works for the support of the colonies. For that reason, and for that reason alone—because he stood at the head of those who worked for the Palestinian Colonies, and afterwards of the Society formed for their support—Pinsker is remembered by his colleagues, the original *Chovevé Zion* of his own country, whose privilege it was to know him personally and to work with him. It is they who have made the anniversary a matter of public interest. If not for this, the new Zionists, whose calendar begins with the birth of political Zionism, would not have remembered the man who, fifteen years before Herzl, worked out the whole theory of political Zionism from beginning to end, with a logical thoroughness and an elevation of style unequalled by any subsequent work.

How indeed should these new Zionists remember him, seeing that they know nothing at all of Pinsker as the author of the theory of political Zionism? And whence should they know of him, if their leaders have never yet told them, explicitly or by implication, in print or on the platform, in Zionist Congresses or outside them, who was the true author of that theory, the real if unacknowledged fountain from which all who came after him have drunk?[1] Pinsker's pamphlet in the original German is already out of print and rare. While a stream of new pamphlets, mostly poor and tasteless *rechauffés*, is daily poured forth and spread among the people with the assistance of the Zionist organisation and with the concurrence of its leaders, for propaganda purposes, this pamphlet of Pinsker's, which is uniquely capable of attracting intelligent Jews in every country to the Zionist idea, has not been honoured with a new edition to this day;[2] and many of the new Zionists, especially in the West, have never seen it, nor even heard of its value.[3] All that they hear is that there were Zionists even before Herzl, but they were poor, simple-minded dreamers, who—incapable of comprehending a great political idea—thought to solve the Jewish problem by founding a few colonies in Palestine and supporting them with halfpence; and as for Pinsker—well, he was the leader of these poor visionaries.[4]

[1] We hear now that Herzl commended Pinsker and his pamphlet—for the first time—at one of the sittings of the Fifth Congress. That Congress met at Basle some weeks after the *Chovevé Zion* in Russia had given prominence to Pinsker's name on the anniversary of his death. This is evidence that the President of the Zionist Congress still sometimes pays attention to the public opinion of Russian Jewry. But, of course, this does not affect what is said above.

[2] [A second edition was published about a year after the appearance of this Essay. —*Tr*]

[3] Here is an incident which illustrates the extent to which the contents of Pinsker's pamphlet have been forgotten, even in Russia. A short time ago, some of the Jewish periodicals in Russia published a letter of Pinsker's dating from 1883, which was found among the papers of the Odessa Committee. The letter contains only a few headings of the ideas which are explained in detail in his pamphlet. But the periodicals were surprised, and found it necessary to remark that it appeared *from this letter* that so long as twenty years ago Pinsker had " foreseen, as it were," the Zionist movement of our day.

[4] In Austria the *Chovevé Zion* used to call themselves " Zionists " long before Herzl's time. I believe that Dr. Birnbaum invented the name in his journal *Selbst-Emanzipation*. Herzl mentions the " Zionists " a few times in his brochure, and satirically represents them as trying to raise a heavy load by the steam of a tea-kettle (*Judenstaat*, p. 4).

I doubt whether the time has yet come to restore to Pinsker the place of honour in the Zionist movement that belongs to him of right.   We are in the thick of the tumult and the shouting, and as yet there is no room for a true and unbiassed judgment.   That must be left for later history, for the time when " the tumult and the shouting dies," and the influence of personality and fleeting circumstance gives place to a national *motif* more general in scope and more permanent in character.   But as the memory of Pinsker is now in the public mind—be it but for a moment—we may not improperly take advantage of the opportunity to recall the message which Pinsker brought to his people, but for which he has not yet received the credit.

That message is, as I have said, the message of *political* Zionism.   Pinsker was the first to lay down a clear theoretical basis for political Zionism.   He was also the first to work out—though only in outline—a definite practical programme for the realisation of the idea.   It is this programme, or the fundamental points in it, that the new Zionists have laid hold on ; it is because of this programme that they call themselves " political," denoting thereby, as they believe, the original feature which distinguishes them from their predecessors.   Pinsker compressed all his teaching, theoretical and practical as well, into his one small pamphlet, which is characterised by conciseness of style and absence of systematic arrangement.   His outraged feelings were too strong for the cold processes of thought, and did not allow him to arrange his ideas systematically.   Pinsker did not write a scientific treatise ; he uttered a loud, bitter, heart-felt cry, fraught with indignation and grief at our external and internal degradation.   For that reason he must be studied with close attention before one can put together the scattered fragments of ideas—some repeated time and again with a wealth of poetic eloquence, others no more than briefly hinted at by the way—and discover the full import of his teaching.

This is what I propose here to attempt. But first of all I must point out—what might not be self-evident to all my readers—that my object is only to explain Pinsker's teaching in its relation to present-day political Zionism. I am not here giving a statement of my own views on political Zionism in general. What I had to say on that subject has been said in various essays, which will be familiar to many of my readers; and these previous utterances absolve me, I think, from the necessity of commenting here on every point with which I am not in agreement. In this essay I take for granted the fundamental standpoint of political Zionism, which was Pinsker's standpoint also, though, as we shall soon see, he gave it a peculiar turn, making it approximate more to that Zionist ideal which is nowadays called " spiritual Zionism."

Pinsker, like all subsequent political Zionists, arrived at the idea of Zionism not through the problem of Judaism—through the necessity of seeking for a new foundation for our national existence and unity, in place of the old foundation, which is crumbling away—but through the problem of Jewry—through a definite conviction that even emancipation and general progress will not improve the degraded and insecure position of the Jews among the nations, and that anti-Semitism will never cease so long as we have not a national home of our own. But it is worth while to examine particularly the way in which he arrived at this conviction of the eternity of the feud between Israel and the nations, because it is a different way from that of the later Zionists, and it is this difference that gives a peculiar colouring to Pinsker's message.

Pinsker finds three principal causes which lead to our being hated and despised more than any other human beings ; and for each of the three there is no remedy except a separate Jewish State.

The first cause is a national one, and its roots lie deep in human psychology. We cannot know whether that great day will ever arrive when all mankind will live in brotherhood and concord, and national barriers will no longer exist ; but even at the best, thousands of years must elapse before that Messianic age. Meanwhile nations live side by side in a state of *relative* peace, which is based chiefly on the fundamental equality between them. Each nation, that is, recognises and admits the national existence of the other nations, and even those which are at enmity or even at war with one another are forced to recognise each other as equals, standing on the same plane of nationhood, and therefore entertain each for the other a certain feeling of respect, without distinction between large nation and small, strong and weak. But it is different with the people of Israel. This people is not counted among the nations, because since it was exiled from its land it has lacked the essential attributes of nationality, by which one nation is distinguished from another—has lacked " that original national life which is inconceivable without community of language and customs and without local contiguity." It is because we lack these attributes that the other nations do not regard us as on the same plane with themselves, as a nation equal to them in integral value. True, we have not ceased even in the lands of our exile to be *spiritually* a distinct nation; but this spiritual nationality, so far from giving us the status of a nation in the eyes of the other nations, is the very cause of their hatred for us as a people. Men are always terrified by a disembodied spirit, a soul wandering about with no physical covering; and terror breeds hatred. This is a form of psychic disease which we are powerless to cure. In all ages men have feared all kinds of ghosts which their imaginations have seen; and Israel appears to them as a ghost—but a ghost which they see with their very eyes, not merely in fancy. Thus the hatred of the nations for Jewish nationality is a psychic disease of the kind known as " demonopathy "; and having been transmitted from generation to generation for some two thousand years, it has by now become so deep-rooted that it can no longer be eradicated. The primary object of this hatred is not Jews as individuals, but Judaism— by which is meant that abstract nationality, that bodiless ghost, which wanders about among the real nations like something apart and different, and arouses their latent faculty of demonophobia. Hence we see on the one hand that individual Gentiles live in peace and amity with their Jewish acquaintances, while retaining their deep-seated animosity against Jews as a people, and on the other hand that, throughout all the periodical changes of national tendencies and international relations, all nations remain at all times the same in their hatred of the Jews, just as they remain always the same in their hatred of the other kinds of ghosts in whose existence they believe.[1]

[1] *Autoemancipation*, pp. 1-7 [7-11 in the second edition, 1903. —*Tr.*]

What, then, must we do to escape from this national hatred?

Assimilate with the nations? If real assimilation be meant—the assimilation that reaches to the very soul and ends in annihilation—that is a kind of death which does not come of itself, and we do not wish to bring it on by our own efforts.[1] But the surface assimilation which is the panacea advocated by a certain section of Jews can only make matters worse for us. Pinsker himself does not draw this conclusion in so many words; but it is a necessary consequence of the idea just mentioned. For, seeing that the source of anti-Semitism lies in our lack of a concrete national existence, which would compel the other nations to recognise in us a nation equal to themselves in status, it follows plainly that the more we assimilate—the more we imitate our surroundings and whittle away our national distinctiveness—the less concrete and the more spiritual will our national existence become; and the more, therefore, will the ghost-fear which begets anti-Semitism grow in intensity.

There remains, then, but one means of destroying anti-Semitism. We must become again a real nation, possessed of all those essential attributes of nationality by virtue of which one nation is the equal of another. These attributes are those mentioned above—a common land, a common language and common customs. It is the combination of these that makes " an original national life."[2]

---

[1] *ib*. p. 15 [17.]

[2] Pinsker died before the days of what is now called " spiritual nationalism," the view which denies the need for a distinct national territory, believing it possible that sooner or later we shall obtain equal rights in the lands of our dispersion *as a nation* : that is, shall be allowed to carry on our distinctive *national* life in these lands, just as we have already obtained equal rights, *as citizens*, in many

The second cause of our degradation is political in character. "Generally speaking," says Pinsker, "we do not find any nation over-fond of the stranger. This is a fact which has its foundation in ethnology, and no nation can be blamed for it." Now since the Jew is everywhere regarded as a stranger by the native population, we should have no right to grumble if our hosts in the various countries treated us like other strangers who settle permanently among them. But in fact we find that people everywhere dislike Jews much more than other strangers. Why is this? For the same reason— replies Pinsker—for which men behave in different ways to a well-to-do guest and to a penniless beggar. The first comes as an equal; he too has a house in which he gives hospitality—no matter whether we ourselves or others enjoy it—and therefore we recognise it as our duty to give him a welcome, even if we are not altogether delighted with his company; while he on his side is conscious that he has a right to demand such treatment as the conventions of polite society dictate, just as in his own house he extends that treatment to others. Not so the homeless mendicant. He on his side is free from the obligations of hospitality, since he has no opportunity of

countries: that is, have been allowed to take part in social and political life like the other inhabitants. But Pinsker lays the foundation for this view, by demanding—for the first time—*national* equality, and substituting the formula of spiritual nationalism: "the same rights for the Jewish *nation* as for the other *nations*" (" die Gleichstellung der jüdischen Nation mit den anderen Nationen "— *Autoemancipation,* p. 7 [11]) for the older formula of the protagonists of emancipation: "the same rights for Jews as for the other citizens." It is, however, fundamental to Pinsker's view that national equality is unattainable so long as we lack the concrete attributes of nationality. A nation which is a nation only in the spiritual sense is a monstrosity which the other nations cannot possibly regard as their compeer; it follows that they cannot recognise its title to demand the same rights as those enjoyed by the real nations.

fulfilling them. Hence his request for our hospitality is a request for pure charity. It is not the appeal of an equal to the principle of equality of rights and duties ; it is the appeal to compassion of one weaker and humbler than ourselves, who can receive but cannot give. Hence, even if we are so compassionate as to welcome the poor man and treat him with affection and respect, like one of ourselves, the equality is only one of external appearance. In our heart of hearts we feel, and he feels too, that we are doing him a kindness, that we are treating him well out of our goodness of heart, and doing something that we might have forborne doing if not for our charitable and benevolent disposition. This feeling alone suffices to create a wide gulf between us, and to lower his worth in our estimation and his own.

Which picture represents Israel among the nations ? Not that of the well-to-do guest ; for Israel has no place of his own where he can fulfil the obligations of hospitality towards other nations. Israel is like the mendicant who goes from door to door, asking others to give him what he does not give to others. And therefore the other nations do not regard the Jew as their equal, and do not recognise any duty to show him that decent behaviour which they practise towards all the other foreigners who live among them. If, then, they are kind enough to make room for him, it is only by an act of charity, which degrades the recipient. When their generosity goes to the furthest extreme, they give the poor visitor the greatest boon that they can give— that of equal rights. But the mere fact that the grant of equal rights is an act of generosity, and not a duty based on the real equality of the two parties, robs the boon of its moral value, and makes it merely a piece of legislative machinery. The giver can never forget that he is the giver, nor the receiver that he is the receiver. For this reason Jewish emancipation in all countries has been and must always remain political only, not social. The Jew enjoys equal rights as a citizen, but not equality as a man, as one who takes his part in the intimate life of society. The non-Jew and the Jew alike are conscious of this fact, and so, despite his equal rights, the Jew remains an inferior even in his own estimation, and in non-Jewish society he endeavours to hide his Judaism, and is grateful to non-Jews when they do not remind him of his origin, but behave as though it were a matter of indifference to them.

The conclusion is that the Jews can never attain to true social equality in Gentile countries unless they cease to be always recipients and rise to the rank of respectable visitors, who can give to others what they ask for themselves. In other words, the Jews must once more possess themselves of a native land of their own, where they will be masters and hosts. Then their place in the estimation of other nations will improve automatically, and wherever they set foot they will be regarded as equals by the natives, who will consider themselves in duty bound to treat the Jews with the same respect which they show to other strangers who come to stay among them.[1]

Besides the two causes explained above, there is a third cause, economic in character, which gives a practical turn to Gentile hatred of the Jew, and brings it into actual operation in the form of physical restriction and persecution.

In the life of civilised nations the struggle for existence

[1] *ib*. pp. 7-10 [11-13]

assumes the form of peaceful competition.   In this
sphere every State distinguishes to a certain extent between the native and the stranger, and gives the native
preference where there is not room for both.   This discrimination is practised even against the honoured
stranger, whom the native regards as his equal; and it
stands to sense that there will be a vastly greater amount
of discrimination against the poor vagrant, whose
existence in the State is tolerated only out of kindness
and charity.   If you have a large house, with room
enough and to spare for your family and for respectable
visitors, you do not begrudge the beggar his corner, but
let him live with you as long as he likes.   But when the
family grows and the house begins to feel cramped you
will at once look askance at the beggar-guests, whom
you are under no obligation to respect or to feed.   And
if you see that they do not squeeze up and make room for
you, but, on the contrary, endeavour to get more elbow-
room for themselves, regardless of the fact that they are
crowding you, then you will resent the impudence with
which they forget their place, and in the heat of anger
you will turn them out neck and crop, or at least drive
them back into their own corner, make it as small as
possible and confine them rigidly to it for the future.
But the respectable guests will still be treated with
deference, and though you may secretly dislike them for
occupying valuable room, you will not permit yourself to
overstep the limits of politeness and to turn them out into
the street, save in exceptional cases where they themselves overstep the mark and your patience gives out.

Thus we find that even where the number of Jews is
small, they bring down on themselves the resentment
and hatred of their neighbours because of their success in

the struggle for existence, and the advantage which
their ability and pertinacity gain for them over their competitors in the various walks of life ; and where the
Jewish settlement is considerable, anti-Semitism finds its
food—even without any success on the Jewish side—in
the mere fact of their existence : for their existence is
bound, poor and cramped though it be, to lead to competition which their neighbours will feel.   In either case
the native population does not consider itself obliged to
restrain its feelings and behave with perfect politeness to
a miserable nation which is allowed to live among the
other nations only on sufferance, and is so ungrateful as
to jostle its benefactors without shame.[1]

This cause also, then, cannot be removed except
through the removal of the other causes mentioned
before.   We must build a house for ourselves, and then,
even in foreign countries, we shall have the position of
respected guests, and our competition with the native
population will not arouse their resentment and jealousy
more than the competition of other strangers.   But the
economic cause differs from the other causes. Our national
and political degradation is a moral fact, and requires
only a moral remedy—that we stand higher in the
estimation of the world, as a nation with a concrete life
of its own, and with a land in which it can extend to
others that hospitality which it receives elsewhere.   But
in order to remove the economic cause we must of
necessity diminish the competition between Jew and non-
Jew in places where that competition is excessive.   For
even the respected guest has economic freedom only
within certain limits.   If he oversteps these limits, and
his competition presses too hard on the native, the native

[1] *ib.* pp. 10-11 [13-14 —*Tr.*]

is forced to protect himself, either by legislative restriction of the foreigner's rights, or sometimes even by force. It follows that if we succeed in establishing a separate State for our people, the two first causes of anti-Semitism will be removed, even if the State is very small, and even if most of the Jews remain where they are, and only a very small minority goes to settle in our State. For the mere fact of the existence of a Jewish State, where Jews would be masters, and their national life would develop on lines of its own in accordance with their spirit—this fact alone would suffice to remove from us the brand of inferiority, and to raise us in the world's estimation to the level of a nation equal in worth to the other nations, sharing alike their privileges and their duties ; and the attitude of the other nations to us would no longer be different from their attitude to each other. But the economic cause, though its working may be mitigated to some extent when the wandering mendicant is transformed into a well-to-do guest, cannot be got rid of until the number of Jews in every country declines to the limit dictated by the economic condition of the native population. Until that time hatred of these foreign competitors will continue, and the native population will continue to persecute them with restrictive laws and even with violence, even though there exist somewhere or other a separate Jewish State, and even though all nations respect the Jewish nationality which has in that State its concrete expression.

Thus we arrive at a further condition of the solution of our problem. What we need is not simply a State, but a State to which the majority of the Jews will emigrate from all their present homes—to such an extent that their numbers in every country will decline to the extent demanded by local conditions—and a State extensive enough and materially rich enough to maintain so large a population.

And here we come to the Achilles' heel of political Zionism.   Granted that we have it in our power to establish a Jewish State : have we it in our power to diminish thereby the number of Jews in every country to the maximum which the economic condition of the country can bear without their arousing anti-Semitism ? This question the opponents of the new Zionism, which promises *to put an end to the Jewish problem* by the establishment of the State, are continually asking : but so far we have not received from the Zionists a clear and satisfactory answer.   During the last twenty years, for instance, at least a million Jews have left Eastern Europe for America and Africa.   That is a very large number, sufficient for the establishment of a Jewish State.   Yet this emigration has had no perceptible effect on the economic condition of the countries from which it has taken place, and the relations between the native population and the Jews in those countries have not improved.   The reason is that the emigration has not in fact lessened the number of Jews in those countries, the loss being always counterbalanced by the natural increase of those who remain.   If, then, Pinsker's idea had been carried out as soon as his pamphlet was published, and all these emigrants had gone not to America or Africa, but to the Jewish State, the State might by now have been successful and flourish-ing, and national life might be developing there in a satisfactory manner, so as to bring great honour to our people wherever Jews are ; but none the less the Jewish problem in the lands whence the emigration proceeded would remain exactly where it was, because economic competition between the Jews and the native population would be just as keen as before, and would still be felt by the latter to an intolerable degree. If, therefore, a Jewish State is really to solve the Jewish problem on its economic side for good and all, then hundreds of thousands must emigrate to it every year from the lands of the Diaspora, so that the diminution in the number of Jews in those lands will be patently perceptible, and their influence on economic life will decrease from year to year, till it ceases to be a cause of hatred and jealousy on the part of the native population. We must therefore ask ourselves first of all, whether it is really possible to transport such a vast number of people in a short time, and to open up for them new sources of livelihood in a new State, wherever it may be. I doubt very much whether any responsible person will answer this question in the affirmative.

But this criticism, which is fatal to the new Zionism, as expounded by Herzl and his followers, does not seriously affect Pinsker's Zionism. The new Zionists make the political and economic problem the be-all and end-all of their strivings. Their primary aim is to improve the hard lot of the Jews *as individuals*. They regard such improvement in exile as out of the question, since Jews are regarded as strangers in every country, and the competition of the stranger exposes him to the resentment of the native population. Hence they demand that the Jews shall establish a separate State for themselves, where they will not be strangers and their competition will not be a crime.[1] But this idea can be justified only if the State is able to improve the lot of all the Jews or most

[1] *Judenstaat*, pp. 24-26.

of them; that is, if all or most of the Jews can leave foreign countries and settle in their State. Unless this condition is fulfilled, the amelioration will be only partial; it will affect only that fortunate minority which succeeds in establishing itself in the Jewish State. The majority will remain as badly off as before—hated and persecuted foreigners in strange lands. Where, then, is the promised annihilation of the Jewish problem through the establishment of the State?

But with Pinsker it is different. The loss which he mourns is primarily the loss of Jewish national dignity. He weeps for a *nation* which is not regarded and re-spected by the other nations as an equal, and whose individual members are·treated everywhere not merely as foreigners, but as beggars in receipt of charity. With him the question of national dignity comes first of all. Of the three causes to which he traces the ill-feeling between Jews and Gentiles, the first one, which lies in the degraded position of the Jews as a nation—a point not mentioned by the new Zionists—is the most impor-tant in his own view, and occupies most of his attention. Next to it stands the political cause; and this cause also, unlike the new Zionists, he regards from the point of view of the problem of national dignity. He is not much troubled by the fact that we are treated as aliens in every country: that fact, no doubt, harms us as individuals, but in·itself it does not imply any contempt or inferiority. The root of the trouble is that we are not treated as aliens in the ordinary political sense, but are regarded as wandering mendicants, as inferior beings, who are not entitled to demand respect and consideration as of right. So with the third cause, the economic one. Its sting lies for Pinsker chiefly in the fact that here also we Jews are differentiated from other aliens—that in consequence of the low esteem in which we are held our competition causes more resentment than that of other aliens.   Pinsker, therefore, has more right than the new Zionists to regard the establishment of a Jewish State as the absolute solution of the Jewish problem—that is, of the problem of the *dignity* of the Jewish nation and of its members, who, even if most of them remain scattered among the nations, and even if they continue to be hated and persecuted in various countries because of their economic competition, will at any rate no longer be exposed to the contempt of their neighbours, and to the taunt that they are not a nation, but a pack of beggars wandering about in a world which is not theirs, and existing only on sufferance.

On the other hand, Pinsker raises another question, which does not trouble the new Zionists very much : the question of the national consciousness.

If we assume, as Herzl does in his pamphlet, that the Jewish State will contain all the Jews, and will offer to every individual Jew the possibility of living comfortably among his people, then we need not be much concerned about the anterior development of the national consciousness as an incentive to the establishment of the State. We have ready to hand another and a stronger incentive in the natural desire of every individual to improve his position.[1]   But if from the outset we accept the fact that even a Jewish State will not absolutely solve the Jewish problem on its economic side, and that the chief purpose for which we need a State is a moral one—to gain for

[1] The question, " What will induce the Jews to found their State and to settle in it?" is answered by Herzl quite simply : " We can trust the anti-Semites to see to that." (*Judenstaat,* p. 59.)

our own nation the respect of other nations, and to create a healthy body for our national spirit—then we are bound to face the question whether the national consciousness is so strong among us, and the honour of our nation so dear to us, that this motive alone, unalloyed by any consideration of individual advantage, will be sufficient to spur us on to so vast and difficult a task.

Now Pinsker, candid here as always, does not conceal from us that, as things are, the national consciousness among us is not nearly strong enough for our purpose. " Our greatest misfortune is that we do not form a nation : we are merely Jews." The *galuth* life has compelled every Jew to put all his strength into his individual struggle for existence ; and in that struggle we have been compelled to use any kind of weapon that came to hand, without enquiring too closely whether it was consistent with our national dignity. Thus, as time went on, both our sense of nationality and our sense of dignity became dulled ; and at last we ceased to feel the need of restoring our dignity, national or individual.[1] We left it to the Deity to perform that ideal task by bringing us the Messiah at the proper time, and buried ourselves in affairs more necessary for our immediate physical survival.[2] Even in modern times, when the breeze of modern culture has blown on us and begun to awaken our dormant sense of dignity, we try to find satisfaction in a strange delusion of our own invention—that the people of Israel has a " mission," for the sake of which it must remain scattered among the nations : " a mission in which nobody believes, a privilege of which, candidly, we should be glad to be rid, if at that price we could wipe

[1] *Autoemancipation*, p. 12 [15].
[2] *ib.* p. 16 [18].

out the name of ' Jew ' as a title of shame."[1] This loss
of self-respect on the one side aggravates the contempt
in which we are held, and on the other side is itself the
greatest stumbling-block on our path of progress. For
what, except a strong national consciousness, can induce
our people to bend all its energies to the task of restoring its national dignity, and to fight unceasingly and
unwearyingly against all the obstacles with which it is
confronted? That those obstacles are many and
serious—this again Pinsker does not conceal from us.
At the best, several generations must elapse before we
can attain our end, " perhaps only after labour too great
for human strength." Only, as we recognise that this is
the one road to our national salvation, we must not turn
back faint-heartedly because of the danger or for
lack of confidence in the success of our efforts.[2]
But such language is intelligible only to a thoroughly
awakened national consciousness, which can intensify
the desire to attain the end in proportion to
the heaviness of the task, can flame up for
one instant in the heart of the whole people, and produce
a " national resolution," a sacred and unbending resolve
to take up the work of revival and to carry it on,
generation after generation, till its completion. And
" where," asks Pinsker, bitterly, " where shall we find
this national consciousness? "

[1] *ib.* p. 19 [20]. As the sequel shows, Pinsker's criticism is aimed
only at those who make the " mission " the moral end of our
dispersion. They think that we can fulfil our mission only if we are
thoroughly scattered : whereas the fact is precisely the reverse. " So
far the world does not regard us as a genuine firm, and allows us
little credit." If, therefore, we really wish to benefit the world by
fulfilling a mission, we must first of all establish our national
position, so as to enhance our credit with the rest of the world.

[2] *ib.* p. 20 [21].

Pinsker found no satisfactory answer to this question. He made this national consciousness a categorical imperative, a *conditio sine qua non;* but he did not show how it was to be supplied.   For this reason the whole of the practical scheme which follows gives one the impression of being formulated conditionally—subject, that is, to the emergence among our people, no matter by what means, of a national consciousness strong enough to enable them to carry out the idea in practice.

Pinsker's practical scheme, as I said above, is only an outline.   But its general lines are very similar to those laid down by Herzl in the pamphlet which is the basis of present-day Zionist policy.

As we cannot hope for another leader like Moses— " history does not vouchsafe such leaders to the same people repeatedly "—the leadership of the movement for national rebirth must be taken by a group of distinguished Jews, men of strong will and generous character, who " by their union will, perhaps, succeed in freeing us from reproach and persecution, no less than did the one great leader.'"   Herzl uses very similar language about this collective *negotiorum gestor,²* and he and Pinsker alike look for its members among the upper-class Jews ; but Herzl has his eye especially on the Jews of England, while Pinsker looks generally to the great organisations already in existence.³   Herzl calls this governing body "the Society of Jews " ; Pinsker calls it " the Directorium."   Herzl pictures the formation of the Society of Jews in a very simple manner.   The best

---

¹ *ib.* p. 26 [25].

² *Judenstaat,* p. 70.

³ He means, apparently, the *Alliance Israélite Universelle* and its sister organisations in England and Austria. The Jewish Colonisation Association had not yet come into existence.

of the English Jews, having approved the project, come
together without any preliminaries, and form a " Society
of Jews." Herzl sees no need to call a National Assembly
first : the general consent which is necessary to give the
Society proper standing with the Governments will come
afterwards spontaneously.[1]   But Pinsker wanted the
various organisations to call " *a National Congress,* of
which they themselves would be the nucleus." Only in
the event of their refusing to do this does he suggest that
they should at least constitute a special " national
institution " called a " Directorium," which should unite
all forces in the national work. The principal and
immediate object of this institution would be " to create
a safe and independent home of refuge for that superfluity of poor Jews which exists as a proletariat in various
countries, and is disliked by the native population."[2] All
other Jews, not merely in the West, " where they are
already naturalised up to a certain point," but also " in
those places where they are not readily tolerated," can
remain where they are. Unlike Herzl, Pinsker does not
think it possible that all the Jews will leave their homes
and go to their own State ; nor is this necessary for his
real object, as I have pointed out above. Economic
pressure is under present conditions causing the " superfluity " to emigrate year by year from every country
where there is a superfluity ; and thousands of Jews leave
their homes because they can no longer maintain themselves. At present these emigrants escape one trouble

[1] Herzl shows, in his pamphlet, no great liking for large meetings,
even for propaganda purposes. " There is no need "—so writes the
founder of the Zionist Congress—" to summon special meetings with
a lot of palaver." (*ib.* p. 57.)

[2] *Autoem.* p. 27 [25-26]. Elsewhere (p. 34 [30]) Pinsker insists that
the home of refuge must be secured by *political* means (" politisch
gesichert.")

to fall into another. They wander from country to country, and find no proper resting-place ; and the large sums of money expended by various organisations on the migration of Jews and their settlement in new homes produce no real benefit, because the new home also is only a temporary lodging. When the number of Jews in the new country reaches the " saturation-point," the journey will have to be resumed ; the Jews must move on to yet other countries. But if we can prepare, while there is yet time, a single secure home of refuge instead of the many insecure ones, the superfluity will gradually find its way thither, and its inhabitants will increase from year to year, till at last it becomes the centre of our national life, though the bulk of the people will remain, as hitherto, scattered in strange lands.

The first act of the " Directorium " would be to send an expedition of experts to investigate and find the territory best suited to our purpose from every point of view. When he wrote his pamphlet Pinsker did not yet regard our historic land as the only possible home of refuge ; on the contrary, he feared that our ingrained love for Palestine might give us a bias and induce us to choose that country without paying regard to its political, economic and other conditions, which perhaps might be unfavourable. For this reason he warns us emphatically not to be guided by sentiment in this matter, but to leave the question of territory to a commission of experts, who will solve it after a thorough and detailed investigation. But on the whole he thinks that the desired territory will be found either in America or in Turkey.[1] In the

---

[1] Herzl also, in his pamphlet, does not decide on a territory ; but he also looks to America and Turkey, and suggests the Argentine or Palestine (*Judenstaat*, p. 29).

latter alternative we shall form a special " Pashalik," the independence of which will be guaranteed by Turkey and the other Great Powers. " It will be one of the principal functions of the Directorium," writes Pinsker, for all the world like an orthodox adherent of " diplomatic " Zionism to-day, " to win for this project the sympathy of the Porte and the other European Governments."[1]

" And then, but not till then," he warns us once again, the Directorium will enter on its work of buying land and organising colonisation. In this work it will need the assistance of " a group of capitalists," who will form " a joint-stock company "—exactly as in Herzl's scheme, where side by side with the Society of Jews there is established the Jewish Company, a company of capitalists, to direct the material affairs of the settle-ment.

Pinsker next proceeds to describe in outline the pro-gress of the new settlement—how the land will be parcelled out in small plots, some to be sold to men with capital, and some to be occupied by men of no means with the assistance of a *National Fund* established to that end ; and so forth. But for our present purpose we need follow him no further. What has been said above will suffice to make it plain to all who wish to see that it was Pinsker who worked out the whole theory of political Zionism, and that his successors, so far from adding any-thing essential to his scheme, actually took away in large measure its ideal basis, and thus so seriously impaired its moral value that they had to have recourse to various promises which they could neither fulfil nor repudiate. This will become abundantly clear to anybody who

[1] *Autoem.* p. 30 [28].

will compare the two pamphlets, Pinsker's and Herzl's.

Pinsker, as we have seen, puts the emphasis on the moral aspect, Herzl on the material. Hence Pinsker wishes to found only a national centre, Herzl promises a complete " ingathering of the exiles " ; Pinsker finds the motive power in a strong national consciousness, Herzl in the desire for individual betterment. For this reason Pinsker does not find it necessary to minimise the difficulties : on the contrary, he repeats many times, with emphasis, that only at the cost of infinite sacrifice will the goal perhaps—mark that "perhaps" !—be reached. Similarly, he recognises that it is not work for one generation alone. " We have to take only the first step ; our successors must follow in our footsteps, with measured tread and without undue haste."[1] Not so Herzl. He is bound to make light of the difficulties, because otherwise he would have to face the question : " If we are looking for betterment as individuals, how can we waste so much energy on a task that will take generations to accomplish, and may not be accomplished at all, when we have so many pressing needs which can be more or less met if we devote that energy to them ? " Hence Herzl is never tired of promising that it will be very easy to carry out his project in a short time, if only we want it. " Let us but begin, and anti-Semitism will at once die down in every country : for this will be our treaty of peace with it. Once let the Jewish Company be established, and the news of it will spread in one day to the ends of the earth, and our position will immediately begin to improve. . . . Thus the work will proceed, rapidly yet

[1] *ib.* p. 35 [31].

without convulsion.''[1] The same difference is evident
in the general scheme of the two pamphlets. Pinsker
devotes most of his pamphlet to showing how low we
have sunk as a nation, and how badly we need a State
of our own to save our dignity. Only at the end does
he explain briefly how he pictures to himself the practical realisation of his idea. This is because from his
point of view the essential thing is that we resolve
that our dignity absolutely demands this course of
action, cost what it may. We have no need to spend
much thought at the outset on the question whether
we shall succeed, or how and when we shall succeed, because, if we suppose that the task is beyond
our strength, we must none the less take it up,
in order to wipe out our reproach. The question of
dignity brooks no calculation. But Herzl deals very
briefly with fundamental principles and reasons,
because, from his materialistic point of view, there is
really no need to enlarge on them. Can anybody doubt
that the position of the Jews in exile is very bad, and
that it would be better for them and for their neighbours
if they went and established a separate State for themselves? Even our "assimilationists" would certainly
agree for the most part, if they only knew with absolute
certainty from the start that the project could be carried
out without too much trouble, "rapidly yet without
convulsion." The root question is, then, whether the
goal can in fact be reached under such comfortable
conditions. For this reason Herzl gives most of his

---

[1] " Eilig und doch ohne Erschütterung " (*Judenstaat*, p. 85). In
one place Herzl says that the emigration of the whole people from
the various countries to its own State will take " some decades "
(p. 27), but does not say how many. Elsewhere he is more definite ;
the emigration will last " perhaps twenty years or perhaps more "
(p. 79).

attention to this question, and explains his practical scheme in minute detail, with the object of showing that it demands no great sacrifices, whether material or spiritual, and that everything from A to Z will be achieved with ease, rapidity and universal satisfaction. All the emigration to the Jewish State, up to the time when the whole people is gathered there, he describes almost as though it were a holiday excursion. And in the State itself everybody lives in comfort and prosperity. Nobody will need to forgo even the minor habits of his ordinary life ; and the immigrant will not even have to miss his friends and relations, because the Jews will leave the different countries in "local groups," and will be settled in their own land on that basis, so that each man can attach himself to the group which is closest to him geographically and spiritually. The working-classes, on whose strength the State will be built up, will work only seven hours a day, and even the Jewish Company, which is to direct the whole work with its capital, will not incur any financial risk, because its investments will be sound and will produce an exceptionally good return.[1]

If, further, we take into account the wide difference between the two pamphlets in style, we may see that Herzl's pamphlet has the air of being a translation of Pinsker's from the language of the ancient Prophets into that of modern journalism.

Yet the name of Pinsker, as the originator of the

[1] It is worth pointing out that Pinsker, too, hints that the company of capitalists, which is to co-operate with his Directorium, may expect a good profit. But as soon as he has mentioned this expectation he adds : " Whether, however, this act of national redemption will be more or less good business or not—that question is not of great moment in comparison with the importance of the undertaking for the future of our people." (pp. 32-33 [30].)

political Zionist theory, is almost forgotten.   He is
mentioned as a rule only in connection with the work of
" petty   colonisation"   in   Palestine,   as   though   his
horizon had been bounded by his activity in that sphere.
Ordinary men, for whom the real is the visible, remember only things that are done : and the thing that
Pinsker did—that to which he devoted all his subsequent work—has really no direct relation to the message
which he began by enunciating.

I have shown elsewhere how it was that Pinsker came
to take part in the work of the *Chovevé Zion,* despite
the political character of his theory.   He understood
perfectly well that their work was very far removed
from the great project of which he dreamt ; but he
understood also that without a "national resolution,"
proceeding from a strong national consciousness, and
without unity and an organisation embracing the whole
people, it would be impossible to carry out his great
idea.   The consent of the Powers, the favour of the
Sublime Porte, even a Charter signed and sealed—all
this cannot help us in the least, so long as we are not a
single people, strong by virtue of our unity and our
indomitable will, penetrated through and through with
a sense of our present national degradation, and prepared to sacrifice our all for a nobler future.   Hence,
when Pinsker saw that national indifference was the
rule in every section of the people ; when he saw how
faint an echo his pamphlet raised in the hearts of the
ruling classes, whom he confidently expected to be the
first to rally to his banner ; and when he saw a small
group of men with insignificant means, or none, put-
ting forth every possible effort to carry out a national
project, small and poor though it was in comparison

with his own ideal—Pinsker could not help lending a hand to those who were engaged in this work, seeing in them the nucleus of an organisation, and the small beginning of the "national resolution." For Pinsker the work done in Palestine was not the beginning of the practical realisation of his programme, but only the beginning of the preparatory stage—the beginning of the revival of the national consciousness, and of the union of the people under the banner of a common ideal. He hoped by means of national action on a small scale to arrive ultimately at that national resolution on the part of the whole people for which he looked in his pamphlet; and then the real work would begin.

It is abundantly clear that this is exactly the course which the new Zionists too are taking to-day, though as yet, it would appear, unconsciously. How great, for instance, is the gulf between the Jewish Company of Herzl's vision—possessing a capital of fifty millions sterling, and undertaking not only to plant the settlers in the Jewish State, but also to sell the property and transact the business of all the Jews in the Diaspora— and the small Bank, with its quarter-of-a-million, which has now been opened, after infinite labour, to carry on some simple and unimportant business operations in Palestine and Russia! Or again, is there any sort of relationship between the Society of Jews which Herzl describes in his pamphlet—a Society which is to stand at the head of the whole people and manage all its national affairs, as Moses did—and the Actions Committee which now stands at the head of the Zionist organisation? And how shall we be brought to the Jewish State—that free State guaranteed by all the Powers—by such minor concessions as it is possible to

obtain now, according to the Zionist leaders, at Yildiz
Kiosk for a certain price? The plain truth is that all
this work, which the new Zionists regard as " political "
work *par excellence,* has as little to do with the theory
of political Zionism as had the petty colonisation work
which Pinsker took up. In the one case as in the
other, the whole value of the work lies in its effect on
the people, which it educates gradually in the direction
of unity, organisation, national resolution. In other
words, we are still, as we were in Pinsker's day, at the
first stage, the preliminary stage of preparatory work.

It must be admitted, however, that in the practical
sphere—even confining that to preparatory work and
propaganda—Pinsker did little, and did not achieve in
his ten years of work half as much as the leader of the
new Zionism has achieved in five years. Pinsker was
purely a theorist : he worked out the theory of Zionism
better and more fully than his successor, but, like all
theorists, he was of little use when it came to practical
work. Men of his type, simple-souled and pure-
minded to a degree, innocent of the tricks and wiles of
diplomacy, knowing nothing but the naked truth—such
men cannot find the way to popular favour. Their
words are too sincere, their actions too straightforward.
Those only can attract the mob and bend it to their will
who can descend to its level, pander to its tastes, and
pipe to it in a hundred tunes, choosing the right one at
the right moment. Pinsker had none of these arts. If,
for example, he had gone to Yildiz Kiosk to negotiate
for the colonisation of Palestine, and had been told
there : " If you have two million pounds you may have
so-and-so ; otherwise—nothing "—what would he have
done? Without a doubt he would have replied at once :

" We have not such a large sum of money, and have at present no prospect of getting it." Then he would have returned home empty-handed, and the public at large would have known nothing of his going or of his returning ; or, if it had been impossible to keep the matter quiet, everybody would have known that "certain steps had been taken " at Yildiz, but had come to nothing. This, of course, would have made a bad impression, and have helped in some degree to weaken the energy of his few supporters. But we all still remember how the Zionist leaders behaved on a similar occasion last year. Leadership on these lines cannot satisfy those who have a liking for the plain truth ; but from a pragmatic point of view it undoubtedly has the advantage. First of all, people heard only the glad news (it " spread in one day to the ends of the earth") that the Sultan had given the Zionist leaders a favour- able reception and made them certain promises, but that the details could not yet be published. This news aroused widespread attention : friends and foes alike waited breathlessly for the curtain to be drawn. Then, after the news had become public property and enlivened the hopes of the Zionists, the leaders made the further announcement that the great promises had been made conditionally, and could not be fulfilled unless they had two million pounds. Everybody who knew the true state of things understood at once—and certainly the leaders understood it, even while they were having audience of the Sultan—that this condition could not be met, so that the promises were mere empty words. And yet the first impression was not altogether effaced, and it served to strengthen in many people the belief that something great could be done if only all sections of the people were ready to put all their strength into it—the kind of belief which is calculated to intensify the energy of the workers, and to spur them on to put forth greater efforts.

In a word : theory and practice are two departments which no doubt depend on each other, but each one needs special abilities and different qualities of mind, which can with difficulty be combined in one man. We must therefore honour every man according to his value in his own department. If I might borrow an illustration from religion, I should say that Pinsker was the originator of the gospel of political Zionism, and Herzl its apostle ; Pinsker brought the new dispensation, and Herzl gave it currency. But it is usual for the apostle to recognise the originator and to acknowledge his greatness : as he spreads the gospel, so he publishes abroad and sanctifies the name of him who brought it. Had the Zionist apostle followed this custom, Pinsker would now have a world-wide reputation, and would be venerated by all whose watchword is Zion. But Herzl would not be satisfied with the practical mission which was in reality his *métier*. He must needs "originate" the gospel itself over again—in an inferior form, it is true—so that it should be all his. Thus the odd result has come about that the further the gospel spreads, the more completely is its true originator forgotten.

But it is not for Pinsker's reputation that I am concerned. In his lifetime he was so far from the desire for notoriety and ascendancy, that I have no doubt that if he were alive to-day, he would rejoice wholeheartedly at the wide vogue given to his idea, and not a shade of displeasure would pass over his face because of the injustice done to himself personally.   My only regret is that Pinsker's wonderful pamphlet has sunk with him, and the Zionist gospel itself has become more superficial and more materialistic.[1] Zionism is a faith, and, like every other faith, it needs one authoritative " Bible," to be conned by the true believers, to be their fountain-head of spiritual influence. At present Zionism has no " Bible." Great as is Herzl's influence with the new Zionists, his pamphlet could not attain that high dignity.   But its general spirit pervades all the other brochures and speeches on which Zionists live, and from which they derive their faith ; and that spirit, as we have seen, is not calculated to raise the masses above material interests, and render them capable of making great sacrifices for a higher national ideal. Pinsker's pamphlet is the only one that is worthy to take the first place in the literature of Zionism, and to be revered by the party as the *fons et origo* of all its views and policies.   If this pamphlet were disseminated among Zionists, and made familiar to them, it would undoubtedly help to educate them in its spirit—a spirit of pure idealism, which sets more store by the dignity of the whole people than by the advantage of the individual, never flinches in the face of danger, is never impatient, and demands no certainty of success.   Then the leaders would not have to be always looking for some means of keeping the fervour up to the required temperature, nor to entangle themselves in exaggerated promises

---

[1] Even in his lifetime Pinsker was not understood, and his pamphlet was not appreciated at its full value. Smolenskin, in his critique, saw nothing in the pamphlet beyond the superficial *Chibbath Zion* which had then a wide vogue in Hebrew literature, and could find nothing to say in its praise except that it was written in German— a language in which " such ideas . . . . . have never been expressed before."

and self-contradictions, which only the blindness of enthusiasm can fail for a moment to detect.

Enthusiasm, however, is a flame which spreads rapidly but does not last. It is only the slow-burning fire, with its steady flame, that can create the enormous strength required for such a national task in many successive generations. For this reason I believe that there will yet come a day when all the external show and parade will no longer satisfy those who thirst for a national ideal; and in that day many will once more remember Pinsker and his pure and lofty message—a message of work without limit and sacrifice without reward, for no other object than to restore the dignity of our people, and to enhance our value for humanity.

SUMMA SUMMARUM*

(1912)

This is a summary not of facts and figures, but of
impressions stored in my mind in the course of sixty
days during which our national work enveloped me in
its atmosphere and engrossed my every thought : ten
days at Basle during the Tenth Congress, and fifty days
afterwards in Palestine.

Fourteen years have passed since I saw a Zionist
Congress (the first), and twelve years since I witnessed
the condition of our work in Palestine. My object in
revisiting both the Congress and the land was not, as
before, to go into details, to collect material, in the
shape of facts and figures, for the solution of certain
practical problems. On this occasion I opened my
mind wide to the different impressions that crowded in
on me from all sides ; I allowed them to enter and to
dissolve of themselves into a single general impression—a kind of mental summary of all that I saw and
heard in connection with our movement and our work in
and out of Palestine. I am of those who stand on the
threshold of age and look back on many long years of
work and struggle, of victories and defeats, of pain and
of joy. A man in this position finds it necessary at
times to turn his thoughts for a while from questions of
detail, and to take a more comprehensive view, so that
he may find for his own satisfaction an answer to that
broad, fundamental question which occasionally disturbs
his sleep : What is the purpose, what the result, of all

*With minor abridgment   125

this work which has occupied your life and consumed your strength?

It was this necessity that took me on this occasion to Basle and to Palestine. And let me confess that it is a long time since I spent such happy days as those of my travels. Not that all is now right with the movement; not that the sun has shone on our work, and driven away the shadows, and spread light and joy everywhere. We are still a long way from such a happy consummation. Even to-day the shadows are many; if they are less in one place, they are more in another. But one fact is becoming increasingly clear: our work is not an artificial product, a thing that we have invented to give the people something to do, as a palliative for the national sorrow. That idea might be entertained if aim and achievement corresponded, if the work were done for the purpose of attaining that result which it is in fact attaining. If that were so, one might doubt whether the attainment of this result were really necessary for the nation, and whether the whole business were not artificial. But that is not the case. Since the beginning of the movement the workers have had one goal in view, and have been unconsciously approaching another. This dualism is the surest sign that the driving force is not reasoning reflection, but something much deeper: one of those natural instincts which work in darkness, and make a man do their will whether he likes it or not, while he believes that his action is directed to the object which his reason has set before him. This driving force is the instinct of national self-preservation. By it we are compelled to achieve what must be achieved for the perpetuation of our national existence; and we follow it—albeit without clear consciousness, and by crooked paths—because follow it we must if we would live. I used to be distressed by this dualism; I used to fear that we might lose the right path—the path of life—through making for a goal to which no path can lead. But now that I have seen the results of the work so far, I have no such fears as to its ultimate fate. What matters it that the work is professedly directed to an object which it cannot attain? *L'homme propose* . . . History does not trouble about our programme; it creates what it creates at the bidding of our " instinct of self-preservation." Whether we ourselves understand the true import and purpose of our work, or whether we prefer not to understand—in either case history works through us, and will reach its goal by our agency. Only the task will be harder and longer if true understanding does not come to our aid.

That is the real state of the case. All that I saw and heard at Basle and in Palestine has strengthened my conviction that the " instinct of self-preservation " slumbers not nor sleeps in the nation's heart. Despite our mistakes, it is creating through our agency just what our national existence requires most of all at present: *a fixed centre for our national spirit and culture, which will be a new spiritual bond between the scattered sections of the people, and by its spiritual influence will stimulate them all to a new national life.*

To miss Basle during the Tenth Zionist Congress was to miss seeing an extraordinary medley of languages and ideas—the result of an internal crisis of which everybody was conscious, but which everybody tried hard not to see. Throughout the Congress there was a struggle between two sections, the " political " and the " practical." You hear the " politicals " declare

that they, too, are really " practical," only that they
do not forget " the political end " ; you hear the "practicals " protest that they, too, are really " political,"
only that they do not forget " the practical means."
And both sections alike protest that the " State " has
really been given up, but the Basle Programme has not
been given up to the extent of a single comma.[1] . . .
In the end the " practicals " won : that is to say, the
essential work of Zionism was pronounced to be the
extension of the Jewish settlement, and the furthering
of education and culture, in Palestine. Thereupon the
victors stood up and promised to guard faithfully the
Basle Programme and " the Zionist tradition developed
during fourteen years."

But all this confusion was only an inevitable consequence of the state of mind in which the two sections
came to the Congress.

The Zionism of the " politicals," most of whom were
brought into the camp not by a heartfelt longing for the
persistence and the development of Jewish nationality,
but by a desire to escape from external oppression
through the foundation of a " secured home of refuge"
for our people—their Zionism is necessarily bound up
with that object, and with that alone : take that away,
and it remains an empty phrase. For this reason they
cannot help seeing that the " practical work " which
their opponents make the basis of Zionism is not calculated to hasten that end which is, for them, the only
end. They still remember the estimate which they

[1] [The first article of the Basle Programme, formulated in 1897,
reads : "Der Zionismus erstrebt für das jüdische Volk die Schaffung
einer öffentlich-rechtlich gesicherten Heimstätte in Palästina." Until
the Ninth Congress (1909) this was generally understood as involving
the creation of an autonomous " Jewish State" in Palestine.—Tr.]

heard in the opening speech of the first Congress : that the colonising work of the *Choveve Zion* will bring the exiled people back to Palestine in nine hundred years ! But the course of events during recent years has destroyed their hope of reaching that goal more quickly by means of that " political" work which is the foundation of " the Zionist tradition." Hence they were in a quandary at this Congress, and did not know how to extricate themselves. They came with empty hands, and professed devotion to an object which there were no means of attaining ; they could only fall back on the hope of a vague future, when external conditions may perhaps become more favourable to " political work." This explains also the excessive shyness which they displayed. They did not go out to battle, as they used to do, with trumpetings and loud alarums ; there was scarcely a mention of those familiar flourishes, which they used to utter with such boldness and vigour, about the salvation which Zionism is to bring to all oppressed and persecuted Jews. Even Nordau, in his speech on the condition of the Jews, changed his tune on this occasion. The whole idea of his speech, which has been given at the opening of every Congress, and has become an essential part of the " Zionist tradition," was to justify Zionism *on the ground of anti-Semitism.* " You see "—such, in effect, used to be his argument— " how perilous is your position all over the world ; there is no way out. And *therefore,* if you wish to be saved, join us, and we will save you." But on this occasion Nordau contented himself with describing the evil, and dealing out reproaches to Jews and non-Jews. The essential thing—the " therefore "—was lacking almost entirely. And throughout the Congress there were heard speeches which openly opposed this Zionism based on anti-Semitism, and the speakers were not shouted down, as they certainly would have been in earlier years.

The " practicals "—mostly Eastern Jews and their Western pupils, for whom national Judaism is the very centre of their being, and who are ruled unconsciously by the " instinct of national self-preservation "—they came to Basle in a very different frame of mind. They brought with them a complete programme of " practical work in Palestine," embracing both colonising and cultural activity ; and they came with a settled conviction that all the various branches of this work were the proper means to the attainment of the end—THE end—the one and only, yet undefined. The "politicals" raised their old question : " Do you honestly believe that the occasional purchase of a small piece of land, the foundation of a tiny colony with infinite pains, a workmen's farm without security of tenure, a school here, a college there, and so forth—that these are the means of acquiring a ' home of refuge ' as understood by the ' Zionist tradition '—a refuge which will end our troubles by ending our exile ? " The " practicals " had no satisfactory answer. None the less, they stood to their guns, and stoutly maintained that work in Palestine is the only road that leads to *the* end : but . . . At this point they broke off abruptly, and did not complete their thought—for a very good reason. They dared not expressly repudiate that article of faith which alone has made Zionism a popular movement—" the redemption of the nation." They dared not recognise and acknowledge that the end of which they speak to-day differs from that of the " Zionist tradition."

What they are working for is not " a home of refuge
for the *people* of Israel," but " a fixed centre for the
spirit of Israel." All branches of the present work in
Palestine, *be it buying land or founding schools,* are
sure means to the attainment of that end, but have
nothing to do with the other. The " practicals " were
inwardly conscious of this truth even while the
" politicals " still had the upper hand, and for this
reason they joined with the " politicals " in fighting it
bitterly and angrily. It was a disturbing factor, of
which they would fain be rid. But now that the star
of " political " Zionism had waned, this conviction had
grown stronger in the minds of the " practicals," and
had become a real driving force. As yet, however, they
lacked the moral courage to intensify this subconscious
whisper into a clear profession of faith. Thus the real
object remained beneath the threshold of consciousness,
while above the threshold there wandered about, like disembodied spirits, here means without an object, there
an object without means ; and imagination tried hard to
combine the two.[1]

But while the " makers of history " inside the Con-

---

[1] It may be worth while to mention here an article written at Basle
during the Congress and printed in the *Jewish Chronicle* (25 Aug.,
1911), as it is a striking example of the confusion of thought which
reigned at this Congress. The writer regards the victory of the "practicals " as an abandonment of the national ideal, and expresses his
surprise that Hebrew occupied so prominent a place at such a Congress. The Herzlian Zionists, he thinks, standing as they do for a
national ideal, naturally desire the revival of the national language ;
but these " practicals," who have turned their backs on the national
ideal, and made Zionism merely a colonising scheme—what interest
have they in the revival of Hebrew? Could not Jews live comfortably in their Colonies in Palestine even if they spoke other languages, like the Jews of the rest of the world?—I should advise those
against whom this argument is directed not simply to dismiss the
paradox with a smile, but to ask themselves how it came about that
their aims could be so misunderstood.

gress Hall were in the dark, it was outside the Hall, among the crowds attracted to Basle by the Congress, that I saw quite clearly what history has really been doing. In the fourteen years since the first Congress we have been joined by a body of Jews of a new kind : men in whom the national consciousness is deep-rooted, and is not measured by *Shekalim*[1] or limited by a Programme, but is an all-pervading and all-embracing sentiment. Jews of this type came to Basle from all the ends of the earth ; they returned to their people out of the gulf of assimilation, most of them yet young in years, able and willing to work for the national revival. When I saw these men—our heirs—outside the Congress Hall, I said to myself : Never trouble about those who are inside ! Let them make speeches and pass resolutions and believe that they are hastening the redemption. The distant redemption may not be any nearer ; but the estranged hearts are drawing near. In spite of all, history is doing its work in this place, and these men are helping, whether they know it or not.

This same historical tendency, dimly discerned at Basle through the dark cloud of words, I found in Palestine clearly revealed in the light of facts. The more I travelled and observed, the more evident it became to me that what is happening in Palestine— despite all the contradictions and inconsistencies—is tending broadly towards a single goal—that goal which I mentioned above. No doubt we have a long journey to travel yet ; but even an untrained eye can see our destination on the distant horizon. If any there be for

---

[1] [The Biblical *Shekel* (plural *Shekalim*) has been adopted as the unit of contribution to the Zionist Organisation. —*Tr.*]

whom the horizon is too narrow, and the goal too petty,
let him go to Zionist meetings outside Palestine : there
he will be shown a wider prospect, with larger aims at
the end of it. But let him not go to Palestine. In
Palestine they have almost forgotten the wider pros-
pects. Realities are too strong for them there : they
can see nothing beyond.

Take the National Bank, which was intended to provide a foundation for " the redemption of the people
and the land " by *political* means. What is the Bank
doing ? Needless to say, its political object has been
abandoned and forgotten. But even in the mere work
of colonisation it neither does nor can achieve great
things. Its business consists—and must consist, if it
wishes to survive—in dealings with local tradesmen,
Jews and non-Jews, and its profits are derived chiefly
from the latter. All that it does for Jewish colonisation,
or all that it could do—if we agree with its critics that
it could do more than it does—without danger to itself,
is so little, that one cannot even conceive any possible
connection between it and the " larger aims," or
imagine it to be moving at all along the road that leads
to the complete " redemption." By this time, apparently, there are many people outside Palestine as well
who have ceased to hope much from the Bank in the
matter of land-settlement; and they now look for the
solution to an Agrarian Bank. But possibly it would
be worth while first of all to examine what little the
existing Bank has done in the way of loans to the
colonies, in order to learn what this experience has to
teach as regards the problems of agrarian credit in
Palestine. It is not enough to adduce examples from
other countries, where the conditions and the people

are different, to demonstrate what agrarian credit can do. Credit is a very useful thing if it succeeds, but a very harmful thing if it fails. Everything depends on local conditions and the character of the people. The existing Bank has followed precedent in its attempts to help the colonies already in existence—and with what success? The colonists will tell you. No doubt I shall be told that I am drawing a false analogy, for such-and-such reasons. But I am not here attempting to express an opinion on this question of an Agrarian Bank, which has already been much discussed, and of which the merits and demerits have been fully canvassed. My purpose is merely to hint at the difficulties of the pro-ject, even if it is carried out on a very modest scale, so as to suggest that it is premature at the present stage, when the Agrarian Bank is not even in sight, to talk about the great things that it is going to do. Our colonisation work in Palestine is carried out under con-ditions of such multifarious difficulty, that even small things have to be done with extreme care, and pre-cedent alone is no safe guide. If the proposed Agrarian Bank is really going to aim high—to aim, that is, at something considerable in relation to " the redemption of the people and the land"—we cannot yet say whether in the end it will help or hurt.'

Then there is the National Fund, and its work for " the redemption of the land " by commercial means, for which purpose it was created. The Fund has already spent a great deal of its money : and how much has it redeemed? How much could it have redeemed if it had spent many times as much? A few scattered pieces of land, lost in the large areas of land not

---

[1] [The Agrarian Bank is still (1921) only a project.]

redeemed. Meanwhile, the price of land in Palestine
is going up by leaps and bounds, especially in districts
where we gain a footing, and the amount of land which
it is in the power of the Fund to redeem with the means
at its command grows correspondingly less and less.
And there is another factor, independent of finance,
which lessens its possibilities still further. Many natives
of Palestine, whose national consciousness has begun
to develop since the Turkish revolution, look askance,
quite naturally, at the selling of land to " strangers,"
and do their best to put a stop to this evil ; while the
Turkish Government—be its attitude to our work whatever it may—is not likely to irritate the Arabs for our
sakes : that would not suit its book. Thus the purchase
of land becomes more and more difficult, and the idea
of " the redemption of the land " shrinks and shrinks,
until no Palestinian whose eyes are open can see in the
National Fund what it was in the imagination of its
founders—the future mistress of all or most of the land
in Palestine. It is clearly understood in Palestine that
many years of hard work, with the help of the National
Fund or by other means, will achieve no more than this :
to win for us a large number of points of vantage over
the whole surface of Palestine, and to make these points
counterbalance by their *quality* the whole of the surrounding area. For this reason, people in Palestine
do not talk much about the coming " redemption" ;
they work patiently and laboriously to add another point
of vantage, and another, and yet another. They do not
ask : " How will these save us? " They all feel that
these points *themselves* are destined to be, as it were,
power-stations *of the national spirit;* that it is not
necessary to regard them as a first step towards " the

conquest of the land " in order to find the result worth all the labour.

Then, again, there are the Colonies already established, which were born in pain and nurtured with so much trouble. They also do not fire the imagination to the pitch of regarding them as the first step towards " the redemption."

Thirty years' experience of the life of the Colonies must finally drive us to the conclusion that while Hebrew Colonies can exist in Palestine, and in large numbers, Hebrew agriculturists—those who are to be the foundation of the " home of refuge "—cannot be made even in Palestine, except in numbers too small to bear any relation to so large an aim. The Jew is too clever, too civilised, to bound his life and his ambitions by a small plot of land, and to be content with deriving a poor living from it by the sweat of his brow. He has lost the primitive simplicity of the real farmer, whose soul is bound up in his piece of ground, whose work is his all, and who never looks beyond his narrow acres : as though a voice from above had told him that he was born to be a slave to the land with his ox and his ass, and must fulfill his destiny without any unnecessary thinking. That agricultural idyll which we saw in our visions thirty years ago has not been and cannot be realised. The Jew can become a capable farmer, a country gentleman—of the type of Boaz—who understands agriculture, is devoted to it, and makes a living out of it : the sort of man who goes out every morning to his field, or his vineyard, to look after his workmen as they plough or sow his land, plant or graft his vines, and does not mind even giving them a hand when he finds it necessary. A man of this type—close to the land and to nature, and very different in character from the Jew of the city—a Jew can become. But at the same time he wants to live like a civilised being; he wants to enjoy, bodily and mentally, the fruits of contemporary culture; the land does not absorb his whole being. This excellent type is being created before our eyes in Palestine, and in time it will certainly reach an uncommon degree of perfection. But of what use is all this for building a "home of refuge"? "Upperclass" farmers of this kind, who depend on the labour of others, cannot be the foundation of such a building. In every State the foundation is the rural proletariat: the labourers and the poor farmers, who derive a scanty livelihood from their own work in the fields, whether in a small plot of their own, or in the fields of the "upper-class" farmers. But the rural proletariat in Palestine is not ours to-day, and it is difficult to imagine that it ever will be ours, even if our Colonies multiply all over the country. As for the present, we all know that the work is done mostly by Arabs from the neighbouring villages, either journeymen, who come in the morning and return home in the evening, or regular labourers, who live in the Colony with their families. It is they who are doing for us the work of the "home of refuge." And as for the future, the number of the Colonies will grow, in so far as it grows, through men of capital, who will found new Colonies of the same "wealthy" type. Colonies for poor men can only be founded by organisations, and their number must be so limited that they can count for nothing in comparison with the need of creating a rural proletariat to cover the whole country and win it by manual labour. Even an Agrarian Credit Bank will not make much difference from this point of view. Such a bank—despite all the great things prophesied for it—will be much better able to help in the foundation of " wealthy " Colonies than to found Colonies for poor men with its own means. Perhaps its inability to increase the number of such Colonies will really be a blessing in disguise. For if they existed in large numbers they must all be full of men quite unfitted for such a difficult task. Only if they are very few can we hope for their survival and development through a process of natural selection, by which the man who has not the necessary qualities will make way for another, and in time these Colonies will gather to themselves all the small body of born agriculturists which is still left among us.[1]

However that may be, this is not the way in which our rural proletariat can be made. It may be said that it will be made in ordinary course in the " wealthy " Colonies, through the natural increase of the inhabitants and the consequent division of the land ; that the sons or grandsons of the farmers will themselves become poor labourers, living by the work of their hands. But experience shows that this, too, is a vain hope. The children who are born in the Colonies have also the cleverness of the Jew. When the son sees that his paternal inheritance will not be sufficient to make him a substantial farmer, and that he is doomed to be one of those pillars of society, the agricultural labourers, he quickly leaves the Colony, and goes to seek his fortune overseas, where he is content to work like a slave, so long as he is free from bondage to the land, and is able to dream of a prosperous future. But it would be doing

---

[1] The Colonies of this type, founded during the last few years, have already been left by many of the first settlers, whose places have been taken by others.

these sons of the Colonies a grievous wrong to imagine
them lacking in love for Palestine. Most of them do
love the country, and long for it, even after they have
left it. Some of them return to it in after years, if they
have succeeded abroad in acquiring enough money to
enable them to settle comfortably in Palestine. But
the trouble is that love of the country alone cannot breed
agriculturists ; for that you must have also love of the
land. The genuine agriculturist feels that leaving the
land is like giving up life. The inherited link between
himself and the land is so strong and deep that he cannot sever it. He therefore prefers to endure poverty
and want, to live all his life like a beast of burden,
rather than to leave the land. But this trait of the
genuine agriculturist disappears gradually even in places
where it exists, so soon as it comes into contact with
a cultured environment. It is clearly impossible to
create it where it does not exist, and most of all in a
people like ours, in which two thousand years of wandering have implanted traits of an exactly opposite character.

There remains, then, only one hope : the young
labourers who come to Palestine with the intention of
devoting their lives to the national ideal, of " capturing
labour "[1] in Palestine and of creating in our existing and
future Colonies that rural proletariat which is so far
non-existent. It is significant that the " labour question " has latterly become almost the central problem
of our colonisation work. It is felt on all hands that
bound up with this question of labour is a still larger
question—that of the whole aim of Zionism. If these

---

[1] [*i.e.*, securing the exclusive employment of Jewish labour on
Jewish-owned land.]

labourers cannot succeed in supplying what is lacking,
that proves that even national idealism is not strong
enough to create the necessary qualities of mind and
heart ; and we must therefore reconcile ourselves to the
idea that our rural settlement in Palestine, even if in
course of time it develops up to the maximum of its
possibilities, will always remain an upper stratum, a
culturally developed minority, with the brains and the
capital, while the rural proletariat, the manual
labourers who form the majority, will still not be ours.
This, of course, involves a complete transformation of
the character and aim of Zionism.   No wonder, then,
that there have been so many suggestions for improving the condition of the labourers. Everybody sees that
so far the labourers have not succeeded very well in
their mission : in recent years many of them have left
the country, while few have arrived there, and the
position of those who remain is insecure.   The general
tendency is to put the blame on certain external
difficulties, and to look for ways of removing those
difficulties—as, by persuading the colonists to give
Jewish a preference over Arab labourers; by making
things more comfortable for the labourers in the matter
of food and lodging ; and many other familiar suggestions.   The Zionist public consoles itself with the
belief that when all these steps are taken the number
of Jewish labourers will steadily increase with the
increase of work, and that as the settlement grows and
the amount of work increases, so will our labouring
rural proletariat increase, and thus the " secure home
of refuge " will be built up by our own hands, from the
foundation to the roof.

Now it seems to me that the time is not very far

distant when the external difficulties will no longer
stand in the way of the labourers, or, at least, will be
reduced to such small proportions that it will no longer
be possible to regard them as an insurmountable barrier.
The National Fund and other institutions are already
trying hard to improve the position of the labourers,
and there is no doubt that little by little everything that
can be done will be done. Even the greatest difficulty—
that of the strained relations between the labourers and
the colonists—is visibly growing less. On the one side,
most of the labourers now see that it is unfair to demand
of any man that he should receive with open arms those
who look down on him and make no attempt to conceal
the hatred and contempt which they feel for him as a
" bourgeois " ; and so they try to adopt a more con-
ciliatory attitude than hitherto. On the other side, the
colonists are beginning to see that it is not only their
duty but also their interest to increase the amount of
Jewish labour in the colonies (there is no need here to
labour this point, which has been often made before) ;
and so we see in the colonies the development of a
certain tendency to employ Jewish labour as far as
possible. It is true that most of the colonies still believe
that the possibilities of employing Jewish labour are
very small (again for reasons too familiar to need explaining here), and an outsider who has paid a brief visit to
Palestine cannot express a definite opinion as to the
soundness of their judgment on this point. Speaking
generally, however, I have no doubt that the more the
colonists become inclined to employ Jewish labour, the
greater will the possibilities automatically become, until
they reach their real limit. But after the removal of
those external difficulties which we ourselves can

remove we shall find out that the way is beset with more
formidable difficulties, which do not depend on our own
will.

In every colony and farm which I visited, I talked a
great deal with the labourers, and listened attentively
to what they said. They expressed many different and
conflicting opinions, and were not always all agreed
even on the most important questions. This notwith-
standing, all these conversations left on my mind one
general impression, and that impression did not
encourage me to believe in the ability of these young
men to accomplish the great task which they had set
before themselves.

These young labourers, who come to Palestine with
the idea of " capturing labour," mostly bring with them
from abroad the hope of becoming independent farmers
after some years of work ; only a few come with the
fixed intention of remaining labourers all their lives.
All alike work for a certain time with enthusiasm and
devotion, but after a while the question of their future
begins to exercise their minds. Those whose hope from
the beginning was to become farmers are, of course,
discouraged when they see how remote is the chance of
attaining their ambition ; that was only to be expected.
But even those who came with the intention of remaining labourers begin to feel that a life such as theirs is
all very well for a time, but is more than they can endure
as a permanency. The civilised man in each one of
them begins to clamour for self-expression, and cannot
reconcile himself to the idea that he must go on digging
or ploughing from morning till evening all his days,
and at best be rewarded for all his toil by a meagre sub-
sistence. So the weaker among them leave the country

with bitterness in their hearts, and the more obstinate remain in the country with bitterness in their hearts; and you may see them wandering from one colony to another, working in one place for a time, then suddenly leaving it for another, not because they want a better job, but because they are restless in spirit and have no peace of mind.

The labourers at present in Palestine may be divided, broadly speaking, into four classes. There are first the unskilled labourers, who do simple work such as digging, and with difficulty earn enough to satisfy their most elementary needs. This class is very far from being contented; many of its members have left the country, many more will leave, and the rest will for the most part pass into the other classes. Secondly, there are labourers who are expert at certain kinds of work (such as grafting) which require skill and care. They earn good money, and their position is not bad. Yet they are mostly anxious to pass into the third class, that of the farmer-labourers, who have each his own small holding in the neighbourhood of some colony, and work on their own land, but eke out a livelihood by working for others in the colony; or—where the holdings are very small—work mostly for others and only a little for themselves. This experiment has been started by various institutions, which have bought land in or near to a colony and have given plots of it to selected labourers. In some places there are labourers who do well with their holdings, and therefore are already hoping that before long they will cease to be labourers and become independent farmers. Fourthly, there are the labourers who have already attained this ideal of becoming independent farmers, and no longer work for others, but are still sometimes counted as labourers because they maintain certain relations with their former "party." The members of this class are few, and most of them are men whom the Jewish Colonisation Association settled in Lower Galilee on the tenant-farmer system. Their holdings are comparatively large, and they have neither time nor need to work for others; on the contrary, they themselves need labour at certain seasons, and then these ex-labourers, having become employers, do not invariably employ Jewish labour!

This last-mentioned phenomenon gave me much food for thought all the time that I was in Palestine. Among these farmers I knew some young men who had previously been regarded as among the pick of the labourers, not only from the point of view of efficiency, but also from that of character and devotion to the national ideal. If these men—I said to myself—could not stand the test, then perhaps it is really impossible for anybody to stand it, and whether it be for the reasons which the farmers suggest, or for other reasons, the fact is there all the same. But when I put this problem to labourers who had not yet become farmers, they replied that these comrades of theirs, when once they had bcome farmers, had lost their proletariat mentality and acquired a different psychology. Then I asked further : " If so, where is the solution ? You yourselves tell me that most of your comrades came to Palestine in the hope of becoming farmers in course of time, and that as this hope grew fainter (because the Jewish Colonisation Association changed its system, and ceased to settle on its land labourers who had not a certain amount of money) the number of new arrivals grew less. But if the labourers come with the hope of becoming farmers,

and then, when they have achieved their ambition, lose
their idealism and employ non-Jews on their own land,
how can you ever 'capture labour,' and what is the
good of your efforts?"

To this question the labourers nowhere gave me a
satisfactory answer! [1]

Such is the condition of "practical work in Palestine,"
and such its relation to " the redemption of the people
and the land." The hope of a future redemption is an
age-long national hope, still cherished by every Jew
who is faithful to his people, whether as a religious
belief or in some other form. Every man can picture
the realisation to himself as it suits him, without regard
to actual present conditions : for who knows what is
hidden in the bosom of the distant future? But if men
set out to achieve the redemption by their own efforts,
they are no longer at liberty to shut their eyes to the
facts. There must be some natural chain of cause and

---

[1] There is a further class of " contractor-labourers," called in
Palestine *k'vutzoth* (groups), who work National Fund land in some
places on a co-operative basis. But the results of this experiment are
not yet clear, and in any case the system cannot be expected to
develop so far as to be able to bring about a radical change in the
labour problem. Recently, too, Yemenite Jews have been coming to
Palestine, settling in the Colonies, and working as labourers ; and
the Zionists are already proclaiming that the Yemenites will build
up the land. But this is another experiment on which judgment cannot yet be passed. Many people in Palestine think that the Yemenites
are not physically strong enough for hard work ; and, moreover, their
level of culture and their mentality are so different from ours that
the question inevitably presents itself whether an increase in their
number will not change the whole character of the settlement, and
whether the change will be for the better.

I have here touched only on the question of the possibility of "capturing labour." But an answer is still awaited to another question—
whether it is proper for us, who are "bottom dog" everywhere, to
aim at a monopoly of labour, and whether they are not right who
maintain that this policy will prove to be our most serious obstacle.

effect between what they do and what they wish to attain. Between " practical work in Palestine " and " the redemption of the people and the land " this chain of causation may be imagined to exist by those who are at a distance ; but in Palestine itself even imagination cannot find it. In Palestine the possibilities of practical work are too clear. It is possible to buy bits of land here and there ; but it is not possible to redeem the land as a whole, or even most of it. It is possible to found beautiful Colonies on the " redeemed" land ; but it is not possible to settle in them more than a very few *poor* Colonists. It is possible to produce in the Colonies an " upper-class " type of agriculturists, whose work is mostly done by others, and perhaps it is possible also to create a small labourer class for the finer kinds of work, which are comparatively easy and well paid ; but it is not possible to create a real rural proletariat, capable of monopolising the rougher, more exacting, and worse-paid kinds of work, which alone can support a rural proletariat with its thousands and tens of thousands.[1]

This being the case, we should expect every visitor to Palestine whose standard is that of the "home of refuge" to return home in grief and despair. Yet every day we find just the opposite. Orthodox Zionists, who wax grandiloquent at home about " the redemption of the people and the land," come to Palestine, see what there is to see there, and return home in joy and gladness, full of inspiration and enthusiasm, as though they had heard Messiah's trumpet from the Mount of Olives.

[1] In Petach-Tikvah, for instance, it is possible for three or four hundred labourers at most to earn a living by the finer kinds of work ; whereas the unskilled labour employs at times thousands.

That is exactly my point. On the surface the Programme is supreme, and all its adherents seem really
to believe that their work is bringing the redemption.
But beneath the surface the unacknowledged instinct of
national self-preservation is supreme, and it is that
instinct that urges them on to work—not for the accom-
plishment of the Programme, but for the satisfaction
of its own demands. When our orthodox Zionist
comes to Palestine, and sees the work and its results,
his whole being thrills with the feeling that it is a great
and a noble thing that is being created there; that
whether it leads to complete redemption or not, it will
be an enormous force for our national preservation in all
the countries over which we are scattered. Then the
" redemption " idea finds its proper level : it becomes
one of those cherished hopes which are not yet ready
to be mainsprings of action ; and the real object, the
object which is actually being attained by practical work
in Palestine, appears large and splendid enough in itself
to provide inspiration and enthusiasm.

My respect for my readers and for myself does not
permit me to explain once more in detail—after more
than twenty years of explanation after explanation—
what exactly is the object to which I allude here. But
I think it no shame to avow that on this occasion I
seemed to myself to see my dream of twenty years ago
in process of realisation in Palestine, though naturally
with differences of detail. What has already been
accomplished in Palestine entitles one to say with confidence that that country will be " *a national spiritual
centre of Judaism, to which all Jews will turn with
affection, and which will bind all Jews together;* a centre
of study and learning, of language and literature, of

bodily work and spiritual purification ; *a true miniature
of the people of Israel as it ought to be* . . . so that every
Hebrew in the Diaspora will think it a privilege to behold
just once the ' centre of Judaism,' and when he returns
home will say to his friends : ' If you wish to see *the
genuine type of a Jew, whether it be a Rabbi or a scholar
or a writer, a farmer or an artist or a business man—
then go to Palestine, and you will see it.' "'[1]

No doubt the time has not yet come, nor will it soon
come, when the traveller returned from Palestine, speaking of the " genuine type of a Jew," can say to his
friends, " Go to Palestine, and you will see it."   But
he *can* say, and generally does, " Go to Palestine, and
you will see it *in the making*." The existing Colonies,
although they depend mainly on non-Jewish labour,
strike the Jew of the Diaspora as so many little generating stations, in which there is gradually being produced a new type of national life, unparalleled in the
Exile. So soon as he enters a Jewish Colony, he feels
that he is in a Hebrew national atmosphere. The whole
social order, all the communal institutions, from the
Council of the Colony to the school, bear the Hebrew
stamp. They do not betray, as they do in the Diaspora,
traces of that foreign influence which flows from an
alien environment and distorts the pure Hebrew form.
Of course, he does not find everything satisfactory and
commendable.   He discovers—if he has eyes to see—
many defects in the communal life and in that of the
individual. Even the schools in the Colonies are still
for the most part very far from perfection ; and even
the much-vaunted predominance of the Hebrew language

---

[1] [The quotation is from an Essay called *Dr. Pinsker and his
Pamphlet*, written in 1892.]

in the Colonies is as yet but half complete—it extends
only to the children.   But everything—he tells himself—is still in its infancy ; the process of free development has only just begun, and it is going on.   Many of
these defects will be remedied in time ; and whatever is
not remedied must be a defect in ourselves, with its
roots in our national character.   If we want to create a
genuine Hebrew type, we must accept the bad with the
good, provided that both alike belong *essentially* to the
type, and that the type itself is not corrupted as in the
Diaspora.   The Jewish visitor travels from Colony to
Colony, and finds them sometimes many hours' journey
from one another, with alien fields and villages in
between.   But the intervening space seems to him
nothing more than an empty desert, beyond which he
reaches civilisation again, and breathes once more the
refreshing atmosphere of Hebrew national life.   Days
pass, or weeks, and he seems to have spent all the time
in another world—a world of the distant past or the
distant future.   When he leaves this world he says to
himself, " If it is thus to-day, what will it be one day,
when the Colonies are more numerous and fully
developed ? "   At such a time he realises that here, in
this country, is to be found the solution of the problem
of our national existence ; that from here the spirit shall
go forth and breathe on the dry bones that are scattered
east and west through all lands and all nations, and
restore them to life.

But from this point of view the term "practical work"
does not apply only to the agricultural colonies.   This
national Hebrew type may have, and indeed has, its
generating stations outside the agricultural settlement.
Many Zionists criticise the Directors of the National

Fund for sinking a good deal of their capital in the building of Jewish quarters in towns (such as Tel-Aviv in
Jaffa). From the point of view of the Programme these
critics are certainly right. The Fund was created for
" the redemption of the land" in the widest sense of
the term, and not for the purchase of small pieces of
urban land, and the erection on them of houses for Jews.
But, as I have said, the work is directed not by the
demands of the Programme but by the promptings of
an instinct. If our visitor from the Diaspora remains
some days in Tel-Aviv, observes its life, and sees the
Hebrew children who are growing up there, he will not
criticise the National Fund for having made it possible
to found such a generating station. He will wish with
all his heart that the Directors would commit the same
fault again, and create similar stations in the other
towns of Palestine.

And need it be demonstrated that the Hebrew schools
in Jaffa and Jerusalem are centres of unremitting activity
in the creation of " the genuine type of a Jew " ? This
educational work, again, does not fit in very well with
the Programme. " What use," it is often asked, " is
there in educating the children in the national spirit,
so long as the land is not redeemed, and the nation does
not come to the land, and many of these very children
may not remain there ? To redeem the land, extend
the settlement, capture labour—that is the way to
realise the Programme. But education ? When the
number of Jews in Palestine is large, national education
will follow as a matter of course. At present we have
no right to use for spiritual purposes the resources
which are needed for more important things." I doubt
whether this criticism can be reasonably and logically

answered on the basis of the Programme.   But what
can logic do when instinct pulls the other way ?   The
very men who promise to bring about the redemption
by means of "practical work in Palestine" are using a
great deal of their energy in educational work in the
country ; and Zionists generally value such work and
turn to it more and more.   To learn why, one has only
to listen to the speeches at a Zionist meeting during a
debate   on   "cultural work" in Palestine.   The
"redeemers" forget for a time the Programme, the
"home of refuge," and all their other catchwords, and
begin to extol "the revival of the spirit," and the
creation of a new Hebrew type.   They prophesy that
this type will in future be a connecting link between all
the scattered parts of the nation.   They point to the
beneficial influence already exerted by the schools in
Palestine on education in the Diaspora.   And so forth,
and so forth.

Eighteen years ago I saw the beginnings of this educational work in Palestine, and I could not then bring
myself to believe that the individual teachers who stood
for the great ideal of a Hebrew education in the Hebrew
language, and had begun to put it into practice with
their limited resources, could really succeed in producing such a spiritual revolution.   But at the same time
I saw how bent they were on the attainment of their
object, and how confident of success : and I said, "Who
knows ?   Perhaps this confidence will be able to work
miracles."[1] Now I have seen that confidence has indeed
worked miracles.   "A Hebrew education in the Hebrew
language" is no longer an ideal in Palestine : it is a

[1] [From the Supplement to an Essay called *Truth from Palestine*
(II), written in 1894. —*Tr.*]

real thing, a natural, inevitable phenomenon ; its disappearance is inconceivable. No doubt there are some
scattered fortresses which have not yet been captured ;
but these, too, will surrender, as others have, to the
demands of the age. Take, for instance, the educational
institutions of the German *Hilfsverein* in Jerusalem,
from the Kindergartens up to the Teachers' Seminary.
All in all, they have sixteen hundred pupils of both
sexes, and these are being trained—despite the still
visible remnant of German education—in the Hebrew
spirit and the Hebrew language. All who know
how things used to be must confess that there has really
been a revolution in Palestine, and that the Hebrew
teacher has won.[1] Of course, there is still much to be
done before the victory can be complete even inter-
nally—that is to say, before Hebrew education can find
the right road in every department, and before its
defects, which are still numerous, can be removed. But
the conqueror has already shown his patience and his
devotion to his ideal ; and we can surely trust him not
to rest until he has so perfected Hebrew education in
Palestine as to make it a worthy model for Jews throughout the world, a standard type of national education, to
which they will endeavour to approximate so far as the
conditions of the Diaspora allow.

Yet another urban generating station of a different kind
has been created of late years, also by the unbounded

---

[1] I cannot refrain from mentioning here a small incident which illustrates the present position excellently. I visited one of the classes of
the Hilfsverein school at Jaffa during the German reading lesson.
The pupils were puzzled by the word *aufheben,* and the teacher tried
to explain it by German synonyms, which they equally failed to
understand. At last the teacher's patience was exhausted, and he
exclaimed angrily, in pure Sephardic pronunciation, "*levatel!*" All
the pupils understood at once !

confidence of an individual; and the Zionists and the
National Fund have not refrained from helping it and
enabling it to live and to develop, although it is very
difficult indeed to bring it within the scope of the Programme. I mean, of course, the Bezalel.[1] True, its
great object—the development of Hebrew art—has so
far been attained only to a slight extent, and it has not
yet touched the higher branches of art. But its achievements in the domain of handicraft justify the belief that
here also confidence will work miracles. Whatever may
happen, the Bezalel has already become the source of a
spiritual influence which makes itself felt in lands far
distant from Palestine. Who can tell how many
estranged hearts have been brought back to their people,
in greater or less degree, by the beautiful carpets and
ornaments of the Bezalel?

All these generating stations, whether in the country
or in the cities, are welded together in our thought, and
appear to us as a single national centre, which even
now, in its infancy, exerts a visible and appreciable
influence on the Diaspora. Hence a man need not
believe in miracles in order to see with his mind's eye
this centre growing in size, improving in character, and
exerting an ever-increasing spiritual influence on our
people, until at last it shall reach the goal set before it
by the instinct of national self-preservation : to restore
our national unity throughout the world through the
restoration of our national culture in its historic home.
This centre will not be even then a " secure home of
refuge " for our people ; but it will surely be *a home of
healing for its spirit*.

And afterwards?

[1] [A Hebrew school of Arts and Crafts in Jerusalem.]

Ask no questions ! In our present state of spiritual disorganisation we have no idea of the volume of our national strength, nor of what it will be able to achieve when all its elements are united round a single centre, and quickened by a single strong and healthy spirit. The generations that are to come afterwards will know the measure of their power, and will adjust their actions to it. For us, we are not concerned with the hidden things of the distant future. Enough for us to know the things revealed, the things that are to be done by us and our children in a future that is near.

AFTER THE BALFOUR DECLARATION

(1920)

When I returned from Palestine in 1912, and my *Summa Summarum* aroused violent anger in various quarters, I wrote an explanatory note by way of supplement to that essay ; and I should like to remind my readers on this occasion of some of the things that I said then, because they seem to me relevant at the present time. ' There must be,' I wrote, ' some natural connection of cause and effect between an object and the means by which its attainment is sought : we must be able to show how this object can be attained by these means. So long as that connection does not exist, so long as we cannot attempt to justify our choice of means except by such vague phrases as " Perhaps . . . . you never can tell . . . . times change . . ."—we may speak of cherished hopes and an ideal for the distant future, but we cannot speak of a *practical* object which can serve as a basis for a systematic plan of work. For every systematic plan of work must necessarily be based on a clear conception (whether intellectual or imaginative) of the chain of cause and effect which connects the various activities one with another, and all of them together with the object. . . . No doubt, we cannot foretell the future ; no doubt it is possible that unforeseen things may happen and may change the face of reality. But a possibility of that kind cannot be made the basis of a systematic plan of work, and we are dealing no longer with an objective of immediate activity, but with a vision of the future.'

About two years after these words were written and
published the world-war began, and led to those results
which we know : ' unforeseen things happened and
changed the face of reality.'   Our own life, too, was
caught in the maelstrom of world-happenings ; and the
face of our own reality, too, was changed as a consequence.   Much might be said, and has already been
said, about the character of these changes, about their
good and their bad side, about their significance both
for the Diaspora and for Palestine.   I cannot now deal
with this subject fully, and I wish for my part only to
say a word or two on one of the principal features of
the changed situation—I mean the widening of the
horizon of our work in Palestine through the famous
Declaration of the British Government, which has
recently been confirmed by the Supreme Council, and
thus has ceased to be merely the promise of a single
Government and has become an international obligation.   This Declaration has provided a new ' basis for
a systematic plan of work,' and has set up ' an objective
of immediate activity '—activity on a large scale, such
as has been hitherto only a theme for the anticipations
of orators and essayists, with no real basis in the
present.   But at the same time the Declaration has
winged anew the imagination of those who were already
accustomed to build castles in the air, without regard
to the realities of this earthly life. That is, I fancy, one
of the reasons why there is still a demand for this book,
though much of its contents does not fit the realities of
to-day.   It is not so much the contents that matter as
the point of view from which I have tried to deal with
the various questions as they arose.   I have tried to
judge not on the basis of that ' you-never-can-tell '

attitude which shrouds itself in the mists of the future,
but on the basis of present realities, or of impending
realities which can be prognosticated from existing conditions. Even to-day this point of view needs reitera-
tion. For once it has happened, as by a miracle, that
what was wildly improbable a short time ago has become
to a certain extent actual : and this 'miracle' has led
those who were always waiting for miracles to claim a
victory, and to insist on maintaining their attitude for
the future also, and on laying down as the one principle
of policy this perverted axiom—that if such a thing has
happened once in exceptional circumstances, its like
may happen again, and we can therefore construct our
world as we please, regardless of present realities, and
relying on a repetition of the miracle when we need it.
There is a Jewish proverb which says : 'A mistake which
succeeds is none the less a mistake.' So a plan of work
which turns its back on realities, and relies on the
possibility that something out of the ordinary may turn
up and change realities to its advantage, is a mistaken
plan, even if it succeeds for once in a way. And if it
goes on banking on the element of chance, which does
in fact interfere occasionally with the normal course of
events, and continues to act accordingly, it will end in
disaster, despite its initial success.

All the details of the diplomatic conversations in
London which led to the Declaration have not yet been
made public ; but the time has come to reveal one
'secret,' because knowledge of it will make it easier to
understand the true meaning of the Declaration.

'To facilitate the establishment in Palestine of a
National Home for the Jewish people '—that is the text
of the promise given to us by the British Government.

But that is not the text suggested to the Government
by the Zionist spokesmen. They wished it to read:
'the reconstitution of Palestine as the National Home
of the Jewish people'; but when the happy day arrived
on which the Declaration was signed and sealed by the
Government, it was found to contain the first formula
and not the second. That is to say, the allusion to the
fact that we are about to *re*build our *old* national home
was dropped, and at the same time the words ' consti-
tution of Palestine as the national home ' were replaced
by 'establishment of a national home in Palestine.'
There were some who understood at once that this had
some significance; but others thought that the difference
was merely one of form. Hence they sometimes attempted
on subsequent occasions, when the negotiations with the
Government afforded an opportunity, to formulate the
promise in their own wording, as though it had not been
changed. But every time they found in the Government's
reply a repetition of the actual text of the Declaration—
which proves that it is not a case where the same
thing may be put equally well in either of two ways, but
that the promise is really defined in this particular form
of words, and goes no further.

It can scarcely be necessary to explain at length the
difference between the two versions. Had the British
Government accepted the version suggested to it—that
Palestine should be reconstituted as the national home
of the Jewish people—its promise might have been
interpreted as meaning that Palestine, inhabited as it
now is, was restored to the Jewish people on the ground
of its historic right; that the Jewish people was to
rebuild its waste places and was destined to rule over it
and to manage all its affairs in its own way, without

regard to the consent or non-consent of its present inhabitants. For this rebuilding (it might have been understood) is only a renewal of the ancient right of the Jews, which over-rides the right of the present inhabitants, who have wrongly established their national home on a land not their own. But the British Government, as it stated expressly in the Declaration itself, was not willing to promise anything which would harm the present inhabitants of Palestine, and therefore it changed the Zionist formula, and gave it a more restricted form. The Government thinks, it would seem, that when a people has only the moral force of its claim to build its national home in a land at present inhabited by others, and has not behind it a powerful army or fleet to prove the justice of its claim, that people can have only what its right allows it in truth and justice, and not what conquering peoples take for themselves by armed force, under the cover of various 'rights' invented for the occasion. Now the historic right of a people in relation to a country inhabited by others can mean only the right to settle once more in its ancestral land, to work the land and to develop its resources without hindrance. And if the inhabitants complain that strangers have come to exploit the land and its population, the historic right has a complete answer to them : these newcomers are not strangers, but the descendants of the old masters of the country, and as soon as they settle in it again, they are as good as natives. And not only the settlers as individuals, but the collective body as a people, when it has once more put into this country a part of its national wealth—men, capital, cultural institutions and so forth—has again in the country its national home, and has the right to extend and to complete its home up to the limit of its capacity. But this historic right does not over-ride the right of the other inhabitants, which is a tangible right based on generation after generation of life and work in the country. The country is at present their national home too, and they too have the right to develop their national potentialities so far as they are able. This position, then, makes Palestine common ground for different peoples, each of which tries to establish its national home there ; and in this position it is impossible for the national home of either of them to be complete and to embrace all that is involved in the conception of a 'national home.' If you build your house not on untenanted ground, but in a place where there are other inhabited houses, you are sole master only as far as your front gate. Within you may arrange your effects as you please, but beyond the gate all the inhabitants are partners, and the general administration must be ordered in conformity with the good of all of them. Similarly, national homes of different peoples in the same country can demand only national freedom for each one in its internal affairs, and the affairs of the country which are common to all of them are administered by all the 'householders' jointly if the relations between them and their degree of development qualify them for the task, or, if that condition is not yet fulfilled, by a guardian from outside, who takes care that the rights of none shall be infringed.

When, then, the British Government promised to facilitate the establishment *in Palestine of a national home* for the Jewish people—and not, as was suggested to it, the reconstitution of Palestine as the national home of the Jewish people—that promise meant two things. It meant in the first place recognition of the historic right of the Jewish people to build its national home in Palestine, with a promise of assistance from the British Government; and it meant in the second place a negation of the power of that right to over-ride the right of the present inhabitants and to make the Jewish people sole ruler in the country. The national home of the Jewish people must be built out of the free material which can still be found in the country itself, and out of that which the Jews will bring in from outside or will create by their work, without overthrowing the national home of the other inhabitants. And as the two homes are contiguous, and friction and conflicts of interest are inevitable, especially in the early period of the building of the Jewish national home, of which not even the foundations have yet been properly laid, the promise necessarily demands, though it is not expressly so stated, that a guardian shall be appointed over the two homes—that is, over the whole country— to see to it that the owner of the historic right, while he does not injure the inhabitants in their internal affairs, shall not on his side have obstacles put in his way by his neighbour, who at present is stronger than he. And in course of time, when the new national home is fully built, and its tenant is able to rely, no less than his neighbour, on the right which belongs to a large population living and working in the country, it will be possible to raise the question whether the time has not come to hand over the control of the country to the 'householders' themselves, so that they may together administer their joint affairs, fairly and justly, in accordance with the needs of each of them and the value of his work for the revival and development of the country.

This and no more, it seems to me, is what we can find in the Balfour Declaration ; and this and no more is what our leaders and writers ought to have told the people, so that it should not imagine more than what is actually there, and afterwards relapse into despair and absolute scepticism.

But we all know how the Declaration was interpreted at the time of its publication, and how much exaggeration many of our workers and writers have tried to introduce into it from that day to this. The Jewish people listened, and believed that the end of the *galuth* had indeed come, and that in a short time Palestine would be a ' Jewish State.' The Arab people too, which we have always ignored from the very beginning of the colonisation movement, listened, and believed that the Jews were coming to expropriate its land and to do with it what they liked. All this inevitably led to friction and bitterness on both sides, and contributed much to the state of things which was revealed in all its ugliness in the events at Jerusalem last April.[1] Those events, in conjunction with others which preceded them, might have taught us how long is the way from a written promise to its practical realisation, and how many are the obstacles, not easily to be removed, which beset our path. But apparently we learned nothing ; and only a short time after the events at Jerusalem, when the British promise was confirmed at San Remo, we began once more to blow the Messianic trumpet, to announce the ' redemption,' and so forth.

---

[1] [The anti-Jewish riots of April, 1920, in which many lives were lost. In a footnote at this point the author recalls that as far back as 1891 he drew attention to the Arab question, and pointed out the folly of regarding the Arabs as " wild men of the desert," who could not see what was going on around them. —*Tr.*]

The confirmation of the promise, as I said above, raised it to the level of an international obligation, and from that point of view it is undoubtedly of great value. But essentially it added nothing, and the text of the earlier promise remains absolutely unaltered. What the real meaning of that text is, we have seen above; but its brevity and vagueness allow those who so wish—as experience in Palestine has shown—to restrict its meaning much more—indeed, almost to nothing. Everything, therefore, depends on the good will of the 'guardian,' on whom was placed at San Remo the duty of giving the promise practical effect. Had we paid attention to realities, we should have restrained our feelings, and have waited a little to see how the written word would be interpreted in practice.

I have dwelt perhaps at undue length on this point, because it is the fundamental one. But in truth we are now confronted with other questions, *internal* questions, which demand a solution without delay; and the solutions which we hear from time to time are as far from realities as are the poles asunder. It will not be long, however, before these visionary proposals, which are so attractive, have to make way for actual *work,* and we have to show *in practice* how far we have the material and moral strength to establish the national home which we have been given permission to establish in Palestine.

And at this great and difficult moment I appear before my readers—perhaps for the last time—on the threshold of this book, and repeat once more my old warning, on which most of the essays in this book are but a commentary :

Do not press on too quickly to the goal, so long as

the actual conditions without which it cannot be reached
have not been created ; and do not disparage the work
which is possible at any given time, having regard to
actual conditions, even if it will not bring the Messiah
to-day or to-morrow.''

THE TRANSVALUATION OF VALUES

(1898)

Amid the confused Babel of voices that are heard in the prevailing chaos of modern Jewry, there is one angry, strident, revolutionary voice which gains the public ear occasionally, and leaves a most extraordinary impression. To most men it is quite unintelligible: they stand amazed for one moment—and go their way. A few there are who understand at least where the voice comes from, and these, because they understand so much, sorrowfully shake their heads, and likewise go their way. But the younger men, ever on the alert, ever receptive of new ideas, drink in the new gospel which this voice proclaims; they are thrilled by it, attracted by it, without inquiring very deeply what is its ultimate worth, or whether the idea which it contains is really a new truth, worth all this enthusiasm.

The new gospel is that of "the transvaluation of values"; and as for the idea which it contains, it is, indeed, no easy task to penetrate the darkness which envelops it, and to state it in clear and definite form; but if we examine the utterances of its votaries, and piece together the shreds and scraps of intelligible speech which sometimes float on the stream of incomprehensibility, we may perhaps describe it thus:

The whole life of the Jews from the time of the Prophets to the present day has been, in the opinion of those who propound this new gospel, one long mistake; and it demands immediate rectification. During all these centuries Judaism has exalted the abstract, spiritual ideal above real, physical force: it has exalted the "book" over the "sword." By this means it has destroyed in the Jews the striving after individual mastery; it has subordinated the reality of life to its shadow; it has made the Jew a sort of appendage to an abstract moral law. In this condition it is impossible for the Jews to live on among the nations; still more impossible for them to restore their national life in their own country. Now, therefore, that the desire for a national rebirth has been aroused in us, it behooves us first of all to trans-valuate the moral values which are accepted among us at present; to overthrow, mercilessly and at a single blow, the historic edifice which our ancestors have left us, seeing that it is built up on this dangerously mistaken idea of the superiority of spirit to matter, and of the subordination of the individual life to abstract moral laws. We must, then, start again from the beginning, and build up a new structure on a foundation of new values. We must put the body above the spirit; we must unfetter the soul, which craves for life, and awaken in it a passion for power and mastery, so that it may satisfy all its desires by force, in unlimited freedom.

Like all the other new gospels which run riot in our literature, this gospel of the "transvaluation of values" is not a home product, nor did it spring into being in response to the demands of our own life. Our literary men found it ready-grown in a strange soil, and thought to give us the benefit of this precious plant, without considering how far, if at all, our own soil was suitable for its reception.

There arose in Germany, in this generation of ours, a philosopher-poet, thinker and seer in one, named

Friedrich Nietzsche, who roused a large section of the youth of Europe to enthusiasm by a new ethical doctrine, based on the "transvaluation of all values" (*Umwertung aller Werte.*). According to him, the function of the human being, like that of all other beings, is to develop and expand unceasingly the powers which Nature has given him, in order that the specific type may attain to the highest of which it is capable. Now, since the perfection of the specific type is only possible through the "struggle for existence" between the individual members of the species, in which the stronger advances ever higher and higher, recking nothing if his upward progress involves crushing and trampling on the weaker, it follows that the moral law is founded on an absolute mistake. It is wrong to regard that as good which brings welfare to the human race in general, and lessens the amount of suffering, and to call that evil which has the reverse effect. The moral law, working on this basis, has turned the world upside down; it has degraded the high, and exalted the low. The few strong men, whose superior endowments of body and mind fit them to rise to the top, and thus carry the specific type nearer to its perfection, are made subordinate to the many weaklings. Not alone are they unable to remove from their path this obstacle to their development: they are actually commanded by morality to *serve* the weak, to treat them with sympathy, to help them, to do them charity—in a word, to forgo the expansion of their own powers and their own individual growth, and to consecrate themselves wholly to the service of others, of the despicable and worthless multitude. The inevitable result is that the human type, instead of striving upwards, instead of producing in each successive generation stronger and nobler examples, and thus approaching nearer and nearer to its perfection, does in fact progress downwards, dragging down even the chosen few of every generation to the low level of the multitude, and thus ever widening the gulf that separates it from its true function. In order, then, to restore the power of self-perfection to the human type, we need a complete change of moral values. We must give back to the idea of good the meaning which it had of old, before "Jewish morality" overthrew Greek and Roman culture. "Good" is to be applied to the strong man, who has both the power to expand and complete his life, and the will to be master of his world (*der Wille zur Macht*), without considering at all how much the great mob of inferior beings may lose in the process. For only he, only the "Superman" (*Ubermensch*), is the fine flower and the goal of the human race; the rest were created only to subserve his end, to be the ladder on which he can climb up to his proper level. But we are not to regard the Superman as a sort of darling child of Nature, to whom she has given the right to satisfy his desires and enjoy all the good things of the world merely for his own pleasure. No: what is honored in him is the human type, which in him progresses and approaches nearer to its perfection. For this reason the development of his powers and the mastery of the world are not only a privilege for the Superman; they are also a high and arduous duty, to which he must sacrifice his personal happiness as he sacrifices the happiness of others; for the sake of which he must be as unsparing of himself as of others. "Deem ye that I take thought for my happiness?" says the Superman (*Zarathustra*); "it is for my work that I take thought." This work, the advancement of the human type in each succeeding generation, though it be but in a few examples, to a higher level than that of the mass of men: this work is in itself a desirable goal, quite independently of its results from the point of view of the happiness or misery, the advantage or disadvantage, of the multitude. And so the moral and cultural value of any period of history does not depend, as is generally supposed, on the level of happiness and culture reached by the generality of men in that period, but precisely on the extent to which the specific type, as manifested in one or more individuals, is raised above the general level.

This is the fundamental idea of the doctrine of the "transvaluation of values" in its original German form.[1] It desires not merely to change morality in certain details—to pronounce some things evil which were regarded as good, and the reverse—but to alter the very foundation of morality, the actual standard by reference to which things are pronounced good or evil. Hitherto the standard has been the lessening of pain and increasing of happiness among the mass of human beings. Everything that was calculated to assist in a greater or lesser degree towards the attainment of that object, whether directly or indirectly, whether at once or in

---

[1] In Nietzsche's own works his teaching is enveloped in a cloud of extravagances and poetic exuberances. They are also full of contradictions in points of detail, so that it is very difficult to extract from them a single coherent system. So far as this is possible, it has been done excellently by that acute philosopher Georg Simmel in his essay "Friedrich Nietzsche," printed in the Zeitschrift für Philosophie und philosophische Kritik, vol. 107, part 2.

the near or distant future, has been good; everything that was calculated from any point of view to produce the reverse effect has been evil. Now we are told that moral qualities and actions are not to be estimated at all by reference to their effects in relation to the mass of men; that there is one thing which is essentially good, which is an end in itself, and needs no testing by any external standard—and that is the free development of individuality in the elect of the human race, and the ascent of the specific type in them to a level higher than that of the generality of men. Thus—as Simmel rightly points out—Nietzsche rendered himself immune from any criticism based on logic or experience. All criticism of that kind must of necessity rest on the old standard which he will not accept. It can only point to the injury which such a theory will inflict on human life in general, to its evil effects on the diffusion of culture, and so forth. But according to the theory in question the whole life and the whole culture of the mass of men cannot weigh against a single Superman.

We see now whence our own literary men got the idea of the "transvaluation of values," and what they have done with it. They found a new doctrine, universal in its scope, and certainly calculated to appeal to men of imagination; and its attraction for them produced a desire to propound a similar new doctrine, of special application to the Jews. So far I have no fault to find with them. The same thing has often been done before, from the Alexandrian period to our own day; and Judaism has more than once been made richer in new conceptions and stimulating ideas. But here, as in every process which demands artistic skill, the essential thing is that the artist should understand the possibilities of his material, and know how to subdue it to the form. He must not be mastered by his material, and let it turn under his hands into a useless piece of ware.

More than a year ago I crossed swords with these young writers, who complain of a spiritual "cleft" in their inner life, and think that they can bridge over the gap by introducing "European" ideas into Hebrew literature; and I said to them at that time: "It is not sufficient for us simply to import the foreign material; we must first of all adapt and assimilate it to our national genius. We see, for example, that the ideas of Friedrich Nietzsche have captured many young Jews, and have come into conflict with their Judaism, and produced a cleft in their inner life. What are we to do? Let us analyze these ideas, and divide them into their constituent parts, in order to discover what it is in them that attracts, and what it is that is at variance with Judaism. This analysis may prove to us at last that there is no essential connection between these two parts—that the first is a human element, while the second is simply German or Aryan, and has become associated with the other only because they happened to fuse in the mind of a particular man who was also a German. Then we shall be able to give these ideas a new form; to free the human element from its subordination to the German form, and subordinate it instead to our own form. Thus we shall have the necessary assimilation, and we shall be importing into our literature ideas which are *new, but not foreign.*" [1]

[1] See the essay called "Good Advice" [not included in this translation.]

If our Ñietzscheans had adopted that course, they would have found that their master's doctrine does, in fact, contain two separable elements—one human and universal, the other merely Aryan; and that the first of these, so far from being opposed to Judaism, actually strengthens Judaism.

The human element in the doctrine of the "transvaluation of values" is that change in the moral standard which I have described above. The end of moral good is not the uplifting of the human race in general, but the raising of the human type in its highest manifestations above the general level. This postulate is, as I have said, one of those fundamental principles which each man admits or denies according to his taste and inclination, and which cannot be met by arguments derived from other premises. But if this postulate cannot be tested by any standard external to itself, that very fact imposes a restriction on those who lay it down. It is impossible for them to define clearly and convincingly the nature of that superior type which they desiderate. Seeing that the goal is the mere existence of the Superman, and not his effect on the world, we have no criterion by which to distinguish those human qualities of which the development marks the progress of the type, from those which are signs of backwardness and retrogression. Here again, as in the case of the postulate itself, we are dependent on our esthetic taste and our moral bent. Nietzsche himself, it is true, exalts physical force and external beauty; he longs for "the fair beast" (*die blonde Bestie*)—the strong, beautiful beast which shall rule the world, and act in all things according to its will. But it is obvious that this conception of the Superman

does not follow by logical necessity from his fundamental postulate. It is no longer the philosopher as
such who speaks; it is the man of Aryan race, who,
with his excessive regard for physical power and
beauty, depicts his ideal according to his own taste.
We are, therefore, at liberty to suppose that this same
Nietzsche, if his taste had been Hebraic, might still
have changed the moral standard, and made the Superman an end in himself, but would in that case have
attributed to his Superman quite different characteristics—the expansion of moral power, the subjuga-
tion of the bestial instincts, the striving after truth and
righteousness in thought and deed, the eternal warfare
against falsehood and wickedness: in a word, that
moral ideal which Judaism has impressed on us. And
what is there to prove that the change in the moral
standard necessarily involves changing the Hebraic
outlook, and substituting the Aryan: that man becomes Superman not through moral strength and the
beauty of the soul, but only through the physical
strength and the external beauty of the "fair beast"?

Those who are at all expert in this matter do not
need to be told that there is no necessity now for the
creation of a Jewish Nietzscheism of this kind, because
it has existed for centuries. Nietzsche, as a German,
may be pardoned for having failed to understand
Judaism, and having confused it with another doctrine,
which sprang out of it and went off on another track.
But his Jewish disciples ought to know that Judaism
has never based itself on mercy alone, and has never
made its Superman subordinate to the mass of men,
as though the whole aim and object of his existence
were simply to increase the happiness of the multi-

tude. We all know the importance of the Zaddik, the "righteous man," in our ethical literature, from the Talmud and the Midrashim to the literature of Hasidism: we know that, so far from his having been created for the sake of others, "the whole world was only created for his sake," and that he is an end for himself. Phrases like this, as is well known, are of frequent occurrence in our literature; and they did not remain mere expressions of individual opinion, mere philosophic tags, but obtained popular currency, and became generally accepted principles of morality.

More than this: if we search deeper, we shall find this idea, in a wider presentation, at the very basis of the Jewish *national* consciousness.

Nietzsche himself complained, in his last book, that hitherto there had been no attempt to educate men deliberately with the object of producing the Superman. If such a man happened occasionally to be produced, this was merely "a happy accident, not the result of conscious will." [1] Indeed, it is easy enough to depict the Superman in lofty poetic images that fire the imagination; but if he is to be a phenomenon of constant occurrence, and not merely an occasional accident, the surrounding conditions of life must be adapted to that end. You cannot get water from a rock, or fruit from the parched soil of the desert. When all is said, man is a social animal; and even the soul of the Superman is a product of society, and cannot wholly free itself from the moral atmosphere in which it has grown and developed. If we agree, then, that the Super*man* is the goal of all things, we must needs agree also that

---

[1] Comp. A. Riehl, "Friedrich Nietzsche" (Stuttgart, 1897), p. 125.

an essential condition of the attainment of this goal is the Super*nation*: that is to say, there must be a single nation better adapted than other nations, by virtue of its inherent characteristics, to moral development, and ordering its whole life in accordance with a moral law which stands higher than the common type. This nation will then serve as the soil essentially and supremely fitted to produce that fairest of all fruits— the Superman.

This idea opens up a wide prospect, in which Judaism appears in a new and splendid light. Many of the "shortcomings" of Judaism, by which strangers judge us, and which our own scholars try to deny or excuse, become, when viewed in the light of this idea, positive superiorities, which are a credit to Judaism, and need neither denial nor excuse.

It is almost universally admitted that the Jews have a genius for morality, and in this respect are superior to all other nations.[1] It matters not how this happened, or in what way this trait developed: we certainly find that in the very earliest times the Jewish people became conscious of its superiority in this respect over the surrounding nations. This consciousness found its expression, in accordance with the spirit of that age, in the religious dogma that God had chosen out Israel "to make him high above all nations." But this election of Israel was not to be a domination based on force, for Israel is "the fewest of all peoples." It was for moral development that Israel was chosen by God, "to be a peculiar people unto Himself . . . . and to keep all His commandments";

[1] Nietzsche himself often admits this: see, for instance, Zur Geschichte-der Moral (Leipzig, 1894), p. 51.

that is, to give concrete expression in every generation to the highest type of morality, to submit always to the yoke of the most exacting moral obligations, and this without any regard to the gain or loss of the rest of mankind, but solely for the sake of the existence of this supreme type.[1] This consciousness of its moral election has been preserved by the Jewish people throughout its history, and has been its solace in all its sufferings. The Jews have never tried, save in exceptional circumstances, to increase their numbers by conversion; not, as their enemies aver, out of jealousy, nor yet, as their apologists plead in excuse, out of tolerance, but simply because it is a characteristic of the superior type "that it will not consent to lower the value of its own duties by making them the duties of all men; that it will not shuffle off or share with others its own responsibility."[2] Judaism does indeed present, in this respect, a unique phenomenon. It distinguishes the Jews from the rest of mankind only in that it imposes on them exacting and arduous obligations; whereas for the non-Jews the yoke is lightened, and they are allowed the reward of a future life for the mere fulfilment of the most elementary moral duties, the so-called "seven commandments given to the sons of Noah." It is only during the last century, since the French Revolution raised the banner of equality and fraternity among all men, and made the general well-being the supreme moral ideal, that Jewish apologists have begun to be ashamed of the

---

[1] Nietzsche says somewhere, that under certain conditions it is possible for whole families, or even whole tribes, to rise to the level of the Superman (Riehl, ibid.).

[2] Nietzsche, Jenseits von Gut und Böse (Leipzig, 1894), p. 264.

idea of Israel's election in its old sense. Finding this
idea opposed to that of absolute equality and the pursuit of the general well-being, they have tried to adapt
Judaism to modern requirements by inventing the
famous theory of "the mission of Israel among the
nations." Thus they reconcile the idea of the national
election with that of human equality, by making the
one a means to the other. Israel is, indeed (so they
argue), the chosen people; but for what end was he
chosen? To spread good will and well-being throughout the world, by teaching mankind the way of life
according to that true Law which was entrusted to
him for this very purpose. Now there is no need to
repeat here the oft-repeated criticism of this compromise, that it has no foundation in actuality, and rests
entirely on a metaphysical dogma. It is enough to
point out that the Jewish people as a whole has always
interpreted its "mission" simply as the performance of
its own duties, without regard to the external world,
and has regarded its election, from the earliest times
to the present day, as the end of all else, and not as a
means to the happiness of the rest of the world. The
Prophets no doubt gave utterance to the hope that
Judaism would exert an influence for good on the
moral condition of the other nations; but their idea
was that this result would follow naturally from the
existence among the Jews of the highest type of
morality, not that the Jews existed solely for the
purpose of striving to exert this influence. It is the
nations who are to say, "Come ye and let us go up to
the mountain of the Lord, ... and He will teach us
of His ways, and we will walk in His paths." We do
not find that Israel is to say, "Come, let us go out to

the nations and teach them the ways of the Lord, that they may walk in His paths."

This idea of Israel as the Supernation might be expanded and amplified into a complete system. For the profound tragedy of our spiritual life in the present day is perhaps only a result of our failure to justify in practice the potentialities of our election. On the one hand, there still lives within us, though it be only in the form of an instinctive feeling, a belief in that moral fitness for which we were chosen from all the nations, and in that national mission which consists in living the highest type of moral life, in being the moral Supernation. But, on the other hand, since the day when we left the Ghetto, and started to partake of the world's life and its civilization, we cannot help seeing that our superiority is potential merely. Actually we are not superior to other nations even in the sphere of morality. We have been unable to fulfil our mission in exile, because we could not make our lives a true expression of our own character, independent of the opinion or the will of others. And so it may even be that many of our latter-day Zionists, who base their Zionism on economic and political grounds, and scoff at the national "election" and the moral "mission"—it may even be that many of these have been driven to Zionism simply by force of this contrast between the possibilities and the actualities of Jewish history: being forced thereby, all unconsciously, to seek some firm resting-place for their people, in order that it may have the opportunity once more of developing its genius for morality, and fulfilling its "mission" as the Supernation.

But enough. I mean no more than to show that the

doctrine of the "transvaluation of values" is really
capable of being assimilated by Judaism, and of enrich-
ing Judaism without doing violence to its spirit, by
introducing "ideas which are new, but not foreign,"
or, rather, by introducing ideas which are not even
essentially new. For, more than eight hundred years
ago there lived a Jewish philosopher-poet, Rabbi
Jehudah Halevi, who recognized the inner meaning
and value of the election of Israel, and made it the
foundation of his system, very much on the lines of
what I have said above, though in a different style.[1]

And now what have our young writers done with
this doctrine?

They have neglected what is essentially original in
it, and have seized only on the new phrase and the
Aryan element which its author introduced: and with
these they come to their own people, as with a medi-
cine to cure the diseases of its old age. For them the
essential thing is not the emancipation of the superior
type from its subservience to the multitude; it is the
emancipation of physical life from its subservience to
the limiting power of the spirit. Such a point of view
as this can never ally itself with Judaism. No wonder,
then, that they feel a "cleft in their souls," and begin
to cry, "Transvaluation! New values! Let the Book
give place to the sword, and the Prophets to the fair
beast!" This cry has become especially prominent
during the last year; and we are told every day that
our whole world must be destroyed root and branch,
and rebuilt all over again. But we are never told how
you can destroy with one breath the national founda-

[1] See his Kuzari, bk. i.

tion of an ancient people, or how you can build up a new life for a nation after destroying the very essence of its being, and stifling its historic soul.

One can understand—and one can tolerate—the individual Jew who is captivated by the Superman in Nietzsche's sense; who bends the knee to Zarathustra, throws off his allegiance to the Prophets, and goes about to regulate his own private life in accordance with these new values. But it is difficult to understand, and still more difficult to tolerate, the extraordinary proceeding of these men, who offer such a new law of life as this to the whole nation, and are simple enough to think that it can be accepted by a people which, almost from the moment of its first appearance in the world's history, has existed only to protest vehemently and unceasingly on behalf of the rights of the spirit against those of the strong arm and the sword; which, from time immemorial to the present day, has derived all its spiritual strength simply from its steadfast faith in its moral mission, in its obligation and its capacity to approach nearer than other nations to the ideal of moral perfection. This people, they fondly imagine, could suddenly, after thousands of years, change its values, forgo its national preeminence in the moral sphere, in order to become "the tail of the lion" in the sphere of the sword; could overthrow the mighty temple which it has built to the God of righteousness, in order to set up in its place a mean and lowly altar (it has no strength for more) to the idol of physical force.

There is a further point that requires mention. These writers go much further than their master in waging war against the Book and all that it contains—

that is, against the laws which set a limit to the supremacy of the individual will—and in lavishing
affection on the dissenters and the rebels of the wilderness, who refused to subordinate the "glory of life"
to abstract laws, and to change the fleshpots of Egypt
for the heavy yoke of moral obligations. Nietzsche
himself, for all his worship of the strong arm and
the glory of physical life, regards righteousness as
the highest perfection attainable on earth: so much
so, that he finds it hard to believe that it is within the
power of man, even of the Superman, to conquer the
feeling of hate and revenge, and to be guided by absolute justice in his relations with friends and foes alike.
Hence he finds it a great advantage that righteousness
should be embodied in fixed abstract laws, which enable a man to test the justice of his actions in relation
to the objective rule, without being compelled to remember, in the moment of his self-examination, the
living enemy, who arouses his passions, so that his
judgment is obscured by his subjective inclinations.[1]

And here I am reminded that these writers of ours
are in the habit of paying me an undeserved honor.
They applaud me because in one of my essays[2] I, too,
have protested against our being "the people of the
Book." To be sure, they think that I am inconsistently
denying my own "heresy" when I couple this protest
with praise of our "national possessions" and their
natural development, and do not demand, as they do,
the complete destruction of the Book. But here again
they have simply found a new phrase and seized on it,
without examining its true inwardness. My regret

---

[1] Genealogie, pp. 82-84.
[2] "The Law in the Soul." [Not included in this translation.]

was not for the existence of the Book in itself, but
for its petrifaction. I lamented the fact that its development has been arrested, that it no longer corresponds to the inner moral feeling, as it used to do, in
the earlier days of Jewish history, when "the voice
of God in the heart of man" used to draw its inspiration direct from the phenomena of life and nature,
and the Book itself was compelled to change its contents little by little, imperceptibly, in order to conform
to the moral consciousness of the people. And so I
was not advocating the dominance of the sword over
the Book; I was pleading for the dominance of that
moral force which was implanted in our people centuries ago, which itself produced the Book, and renewed the spirit of the Book in each successive period,
according to its own needs. It was only after a long
spell of exile that much suffering quelled the spirit,
and the moral feeling practically ceased to develop,
so that there were no further changes made in the
contents of the Book, and the people became absolutely enslaved to a series of lifeless letters. And
it is in accordance with this view, and not in contradiction to it, that I maintained in the essay in
question, as I always maintain, that there is no call for
uprooting, or for proclaiming the change of values
with the blare of trumpets; but only for the introduction of what I have called "a new current of life" into
our spiritual world: this new current being "a living
desire for the unity of the nation, for its rebirth, and
its unfettered development along its own lines, as one
of the social units of humanity." This new current
would bring fresh life to our people, and would restore
to it the faculty of moral self-development; and then,

as a natural consequence, the Book, too, would develóp once more, responding to the true needs and demands of the national spirit, and not to the shrieks of a few imaginative young men, who have eaten the sour grapes of a foreign philosophy, and want the whole nation's teeth to be set on edge.

On more general grounds, too, these writers of ours should have studied the laws of historical evolution a little more deeply before trying their hands at pulling down and building up. It is true that Nietzsche himself hated historians, and stigmatized Darwin and Spencer, the authors of the evolutionary theory, as mediocrities. But this did not prevent even him from inventing historical hypotheses in order to explain the progress of morality, or from taking the cornerstone of his new system from Darwin. These writers of ours seem to regard the moral code of each nation as something external, manufactured from beginning to end by certain individuals, who were fully conscious of what they were doing, and had a definite end in view. In order, therefore, that this moral code may be changed—or, rather, in order that it may be utterly destroyed, and another set up in its place—all that is needed is that certain other individuals should proclaim, loudly and savagely, that a change of values is imperative. An idea of this kind was all very well years ago, in the time of Rousseau and his school. But these modernest of modern writers, who consider themselves the writers of the *future,* ought to know that you cannot manufacture a new moral code for a nation, any more than you can manufacture it a new language. The laws of morality, like those of language, are an outcome of the national character; they are a fruit which ripens little by little through the ages, under the influence of innumerable causes, some permanent, some transient, not in accordance with a system laid down and defined at the outset. Hence it results that in both cases logical contraditions abound, the norm and the exception live side by side. No man has the power to pull them down and build them up according to his desire and taste: they change constantly of their own accord, reflecting the changes in the nation's circumstances, character, and needs. Now, despite all this, Volapük as a language has some value; it may serve as an artificial aid in time of need. But a moral Volapük is a piece of utter fatuity, as unprofitable as it is unnecessary; it serves no purpose but to waste time, and to confuse ardent young men who are athirst for exciting novelties. The inventor of Volapük, wishing his language to be accepted universally, found it necessary to expunge the letter *r* from his alphabet, because it cannot be pronounced by—the Chinese. But the authors of our moral Volapük do not trouble to inquire as to the capabilities of the nation for which they are building: they hold a pistol to your head, and offer you the blessing of a new law, against which every fibre of your being revolts, without first inquiring whether you can accept it.

"It is a thing of the highest importance to instil into the minds of the people . . . . that feeling of reverence which will teach them that there are certain things which they may not touch, certain sanctuaries which they may not approach without removing their shoes, which must be preserved from the hand of profanation. . . . And, on the other side, when we consider the so-called 'men of culture,' those who believe in 'modern ideas,' there is nothing that so disgusts us as their apparent lack of a sense of shame, and that easy effrontery of hand and eye with which they maul and finger everything."

That is a hard saying, but it is not one for which I need ask pardon of our Nietzscheans. The saying is not mine: it comes from their own Bible. It was Nietzsche who wrote these words; and they were directed against those who lay irreverent hands on the Hebrew Book—on the Scriptures. "Such books as this," he adds, "with their fathomless depth and their priceless worth, need an external authority, backed by force, to protect them, in order that they may remain in existence for all the thousands of years which are necessary before their wealth can be exhausted."[1]

These are the master's words. Hearing, after this, the words of his Jewish pupils, one cannot resist the thought that it is better for our children to wander abroad themselves, and draw the noxious water from the fountainhead, than to get it at second hand in this Hebrew "cleft" literature, which promises to reconcile the claims of Judaism with those of human life in general.

[A criticism of the foregoing essay appeared in Ha-Shiloah, to which Ahad Ha'am replied in the same journal. The following paragraph from his reply puts very clearly the point at issue between the "young men" and himself.]

I have never yet discovered what phraseology or what style must be used to convince people of the truth that a belief in the fundamental morality of the Jewish spirit is not in the least opposed to the ideal of the national revival, but rather affords the true historical basis and logical substructure of that ideal.

[1] Jenseits, p. 254.

Times beyond number, in all shapes and forms, have I urged this view. Indeed, if I mistake not, I was one of the first to point out the absolute necessity of awakening our dormant genius for morality in order to overcome the petrifaction which has seized on our life, and to give us an immediate link with nature, without the intervention of "the Book." As regards the very point on which the author of this article attacks me, I have explained again and again that there is no inconsistency between the striving after a healthy national life and the cultivation of our moral strength. And yet the champions of our "young men" can still go on repeating that "we must pay attention also to our physical resources, and strive after a national life like all other nations." As though that were anything new! What they have discovered is not the *need* for a change, for a return to nature: that idea they found ready-made in books of the old-fashioned moral school. The real foundation of their theory is the antithesis between this need and the bent towards morality, which has been characteristic of the Jewish spirit since the Jews existed. Consequently, those who wish to defend them, and to reply to the criticisms of their opponents, are bound to demonstrate the reality of that antithesis, and the necessity for the destruction of this moral bent. To come and argue, on behalf of the "young men," simply that we stand in need of a healthy national life, like all other nations, is merely to bring coals to Newcastle; and to add naïvely that the existence of this need proves "the moral theory of Rabbi Jehudah Halevi" obsolete—this shows that the critic is unacquainted with what he is criticising. For the whole object of my arguments has been to show that there is no incompatibility between the need for a national revival and the "moral" theory of Judaism, and that this theory does not necessarily involve acceptance of the point of view indicated by such phrases as "the people of the Book," and "exceptions to all historical laws." It is, on the contrary, actually opposed to that point of view, because it attempts to apply universal historical laws to Jewish life, and for that very reason cannot stomach the ideas of our "young men," who ride roughshod over history and its universal laws.

FLESH AND SPIRIT

(1904)

Asceticism may be defined as the psychological tendency, frequently manifested both in individuals and in whole societies, to turn from the pleasures of the world with hatred and contempt, and to regard every material good thing of life as something evil and degraded, to be avoided by him who cares for his soul's health.

Asceticism, so defined, is not a descriptive term for certain outward practices, but a name for the inner spring of conduct which prompts those practices; and thus we exclude all those phenomena which have an external similarity to asceticism, but are of an essentially different character. A man may renounce pleasure, or even mortify his flesh of set purpose, and yet not deserve the name of ascetic, because, so far from despising the life of the body, he actually sets store by it, and only refrains from pleasure in order to avoid danger to his health, or physical pain: as when a man avoids wine and other luxuries by order of his doctor, for the sake of his health; or when, in anticipation of a long and difficult journey, a man reduces his allowance of food and sleep, so as to be able to bear privation in time of need without detriment to his health or undue suffering; and so forth. Further, even when abstinence and self-denial are prompted by religious motives, they are not always due to asceticism in the strict sense. In almost all primitive religions fasting and similar "afflictions of the soul" were considered

an important part of the service of God, and the priests
were accustomed, when performing their sacred duties,
"to cut themselves with swords and knives till the
blood flowed." But there is here no asceticism, because
the motive is not hatred of the body, but excessive
love of the body. Primitive man had a rooted belief
that his god, like the head of his tribe, could be pro-
pitiated by a costly offering of his most valuable possession, and especially of flesh and fat and blood, which
are the dainties most palatable to the savage. Now,
the greater the value of the offering in the opinion of
the bringer, the greater, clearly, would be his confidence in its acceptability to the god as a proof of his
true service and fidelity. It was, then, by this process
of reasoning, which followed inevitably from the fundamental belief just mentioned, that men were led to
sacrifice even their offspring to their gods in time of
trouble; and the same reasoning was responsible for
the unnatural idea of sacrificing part of a man's own
body, his fat and blood, as the most precious of his
possessions. Thus religion produced, together with
the idea of sacrifices in general, that of fasting and
mortification, not from a desire to turn men away from
the flesh, but because fasting and mortification seemed
to be the greatest sacrifice of which flesh and blood
was capable, and therefore the most certain means of
propitiating God and gaining His grace. Hence it is
that in all ages this method has been most used in times
of acutest distress, when it was necessary "to cry
mightily unto God," and avert His anger by every
possible means.

But true asceticism, as I have said, is that which
has its source in hatred and contempt for the flesh. It

makes war on the flesh not for the sake of some further end, but because the flesh in itself is unworthy and despicable, and degrades man, who is the flower of creation. For asceticism there is no more important concern in life than this eternal war on the flesh, with all its desires and its pleasures; there is no higher victory for man than the killing of the flesh, the extinction of its desires, and the refusal of its pleasures.

Isolated instances of such asceticism are found at all times and in all places; but as a constant phenomenon, as a sovereign rule of life governing large masses of men for generation after generation, we meet with it first of all in India, among the Buddhists, and much later among Christian nations also. The history of European culture, especially from the fourth century till the end of the Middle Ages, is full of strange and almost incredible stories, which show with abundant clearness how this revolt against the flesh, this desire to wage a ruthless war of extermination on the flesh, can gain ascendancy over the human mind, and how this revolt can spread, like an epidemic, from place to place, from man to man, without limit to its growth.

We stand aghast at this phenomenon, utterly opposed as it is to those general principles which are accepted in our day as laws of history. The whole of civilization, according to these principles, is simply a result of the ineradicable desire, which man shares with the rest of the animal world, to prolong life, to lighten its hardships, to make it smooth and pleasant. The ceaseless warfare, now physical, now spiritual, between man and man, between nation and nation, has its real cause in the desire of every man or nation to add to the number of his and its possessions, material or spiritual,

so as to secure the greatest possible fulness and com-
pleteness of life, by reducing pain to the minimum
and increasing pleasure to the maximum. So far the
laws of history. And now, in the very heart of this
all-devouring ocean of selfishness, behold one solitary
stream making its lonely way *against* the flowing tide.
The current of the whole world is set towards the
broadening of life; every living thing struggles to
drink its fill from every spring of enjoyment and happiness: and here are these mortals deliberately narrow-
ing their lives, and running away from enjoyment and
natural happiness as from the plague. Whence and
in what way can a man get this unnatural impulse, so
utterly opposed to the universal law of life?

This is no new problem, and I am not here concerned
primarily with its solution. I will only indicate briefly
the solution that seems to me most satisfactory, confining myself to what is necessary to my present purpose.

Since man emerged from the darkness of barbarism,
and became a civilized being, striving after self-knowl-
edge and knowledge of the outside world, he has developed two fundamental demands: the demand for the
cause and the demand for the *end*. Turn where he will,
he meets with perplexing phenomena, which force him
to stop and ask himself: Where and whither? What
is the cause that produced these things? and what is
the end, the object, of their existence? But there is a
great difference between these two demands. The
problem of the cause is a logical one, and the demand
for its solution is therefore absolute and common to
all human beings; whereas the problem of the end
is a moral one, and the demand for its solution is

accordingly relative, varying with the degree of moral development in the individual. The laws of knowledge, which govern our reason, require absolutely that every fact shall have a cause; anything without a precedent cause is inconceivable. We might, however, conceive the whole world as simply the inevitable result of certain causes, without reference to any particular end, were it not that our moral sense is up in arms against this conception, and a world without any end is in our view mere vanity and emptiness, as though it had reeled back into chaos. And the demand for an end is especially strong in the case of the individual's own life. For the most part life is a hard and bitter thing, full of troubles and sufferings that have no compensation; and, however clearly we recognize the causes, natural and social, that produce this result, we are still not satisfied or relieved. The moral sense still complains and still questions: To what end?

No doubt there are men who are driven to despair by their failure to find an answer to this question, and bitterly resolve that "the superiority of man over the beasts is nothing," and that the whole aim and object of our being is to "eat and drink, for to-morrow we die." For man, as for all the animals, there is nothing more. Have you had the luck to feast well at life's table? Then rejoice in your good fortune, and die in peace. Have you failed of this happiness? Then suffer in silence. There is no right, no purpose, no end in the government of the world; it is just a chain of cause and effect.

But most men cannot be satisfied with this philosophy of despair, which robs life of its glamor. Their desire for existence will not let them find comfort for to-day's troubles in the thought of to-morrow's death. On the contrary, it forces them to seek consolation not only against the sufferings of the life that is theirs to-day, but also against the bitterness of the death that to-morrow will bring. Not finding what they want in the real world, they arrive finally at the idea of a world beyond nature, and transfer the centre of gravity of their Ego from the body to the soul. This flesh, condemned to suffer and finally to rot, is but a temporary external garment of the real, eternal Ego, that spiritual essence which lives independently of the body, and does not die with the body; this spiritual self alone is the real man, with a future and a lofty purpose in a world where all is good. This fleeting life in the vale of tears, bound up with the mortal flesh, is nothing but a shadow, and like a shadow it will pass, with all its sufferings. Now, when once a man has got so far as to divide himself into two, and regard his body as something external, which is not himself, he has no difficulty in going further. He follows out this idea till he regards the body as the *enemy* of his eternal Ego, keeping him from his true life by its constant demands and numerous ailments. So it follows that my Ego is bound to fight this enemy, to subdue it and weaken it as far as possible, so that it may not be a hindrance to my real life, and may not drag me at its heels into the morass of its own degraded existence, with all its bestiality and its utter worthlessness.

Since this philosophy is essentially intended as a consolation for those who are harassed by life's troubles, it is no wonder that, as these troubles grow, the hatred of the flesh grows also, and the desire to destroy it root and branch becomes more strong. It is a matter of everyday experience that when a man is troubled by pain in some part of his body which is not vital, say a tooth, he is seized with violent hatred of the particular member, and wants to have his revenge on it. The same thing happens in regard to the body as a whole. Once let a man look on his body as an external garment, on which his real life in no way depends, and he will come to hate these undesirable earthy wrappings in proportion as they cause him trouble. Hence we find the tendency to asceticism and mortification of the flesh increasing most markedly in dark and unhappy periods, when misery stalks abroad, and men suffer without knowing how to find relief. Then it is that they fall savagely on their tortured flesh as the seat of all the pain.

Thus the troubles of this life have given rise to two sharply opposed theories. On the one side there is the materialist view, which makes the flesh supreme, and sees no aim for human life but to enjoy the pleasure of the moment, until death shall come and put a stop to the silly game. On the other side we have the spiritual theory, which aims at killing the flesh, so that the spirit may be freed from its foe, and man may be brought nearer to his eternal goal.

But Judaism in its original form held equally aloof from either extreme, and solved the problem of life and its aim in quite a different way.

In the period of the first Temple we find no trace of the idea that man is divisible into body and soul. Man, as a living and thinking creature, is one whole of many parts. The word *Nefesh* (translated "soul") includes everything, body and soul and all the life-processes that depend on them. The *Nefesh*, that is, the individual man, lives its life and dies its death. There is no question of survival. And yet primitive Judaism was not troubled by the question of life and death, and did not arrive at that stage of utter despair which produced among other nations the materialist idea of the supremacy of the flesh and the filling of life's void by the intoxication of the senses. Judaism did not turn heavenwards, and create in Heaven an eternal habitation of souls. It found "eternal life" on earth, by strengthening the social feeling in the individual, by making him regard himself not as an isolated being, with an existence bounded by birth and death, but as part of a larger whole, as a limb of the social body. This conception shifts the centre of gravity of the Ego not from the flesh to the spirit, but from the individual to the community; and, concurrently with this shifting, the problem of life becomes a problem not of individual but of social life. I live for the sake of the perpetuation and the happiness of the community of which I am a member; I die to make room for new individuals, who will mould the community afresh and not allow it to stagnate and remain forever in one position. When the individual thus values the community as his own life, and strives after its happiness as though it were his individual well-being, he finds satisfaction, and no longer feels so keenly the bitterness of his individual existence, because he sees the end for which he lives and suffers. But this can only be so when the life of the community has an end of such importance as to outweigh, in the judgment of the individual, all possible hardships. For otherwise the old question remains, only that it is shifted from the individual to the community. I bear with life in order that the community may live: but why does the community live? What value has its existence, that I should bear my sufferings cheerfully for its sake? Thus Judaism, having shifted the centre of gravity from the individual to the community, was forced to find an answer to the problem of the communal life. It had to find for that life some aim of sufficient grandeur and importance to uplift the individual, and to give him satisfaction at a time when his own particular life was unpleasant. So it was that Israel as a community became "a kingdom of priests and a holy nation," a nation consecrated from its birth to the service of setting the whole of mankind an example by its Law.

Thus Judaism solved the problem of life, and had no place for the two extreme views. Man is one and indivisible; all his limbs, his feelings, his emotions, his thoughts make up a single whole. And his life is not wasted, because he is an Israelite, a member of the nation which exists for a lofty end. Since, further, the community is only the sum of its individual members, it follows that every Israelite is entitled to regard himself as the cause of his people's existence, and to believe that he too is lifted above oblivion by his share in the nation's imperishable life. Hence in this early period of Jewish history we do not find any tendency to real asceticism, that is to say, to hatred and annihilation of the flesh. That tendency can only arise when life can find no aim in this world, and has to seek its aim in another. There were no doubt Nazarites in Israel in those days, who observed the outward habits of the ascetic; but all this, as I have said, was simply part and parcel of the practice of sacrifice. How far the Nazarites were removed from hatred of the flesh we may see from the fact that even Samson was regarded as a Nazarite.

This philosophy of life, which raises the individual above all feelings of self-love, and teaches him to find the aim of his life in the perpetuation and well-being of the community, has been condemned by many non-Jewish scholars as being too materialistic, and has been regarded as a proof of the inferiority of Judaism, which does not promise immortality to every individual, and a reward to the righteous after death, as other religions do. So great is the power of hatred to blind the eyes and pervert the judgment!

But a change came after the destruction of the first Temple, when the national disaster weakened the nation's belief in its future, and the national instinct could no longer supply a basis for life. Then, indeed, Judaism was forced to seek a solution for the problem of life in the dualism which distinguishes between body and soul. But the deep-rooted partiality to the body and material life was so strong that even the new theory could not transform it entirely. Hence, unlike other nations, the Jews of that period did not eliminate the body even from the future life, but left it a place beyond the grave by their belief in the "resurrection of the dead." The end of man's life was now, no doubt, the uplifting of the spirit, and the bringing it near to "the God of spirits"; but the body was regarded not as the enemy of the spirit, but as its helper and ally. The body was associated with the spirit in order to serve it, and enable it to achieve perfection by good actions. And therefore, even in this period, Judaism did not arrive at the idea of the annihilation of the flesh. It regarded such annihilation not as righteousness, but as a sin. The two elements in man, the physical and the spiritual, can and must live in perfect accord, not as enemies; and this accord is not a truce between two opposing forces, based on a compromise and mutual accommodation, but a real inner union. The spiritual element is to penetrate into the very heart of the material life, to purify it and cleanse it, to make all its complex fulness a part of the spiritual life. Such union does not degrade the spirit, but uplifts the flesh, which is irradiated by the spirit's sanctity; and their joint life, each linked with and completing the other, brings man to his true goal.

Talmudic literature is full of utterances which confirm the view here put forward. It is sufficient to mention, by way of example, Hillel's saying about the importance of the body,[1] and the repeated condemnations of those who mortify the flesh, especially the familiar saying: "Every man will have to give an account of himself for every good thing which he would have liked to eat, but did not."[2]

Even the two non-conformist sects, the Sadducees and the Essenes, which might seem at first sight to have stood for the two extreme views, really based themselves on Jewish teaching, and developed no extravagant theories about the life of the individual. The Sadducees did not incline towards the sovereignty of the flesh, nor the Essenes towards its annihilation. The truth is that the Sadducees, who endeavored in all things to revive the older Judaism, held to the Scriptural view in this matter as in others, that is, that

[1] Vayikra Rabba, 34.
[2] Jerusalem Talmud, end of Kiddushin.

the individual has only his life on earth, and eternal life belongs solely to the nation as a whole, to which the individual must subordinate his existence. The Essenes, on the other side, starting from the eternity of the individual spirit as the most fundamental of all principles, endeavored to hold aloof from everything that distracts attention from the spiritual life. But they never despised or hated the flesh; and Philo says of them that "they avoided luxuries, because they saw in them injury to health *of body and soul.*"

In the Middle Ages, no doubt, Judaism did not escape the infection of alien theories based on hatred of the flesh; but the best Jewish thinkers, such as Maimonides, tried to stem the tide of foreign influence. They remained true to the traditional Jewish standpoint, and taught the people to honor the body, to set store by its life and satisfy its legitimate demands, not to set body and spirit at odds. It was only after the expulsion from Spain, when the Jews were persecuted in most countries of the Diaspora, that the Cabbalists, especially those of Palestine, succeeded in obscuring the light, and won many converts to asceticism in its grimmest form. But their dominance was not of long duration; it was overthrown by a movement from within, first by the sect of Sabbatai Zebi and later by Hasidism. The ground was cut from under their asceticism, and material life was restored to its former esteem and importance.

And yet we do find even in Jewish history traces of these two extreme views—the sovereignty of the flesh and its annihilation. But that characteristic tendency, which we have already noticed, to transfer the centre of gravity from the individual to the national

life, is evident here also; and so the Jews applied to the
national life those ideas which other nations applied to
the life of the individual.

In the very earliest times there was in Israel a considerable party which adopted the materialistic view of
the national life. The whole aim of this party was to
make the body politic dominant above all other interests, to win for the Jewish State a position of honor
among its neighbors, and to secure it against external
aggression. They neither sought nor desired any
other end for the national life. This party was that
of the aristocrats, the *entourage* of the king, the military leaders, and most of the priests: in a word, all
those whose private lives were far removed from
human misery, which demands consolation. The
spiritual aspect of the national life had no meaning for
them. They were almost always ready to desert the
spiritual heritage of the nation, "to serve other gods,"
if only they thought that there was some political advantage to be gained. Against this political materialism the Prophets stood forward in all their spiritual
grandeur, and fought it incessantly; until at last it
vanished automatically with the overthrow of the
State. But certain modern historians are quite wrong
when they assert that the Prophets hated the State as
such, and desired its destruction, because they regarded its very existence as essentially inconsistent
with that spiritual life which was their aim. This
political asceticism, this desire for the annihilation of
the flesh of the national organism as a means to the
strengthening of its spirit, was in reality quite repug-
nant to the view of the Prophets. We have only to
read those passages in which the Prophets rejoice in

the victories of the State—in the time of Sennacherib, for instance—or bewail its defeats, to see at once how they valued the State, and how essential political freedom was, in their view, to the advancement of the very ideals for which they preached and fought. But at the same time they did not forget that only the spirit can exalt life, whether individual or national, and give it a meaning and an aim. Hence they demanded emphatically that the aim should not be subordinated to the means, that the flesh should not be made sovereign over the spirit. The Prophets, then, simply applied to the national life that principle which Judaism had established for the life of the individual: the unity of flesh and spirit, in the sense which I have explained.

The real ascetic view was applied to the national life only in the time of the second Temple, and then not by the Pharisees,[1] but by the Essenes. So far as the individual was concerned, the Essenes, as I have said, had no leaning towards hatred of the flesh. But they did adopt that attitude as regards the body politic. These spiritually-minded men saw corruption eating at the very heart of the Jewish State; they saw its rulers, as in the time of the first Temple, exalting the flesh and disregarding all but physical force; they saw the best minds of the nation spending their strength in a vain effort to uplift the body politic from its internal decay, and once more to breathe the

---

[1] [The word "Pharisee" is derived from the root *parosh*, which means "to separate," and is therefore usually regarded as meaning a man "separated" from the concerns of everyday life, i. e., a sort of hermit or ascetic. The author seems to accept this explanation. Others, however, regard the Pharisees as having stood for *national* separateness; others, again, derive the name from a secondary sense of the same root, "to explain, expound," and make the Pharisees the "expounders of the Law." —*Tr.*]

spirit of true Judaism into this corrupt flesh, now
abandoned as a prey to the dogs. Seeing all this, they
gave way to despair, turned their backs on political life
altogether, and fled to the wilderness, there to live out
their individual lives in holiness and purity, far from
this incurable corruption. And in this lonely existence,
removed from society and its turmoil, their hatred
of the State grew stronger and stronger, until even in
its last moments, when it was hovering betwixt life
and death, some of them actually did not conceal their
joy at its impending destruction.

But these political ascetics had no great influence
over the popular mind. It was not they, but another
sect, called Pharisees, although they had no vestige
of real asceticism,[1] who were the teachers and guides
of the people, and who upheld the Jewish view which
was handed down from the Prophets: that is, the combination of flesh and spirit. They did not run away
from life, and did not wish to demolish the State.
On the contrary, they stood at their post in the very
thick of life's battle, and tried with all their might
to save the State from moral decay, and to mould
it according to the spirit of Judaism. They knew full
well that spirit without flesh is but an unsubstantial
shade, and that the spirit of Judaism could not develop
and attain its end without a political body, in which
it could find concrete expression. For this reason the
Pharisees were always fighting a twofold battle: on
the one hand, they opposed the political materialists
within, for whom the State was only a body without
an essential spirit, and, on the other side, they fought

[1] [See the previous footnote.]

together with these opponents against the enemy without, in order to save the State from destruction. Only at the very last, when the imminent death of the body politic was beyond all doubt, did the root difference between the two kinds of patriots, who stood shoulder to shoulder, necessarily reveal itself; and then the separation was complete. The political materialists, for whom the existence of the State was everything, had nothing to live for after the political catastrophe; and so they fought desperately, and did not budge until they fell dead among the ruins that they loved. But the Pharisees remembered, even in that awful moment, that the political body had a claim on their affections only because of the national spirit which found expression in it, and needed its help. Hence they never entertained the strange idea that the destruction of the State involved the death of the people, and that life was no longer worth living. On the contrary: now, now they felt it absolutely necessary to find some temporary means of preserving the nation and its spirit even without a State, until such time as God should have mercy on His people and restore it to its land and freedom. So the bond was broken: the political Zealots remained sword in hand on the walls of Jerusalem, while the Pharisees took the scroll of the Law and went to Jabneh.[1]

And the work of the Pharisees bore fruit. They succeeded in creating a national body which hung in mid-air, without any foundation on the solid earth,

[1] [Rabbi Johanan ben Zakkai obtained permission from the victorious Romans to retire with his disciples to Jabneh, where he kept alight the lamp of Jewish study, and thus secured the continuance of Judaism despite the overthrow of the Jewish State.]

and in this body the Hebrew national spirit has had its abode and lived its life for two thousand years. The organization of the Ghetto, the foundations of which were laid in the generations that followed the destruction of Jerusalem, is a thing marvellous and quite unique. It was based on the idea that the aim of life is the perfection of the spirit, but that the spirit needs a body to serve as its instrument. The Pharisees thought at that time that, until the nation could again find an abode for its spirit in a single complete and free political body, the gap must be filled artificially by the concentration of that spirit in a number of small and scattered social bodies, all formed in its image, all living one form of life, and all united, despite their local separateness, by a common recognition of their original unity and their striving after a single aim and perfect union in the future.

But this artificial building stood too long. It was erected only to serve for a short time, in the days when men firmly believed that to-day or to-morrow Messiah would come; but at last its foundations decayed, and its walls cracked and gaped ever more and more.

Then there came again spiritually-minded men, who revived the political asceticism of the Essenes. They saw at its very worst the scattered and enslaved condition of the dispossessed nation; they saw no hope of a return to the land; they saw, too, the organization of the Ghetto, in which there was at least some shadow of a concrete national life, breaking up before their eyes. Despair took hold of them, and made them absolutely deny bodily life to their nation, made them regard its existence as purely spiritual. Israel, they said, is a spirit without a body; the spirit is not only the aim of Jewish life, it is the whole life; the flesh is not merely something subsidiary, it is actually a dangerous enemy, a hindrance to the development of the spirit and its conquest of the world.

We need not be surprised that this extreme view produced its opposite, as extreme views always do, and that we have seen a recrudescence of that political materialism which confines the life of Israel to the body, to the Jewish State.

This phenomenon is still recent, and has not yet reached its full development. But past experience justifies the belief that both these extreme views, having no root and basis in the heart of the nation, will disappear, and give place to the only view that really has its source in Judaism, the view of the Prophets in the days of the first State, and that of the Pharisees in the days of the second. If, as we hope, the future holds for Israel yet a third national existence, we may believe that the fundamental principle of individual as of national life will be neither the sovereignty of the flesh over the spirit, nor the annihilation of the flesh for the spirit's sake, but the uplifting of the flesh by the spirit.

MOSES

(1904)

The influence of great men on the history of the human race is a subject of much discussion among philosophers. Some maintain that the great men create history, and the masses are nothing more than the material on which they work. Others assert that the masses are the moving force, and the great men of every age are only inevitable products of that age and its conditions. Such discussions make one reflect on the tendency of philosophers to shut their eyes to what lies in front of them, and to seek by roundabout paths what is really so near. Surely it is obvious that the real great men of history, the men, that is, who have become forces in the life of humanity, are not actual, concrete persons who existed in a certain age. There is not a single great man in history of whom the popular fancy has not drawn a picture entirely different from the actual man; and it is this imaginary conception, created by the masses to suit their needs and their inclinations, that is the real great man, exerting an influence which abides in some cases for thousands of years—this, and not the concrete original, who lived a short space in the actual world, and was never seen by the masses in his true likeness.

And so it is when learned scholars burrow in the dust of ancient books and manuscripts, in order to raise the great men of history from the grave in their true shapes; believing the while that they are sacrificing their eyesight for the sake of "historical truth."

It is borne in on me that these scholars have a tendency to overestimate the value of their discoveries, and will not appreciate the simple fact that not every archeological truth is also an historical truth. Historical truth is that, and that alone, which reveals the forces that go to mould the social life of mankind. Every man who leaves a perceptible mark on that life, though he may be a purely imaginary figure, is a real historical force; his existence is an historical truth. And on the other hand, every man who has left no impress on the general course of life, be his concrete existence at a particular time never so indisputable, is only one of the million: and the truth contained in the statement that such an one existed is a merely literal truth, which makes absolutely no difference, and is therefore, in the historical sense, no truth at all. Goethe's Werther, for instance, was a pure fiction; but his influence on that generation was so immense as to cause a large number of suicides: and therefore he is, in the historical sense, much more truly a real person than this or that actual German of the same period, who lived an actual concrete life, and died, and was forgotten, and became as though he had never been. Hence I do not grow enthusiastic when the drag-net of scholarship hauls up some new "truth" about a great man of the past; when it is proved by the most convincing evidence that some national hero, who lives on in the hearts of his people, and influences their development, never existed, or was something absolutely unlike the popular picture of him. On such occasions I tell myself: all this is very fine and very good, and certainly this "truth" will erase or alter a paragraph of a chapter in the book of archeology; but it will not make history erase the name of its hero, or change its attitude towards him, because real history has no concern with so-and-so who is dead, and who was never seen in that form by the nation at large, but only by antiquarians; its concern is only with the living hero, whose image is graven in the hearts of men, who has become a force in human life. And what cares history whether this force was at one time a walking and talking biped, or whether it was never anything but a creature of the imagination, labelled with the name of some concrete man? In either case history is certain about his existence, because history feels his effects.

And so when I read the Haggadah on the eve of Passover, and the spirit of Moses the son of Amram, that supremest of heroes, who stands like a pillar of light on the threshold of our history, hovers before me and lifts me out of this nether world, I am quite oblivious of all the doubts and questions propounded by non-Jewish critics. I care not whether this man Moses really existed; whether his life and his activity really corresponded to our traditional account of him; whether he was really the savior of Israel and gave his people the Law in the form in which it is preserved among us; and so forth. I have one short and simple answer for all these conundrums. This Moses, I say, this man of old time, whose existence and character you are trying to elucidate, matters to nobody but scholars like you. We have another Moses of our own, whose image has been enshrined in the hearts of the Jewish people for generations, and whose influence on our national life has never ceased from ancient times till the present day. The existence of this Moses, as a historical fact, depends in no way on your investigations. For even if you succeeded in demonstrating conclusively that the man Moses never existed, or that he was not such a man as we supposed, you would not thereby detract one jot from the historical reality of the ideal Moses—the Moses who has been our leader not only for forty years in the wilderness of Sinai, but for thousands of years in all the wildernesses in which we have wandered since the Exodus.

And it is not only the existence of this Moses that is clear and indisputable to me. His character is equally plain, and is not liable to be altered by any archeological discovery. This ideal—I reason—has been created in the spirit of the Jewish people; and the creator creates in his own image. These ideal figures, into which a nation breathes its most intense aspirations, seem to be fashioned automatically, without conscious purpose; and therefore, though they cannot, of course, escape a certain superfluous and inharmonious embroidery, and though we cannot insist that every detail shall be organically related to the central idea, yet the picture as a whole, if we look at its broad outlines, does always represent that idea which is the cause of its existence, and as it were the seed from which the whole tree has grown.

I take, therefore, a comprehensive view of the whole range of tradition about Moses, and ask myself first of all: What essentially is Moses? In other words, what manner of thing is the national ideal which has its embodiment in Moses? There are heroes and heroes—heroes of war, heroes of thought, and so forth; and when we examine an ideal picture we must first be clear as to the essential nature of the ideal which the artist had in his mind and attempted to portray.

And as I look at the figure of Moses I go on to ask:
Was he a military hero?

No! The whole canvas betrays no hint of physical
force. We never find Moses at the head of an army,
performing feats of valor against the enemy. Only
once do we see him on the battlefield, in the battle
with Amalek; and there he simply stands and watches
the course of the fighting, helping the army of Israel
by his *moral* strength, but taking no part in the actual
battle.

Again: Was he a statesman?

Again, no! When he had to confront Pharaoh and
discuss questions of politics with him, he was helpless
without his brother Aaron, his mouthpiece.

Was he, then, a lawgiver?

Once more, no! Every lawgiver makes laws for
his own age, with a view to the particular needs of
that time and that place in which he and his people
live. But Moses made laws for the future, for a
generation that did not yet exist, and a country not
yet conquered; and tradition has made no secret of
the fact that many laws attributed to Moses only came
into force after several generations, while others have
never been put into practice at all.

What, then, was Moses?

Tradition answers in the most explicit terms:
"There arose not a *Prophet* since in Israel like unto
Moses." This, then, is what Moses was: a Prophet.
But he was different from the other Prophets, whose
appearance in our history, as a specific type, dates
only from the period of the monarchy. He was,
as later generations learned to call him, "the lord of
the Prophets," that is, the ideal archetype of Hebrew

prophecy in the purest and most exalted sense of the word.

Again I take a comprehensive glance at what reading and reflection have taught me about the nature of Hebrew prophecy, and try to define its essential characteristics.

The Prophet has two fundamental qualities, which distinguish him from the rest of mankind. First, he is *a man of truth*. He sees life as it is, with a view unwarped by subjective feelings; and he tells you what he sees just as he sees it, unaffected by irrelevant considerations. He tells the truth not because he wishes to tell the truth, not because he has convinced himself, after inquiry, that such is his duty, but because he needs must, because truth-telling is a special characteristic of his genius—a characteristic of which he cannot rid himself, even if he would. It has been well said by Carlyle that every man can attain to the elevation of the Prophet by seeking truth; but whereas the ordinary man is able to reach that plane by strength of will and enormous effort, the Prophet can stand on no other by reason of his very nature.

Secondly, the Prophet is an *extremist*. He concentrates his whole heart and mind on his ideal, in which he finds the goal of life, and to which he is determined to make the whole world do service, without the smallest exception. There is in his soul a complete, ideal world; and on that pattern he labors to reform the external world of reality. He has a clear conviction that so things *must* be, and no more is needed to make him demand that so they *shall* be. He can accept no excuse, can consent to no compromise, can never cease thundering his passionate denunciations, even if the whole universe is against him.

From these two fundamental characteristics there results a third, which is a combination of the other two: namely, the supremacy of absolute *righteousness* in the Prophet's soul, in his every word and action. As a man of truth he cannot help being also a man of justice or righteousness; for what is righteousness but truth in action? And as an extremist he cannot subordinate righteousness (any more than he can subordinate truth) to any irrelevant end; he cannot desert righteousness from motives of temporary expediency, even at the bidding of love or pity. Thus the Prophet's righteousness is absolute, knowing no restriction either on the side of social necessities or on that of human feelings.

The Prophet, then, is in this position: on the one hand, he cannot altogether reform the world according to his desire; on the other hand, he cannot cheat himself and shut his eyes to its defects. Hence it is impossible for him ever to be at peace with the actual life in which his days are spent. There is thus a grain of truth in the popular idea of the Prophet as above all a man who predicts the future; for, in truth, the whole world of the Prophet consists of his heart's vision of what is to come, of "the latter end of days." This is his delight and his comfort whenever the cup of sorrows is full to the brim, and he has no strength left to pour out his soul in bitter outcry against the evil that he sees around him.

But just as the Prophet will not bow to the world, so the world will not bow to him, will not accept his influence immediately and directly. This influence must first pass through certain channels in which it becomes adapted to the conditions of life. Then only can it affect mankind. These channels are human channels. They are men who cannot rise to the Prophet's elevation, and have no sympathy with his extremism, but are none the less nearer to him in spirit than the mass of men, and are capable of being influenced by him up to a certain point. These men are the *Priests* of the prophetic ideal. They stand between the Prophet and the world, and transmit his influence by devious ways, adapting their methods to the needs of each particular time, and not insisting that the message shall descend on the workaday world in all its pristine purity.

Thus I picture the Prophet in his purest form.[1] Such, in essentials, were all the true Prophets of Israel, from Hosea and Amos to Jeremiah and Ezekiel; but the type is most perfectly realized in the ideal picture of "the lord of the Prophets."

When Moses first leaves the schoolroom and goes out into the world, he is at once brought face to face with a violation of justice, and unhesitatingly he takes the side of the injured. Here at the outset is revealed the eternal struggle between the Prophet and the world.

"An Egyptian smiting a Hebrew," the strong treading scornfully on the weak—this every-day occurrence is his first experience. The Prophet's indignation is aroused, and he helps the weaker. Then "two Hebrews strove together"—two brothers, both weak, both slaves of Pharaoh: and yet they fight each other.

[1] See the essay "Priest and Prophet" [p. 125].

Once more the Prophet's sense of justice compels him, and he meddles in a quarrel which is not his. But this time he discovers that it is no easy matter to fight the battle of justice; that the world is stronger than himself, and that he who stands against the world does so at his peril. Yet this experience does not make him prudent or cautious. His zeal for justice drives him from his country; and as soon as he reaches another haunt of men, while he is still sitting by the well outside the city, before he has had time to find a friend and shelter, he hears once more the cry of outraged justice, and runs immediately to its aid. This time the wranglers are not Hebrews, but foreigners and strangers. But what of that? The Prophet makes no distinction between man and man, only between right and wrong. He sees strong shepherds trampling on the rights of weak women—"and Moses stood up and helped them."

This is the sum of our knowledge about Moses' life till the time when he stood before Pharaoh—and he was then "eighty years old." Of all that long stretch of years, and what happened in them, tradition takes no account, because they were only the preface, only the preparation for the real work of the Prophet. If an exception was made in the case of these three events, which happened to the Prophet at the outset of his life's journey, and if we see that all three have the same characteristic, that of the Prophet standing up against the world in the name of righteousness, we may believe that the object of the tradition was to throw this conflict into relief, and to show how the Prophet displayed the essential qualities of his kind from the very first. We may therefore infer that throughout the whole of that period, in all his wanderings, he never ceased to fight the battle of justice, until the day came when he was to be the savior of his people, and teach the world justice, not for his own time merely, but for all eternity.

That great moment dawned in the wilderness, far away from the turmoil of the world. The Prophet's soul is weary of his ceaseless battle, and he would fain rest in peace. He turns his back on men for the shepherd's life, and takes his sheep into the wilderness. There "he came to the mountain of God, unto Horeb." But even here there is no rest for him. He feels that he has not yet fulfilled his mission; a secret force in his heart urges him on, saying, "What doest thou here? Go thou, work and fight: for to that end wast thou created." He would like to disregard this voice, but cannot. The Prophet hears "the voice of God" in his heart, whether he will or not: "and if I say, I will not make mention of him. . . . . then there is in mine heart as it were a *burning fire* shut up in my bones, and I am weary with forbearing, and I cannot contain."

And the Prophet remembers that in his youth, at his first encounter with life, the same fire burnt in his heart and gave him no rest. From that day to this he has done all in his power to make justice supreme in the world: and the fire is still burning. The best of his years, the flower of his strength, have been consumed in the battle; and victory is not his. Now old age has come upon him; yet a little, and he will be sapless as a withered and barren tree—even like this bush before him. Can he still find new means of reaching his goal? Can his old age succeed where his youth has failed?

What is there to do that he has not done? Why should the fire still burn within him, still disturb his soul's peace?

Suddenly he hears the inner "voice of God"—the voice that he knows so well—calling to him from some forgotten corner of his heart:

"I am the God of thy father . . . . I have surely seen the affliction of my people which are in Egypt . . . . Come now, therefore, and I will send thee unto Pharaoh, that thou mayest bring forth my people, the children of Israel, out of Egypt."

"The God of his father," "the affliction of his people"—how can he have forgotten all this till now? Faithfully has he served the God of the Universe, fighting a hero's battle for universal justice. In Midian, in every country in which he set foot, he has striven always to deliver the oppressed from the oppressor, has preached always truth and peace and charity. But the God of his father he has forgotten; his people he has not remembered; the affliction wherewith the Egyptians afflict his people—of that he has taken no thought.

Now a new hope springs up in the Prophet's heart, and grows stronger each moment. With this hope, he feels, his strength increases, and the days of his youth are renewed. Now he knows the right way to the goal which he has striven after all his life. Hitherto he has consumed his strength among strangers, who looked on him as an alien even after he had spent years among them; who took no account of him, and paid no heed to his teaching; who would not believe him even if he called on the name of their own gods. But now, now he will go to his own breth-

ren, his own people, and will speak to them in the name
of the God of his fathers and theirs. They will know
and respect him; they will listen to all that he says,
will listen and obey: and the sovereignty of righteousness, hitherto nothing more than his heart's ideal,
will be established in the world by this his people,
which he will bring forth out of the house of bondage.

Under the spell of this noble idea the Prophet for-
gets for a moment all the obstacles in his path, and
in fancy sees himself already in Egypt among his
people. To Pharaoh, indeed, he will not go alone.
He knows beforehand that such a man as he, unskilled
to speak smooth words, cannot bend the hearts of kings
to his desire. But he will approach first of all his own
people; he will assemble the "elders of Israel," men
who are known in the royal house; to them first he
will reveal the great tidings, that God has visited them.
And these men, the flower of the people, will understand him and "hearken to his voice." They will go
with him to Pharaoh, and give God's message to the
king in a language which he understands.

But how if even they, the elders of Israel, "will not
hearken to his voice," "will not believe" in his mission?

In that case he knows what to do. Not for nothing
was he brought up in Pharaoh's house on the knees
of the magicians. "Enchantments" are an abomina-
tion to him; but what can he do if the "elders of
Israel" believe only in such things, and are open to
no other appeal?

Even the "sons of God" have been known to fall
from Heaven to earth; and even the Prophet has his
moments of relapse, when the spirit of prophecy de-

serts him, and his mortal elements drag him down into the mire of the world. But only for a moment can the Prophet cease to be what he ought to be, and needs must be—a man of truth. Scarcely has Moses conceived this idea of gaining credence by means of magic enchantments, when the Prophet in him rises up in arms against this unclean thought. Never! Since first he began to hear "the voice of God" his tongue has been a holy instrument, the outer vesture of that Divine voice within him; but "a man of words," a man whose words are only means to the attainment of his desires, not genuinely connected with his thought —such a man he has never been "heretofore," nor will ever be. This is a price which he will not pay even for the redemption of his people. If there is no way but through enchantments, then let the redemption be achieved by others, and let him alone in his spotless truth, alone in the wilderness:

"Oh, Lord, send, I pray thee, by the hand of him whom Thou wilt send."

But it is not easy for the Prophet to remain in the wilderness. The burning fire which has just roused all his spiritual forces to action has not yet been quelled; it will give him no rest till he find some way to carry out his thought.

So, at last, the Prophet finds the necessary "channel" through which his influence shall reach the people. He has a brother in Egypt, a man of position, a Levite, who knows how to shape his words to the needs of the time and the place. His brother will need no enchantments to gain him allegiance. He, the "Priest" of the future, will go with the Prophet to the elders and to the king himself. Nay, he will know how to find a way into the hearts of all of them:

"And thou shalt speak unto him . . . . and he shall be thy spokesman unto the people: and it shall come to pass, that he shall be to thee a mouth, and thou shalt be to him as God."

So the *immediate* goal is reached. Pharaoh and all his host lie at the bottom of the Red Sea, and Moses stands at the head of a free people, leading them to the land of their ancestors.

"Then sang Moses . . ." In this hour of happiness his heart overflows with emotion, and pours itself out in song. He does not know that he is still at the beginning of his journey; he does not know that the real task, the most difficult task, has still to be commenced. Pharaoh is gone, but his work remains; the master has ceased to be master, but the slaves have not ceased to be slaves. A people trained for generations in the house of bondage cannot cast off in an instant the effects of that training and become truly free, even when the chains have been struck off.

But the Prophet believes in the power of his ideal. He is convinced that the ideal which he is destined to give to his people will have sufficient force to expel the taint of slavery, and to imbue this slave-people with a new spirit of strength and upward striving, equal to all the demands of its lofty mission.

Then the Prophet gathers his people at the foot of the mountain, opens the innermost heavens before them, and shows them the God of their fathers in a new form, in all His universal grandeur.

"For all the earth is Mine," so speaks the voice of the God of Israel "out of the midst of the fire." Hitherto you have believed, in common with all other

nations, that every people and every country has its
own god, all-powered within his boundaries, and that
these gods wage war on one another and conquer one
another, like the nations that serve them. But it is
not so. There is no such thing as a God of Israel and
a different God of Egypt; there is one God, who was,
is, and shall be: He is Lord of *all* the earth, and Ruler
over *all* the nations. And it is this universal God who
is the God of your fathers. The whole world is His
handiwork, and all men are created in His image; but
you, the children of His chosen Abraham, He has
singled out to be His peculiar people, to be "a kingdom
of priests and an holy nation," to sanctify His name in
the world and to be an example to mankind in your
individual and in your corporate life, which are to be
based on new foundations, on the spirit of Truth and
Righteousness.

"Justice, justice shalt thou follow." "Keep thee
far from a false matter." You shall not respect the
strong; "and a stranger shalt thou not wrong. . . . .
Ye shall not afflict any widow, or fatherless child."
But neither shall you wrest justice on the side of the
weak: "Neither shalt thou favor a poor man in his
cause." The guiding rule of your lives shall be neither
hatred and jealousy, nor yet love and pity, for all alike
pervert the view and bias the judgment. "Justice,
justice"—that alone shall be your rule.

"Did ever people hear the voice of God speaking
out of the midst of the fire" such lofty and majestic
words? And the nation that has heard this message,
though it may have been sunk for centuries in the
morass of slavery and degradation, how can it fail to

rise out of the depths, and feel in its innermost soul the purifying light that streams in upon it?

So thinks the Prophet; and the people confirm his belief, as they cry ecstatically, with one voice, "All that the Lord hath spoken we will do."

So the Prophet leaves the camp in peace of mind, and withdraws into solitude on the top of the mountain, there to perfect and complete the law of righteousness. But before he has been many days out of sight the Egyptian bondman rears his head, and in a moment overturns the dream-castle which the Prophet has built on the foundation of his faith in the power of the ideal. "The voice of God" is drowned by "the noise of the people as they shouted"; and the Priest, whom the Prophet trusted, who was his mouthpiece before Pharaoh and the people, this very Priest is carried away by the mob, and makes them "gods" after their own heart, and builds an altar . . . . This, in his view, is what the hour demands: and the Priest is above all a man of the hour.

The Prophet's grief knows no bounds. All his work, all his visions of his people's glorious mission, all the hope which comforted him in his arduous path, all is vanished into nothing. He is seized by impotent despair. "The tablets of the Covenant" fall from his hand and are broken; his faith in himself and his work is shaken. Now he sees how hard it is to create a "peculiar people" out of such warped material, and for one moment he thinks of abandoning this "obstinate people," and entrusting his tablets to the remnant who are faithful to his covenant. They will observe his law, and win over little by little the best of mankind, till they become "a great nation"; and he will return to his shepherd's life in the wilderness.

But the Prophet is not a Priest: it is not for him to bow to circumstances without a struggle, and to change his way of thought at their bidding. The first impulse passes away, and the Prophet returns to his mission, and resolves to go forward, come what may. Now he realizes the hard task that lies before him. He no longer believes in a sudden revolution; he knows that signs and wonders and visions of God can arouse a momentary enthusiasm, but cannot create a new heart, cannot uproot and implant feelings and inclinations with any stability or permanence. So he summons all his patience to the task of bearing the troublesome burden of his people and training it by slow steps till it is fit for its mission.

Thus the first period passes away. The Prophet teaches, trains, bears, and forgives, borne up by the hope of seeing the fruits of his labor at no distant day, when his people's mission will be fulfilled in their own land.

And then comes the incident of the spies. Here is a nation on its way to conquer a country by force, and there build up its own distinctive national life, which is to be an example to the world: and at the first unfavorable report despair sets in, and the glorious future is forgotten. Even the Prophet's heart fails him at this evidence of utter, fathomless degradation.

Moses now sees, then, that his last hope is groundless. Not even education will avail to make this degraded mob capable of a lofty mission. Straightway the Prophet decrees extinction on his generation, and resolves to remain in the wilderness forty years, till all

that generation be consumed, and its place be taken
by a new generation, born and bred in freedom, and
trained from childhood under the influence of the
Law which it is to observe in the land of its future.

It requires unusual courage to go out boldly to meet
danger, to fall single-handed on an enemy of vastly
superior strength, to plunge into a stormy sea. But
far greater heroism is demanded of the man who goes
about consciously and deliberately to tear out of his
heart a splendid hope, which has been the very breath
of his life; to stop half-way when all his feelings
tumultuously impel him on towards the goal which
seemed so near. With such heroism has this Hebrew
tradition endowed its Superman, the prince of its
Prophets. In vain do his followers, now conscious
of their error, urge him to take up the work again, and
lead them to their inheritance; in vain is their entreaty,
"Lo, we be here, and will go up"! The Prophet has
decreed, and will not, nay cannot, retract. He is convinced that "this evil congregation" can be of no use for
his purpose, and no entreaty will induce the Prophet
to act against his convictions. He mourns with
them and makes their grief his own; but for their sup-
plications he has one stern answer, "Go not up, for
the Lord is not among you."

So the Prophet remains in the wilderness, buries
his own generation and trains up a new one. Year
after year passes, and he never grows weary of repeating to this growing generation the laws of righteousness that must guide its life in the land of its
future; never tires of recalling the glorious past in
which these laws were fashioned. The past and the
future are the Prophet's whole life, each completing

the other. In the present he sees nothing but a wilderness, a life far removed from his ideal; and therefore he looks before and after. He lives in the future world of his vision, and seeks strength in the past out of which that vision-world is quarried.

Forty years are gone, and the new generation is about to emerge from its vagabond life in the wilderness, and take up the broken thread of the national task, when the Prophet dies, and another man assumes the leadership, and brings the people to its land.

Why does the Prophet die? Why is it not vouchsafed to him to complete his work himself? Tradition, as we know, gives no sufficient reason. But tradition recognized, with unerring instinct, that so it needs must be. When the time comes for the ideal to be embodied in practice, the Prophet can no longer stand at the head; he must give place to another. The reason is that from that moment there begins a new period, a period in which prophecy is dumb, a period of those half-measures and compromises which are essential to the battle of life. In this period reality assumes gradually a form very different from that of the Prophet's vision; and so it is better for him to die than to witness this change. "He shall see the land before him, but he shall not go thither." He has brought his people to the border, fitted them for their future, and given them a noble ideal to be their lodestar in time of trouble, their comfort and their salvation; the rest is for other men, who are more skilled to compromise with life. Let them do what they will do and achieve what they will achieve, be it much or little. In any case they will not achieve all that the Prophet wished, and their way will not be his way.

As for him, the Prophet, he dies, as he has lived, in his faith. All the evil that he has seen has been powerless to quench his hope for the future, or dim the brightness of the ideal that illumined his path from afar. He dies with gladness on his face, and with words of comfort for the latter days on his lips: dies, as tradition says, "in a kiss," embracing, as it were, the ideal to which he has consecrated his life, and for which he has toiled and suffered till his last breath.

When Heine wanted to describe the greatness of the prince of Hebrew poets, Jehudah Halevi, he said that "he was born with a kiss." But that idea is foreign to the Jewish spirit. When the national tradition wishes to describe the greatness of the prince of Prophets, it makes him die, not come to life, with a kiss. That death-kiss is the crown of a work completed and a duty fulfilled to the uttermost, of a life whose burden has been borne from first to last with the steadfastness of a sea-girt rock, which flinches not nor bows, but bears unmoved the onset of the devouring waves.

"The creator," I have said, "creates in his own image." And in truth, our people has but expressed *itself*, at its highest, in this picture of Moses. Well have the Cabbalists said that "Moses is reincarnated in every age." Some hint of Moses has illumined the dark life of our people, like a spark, in every generation. This needs no lengthy proof. We have but to open our Prayer Book, and we shall see almost on every page how constant has been the striving after the realization of the prophetic ideal in all its world-embracing breadth, constant throughout the blackest periods of the Jew's history, when his life has been

most precarious, and persecution has driven him from
country to country. Israel has never lived in the present. The present, with its evil and its wickedness, has
always filled us with anguish, indignation, and bitterness. But just as constantly have we been inspired
with brilliant hopes for the future, and an ineradicable
faith in the coming triumph of the good and the right;
and for these hopes and that faith we have always
sought and found support in the history of our past,
whereon our imagination has brooded, weaving all
manner of fair dreams, so as to make the past a kind
of mirror of the future. Our very Hebrew language,
the garment of the Jewish spirit, has no present tense,
but only a past and a future. The question has been
much debated, whether the fundamental characteristic
of the Jewish spirit is optimism or pessimism; and extreme views have been propounded on both sides. But
all such discussion is futile. The Jew is both optimist
and pessimist; but his pessimism has reference to the
present, his optimism to the future. This was true of
the Prophets, and it is true of the people of the
Prophets.

There has, indeed, been one short period in modern
Jewish history when Israel grew utterly weary of toil
and trouble, and began to long for solace in the present, taking pleasure in the fleeting hour, as other nations do, and demanding no more of life than what it
can give. And when once this longing was aroused,
and became Israel's ideal (despite its fundamental opposition to the prophetic outlook), the prophetic characteristic at once manifested itself here also: the ideal
was pursued to extreme lengths, without any regard to
'e obstacles that lay in the way of its attainment.

The Jews of that period had no pity on the vision of a
great future, to which their ancestors clung throughout history. They wiped it out at a single stroke, as
soon as its abandonment seemed to be a necessary step
to the attainment of the ideal of to-day. And with the
future the past necessarily went, seeing that it had no
meaning except as a mirror of the future. But we all
know the end of the story. The ideal of to-day was
not attained; and all the labor of that period, its attempt to destroy one world and build another, left
nothing but ruin and the bitterness that comes of
wasted effort.

But this was a mere passing phase, a sort of faint-
ing-fit, a temporary loss of consciousness. The prophetic spirit cannot be crushed, except for a time. It
comes to life again, and masters the Prophet in his
own despite. So, too, the prophetic people regained
consciousness in its own despite, and we see once again
some beginning of the "reincarnation of Moses." The
Spirit which called Moses thousands of years ago and
sent him on his mission, against his own will, now
calls again the generation of to-day, saying,

"And that which cometh into your mind shall not
be at all; in that ye say, we will be as the nations . . .
as I live, saith the Lord God, surely with a mighty
hand . . . . will I be king over you."

THE SUPREMACY OF REASON

(TO THE MEMORY OF MAIMONIDES)

(1904)

At last, after the lapse of seven hundred years,[1] the anniversary of Maimonides' death has been raised to the dignity of an important national day of memorial, and has been honoured throughout the Diaspora. In earlier centuries our ancestors do not apear to have remembered that so-and-so many hundred years had passed since the death of Maimonides ; still less did they make the anniversary a public event, as we do now, although they were in much closer sympathy with Maimonides than we are—or, to be more correct, *because* they were in much closer sympathy with him than we are. They did not feel it necessary to commemorate the death of one whom in spirit they saw still living among them— one whose advice and instruction they sought every day in all their difficulties of theory and practice, as though he were still in their midst. In those days it was almost impossible for an educated Jew (and most Jews then were educated) to pass a single day without remembering Maimonides : just as it was impossible for him to pass a single day without remembering Zion. In whatever field of study the Jew might be engaged—in *halachah*,[2] in ethics, in religious or philosophical speculation—inevitably he found Maimonides in the place of

---

[1] [Maimonides died on the 13th December, 1204.]
[2] [Jewish Law.]

honour, an authority whose utterances were eagerly
conned even by his opponents. And even if a man
happened to be no student, at any rate he would say
his prayers every day, and finish his morning prayer
with the " Thirteen Articles" : how then could he forget the man who formulated the Articles of the Jewish
religion ?

But how different it is to-day ! If a Jew of that
earlier time came to life again, and we wanted to bring
home to him as forcibly as possible the distance between
ourselves and our ancestors, it would be enough, I think,
to tell him that nowadays one may spend a great deal
of time in reading Hebrew articles and books without
coming across a single reference to Maimonides. And
the reason is not that we have satisfactory answers to
all the spiritual questions which troubled our ancestors,
and have therefore no need for the out-of-date philosophy of Maimonides. The reason is that the questions
themselves are no longer on our agenda : because we
are told that nowadays men of enlightenment are concerned not with spiritual questions, but only with politics
and hard, concrete facts. If Maimonides in his day
accepted the dictum of Aristotle that the sense of touch
is a thing to be ashamed of, we in our day are prone to
accept the dictum that " spirituality " is a thing to be
ashamed of, and nothing is worth notice except what
can be touched and felt. When, therefore, we were
reminded this year that seven hundred years had elapsed
since the death of the man with whom the spiritual life
of our people has been bound up during all the intervening period, the fact made a profound impression
throughout the length and breadth of Jewry. It was as
though our people were quickened by this reminder, and

stirred suddenly to some vague yearning after the past—
that past in which it was still capable (despite all the
Judennot[1]) of looking upwards and seeking answers to
other questions than those of bread and a *Nachtasyl*.[1]

Be that as it may, Maimonides has become the hero
of the moment and a subject of general interest. Many
an address has been delivered, many an article has been
written in his honour this year; but nobody, so far as I
have seen, has yet used the occasion to unearth, from
beneath that heap of musty metaphysics which is so
foreign to us, the central idea of Maimonides, and to
show how there sprang from this central idea those
views of his on religion and morality, which produced
a long period of unstable equilibrium in Judaism, and
have left a profound impression on the spiritual development of our people. Since none else has performed
this task, I am minded to try my hand at it. If even
those who are expert in Maimonides' system find here
some new point of view, so much the better; if not, no
harm is done. For my purpose is not to discover something new, but to rehearse old facts in an order and a
style that seem to me to be new, and to be better
adapted to present the subject intelligibly to modern
men, who have not been brought up on medieval literature.

I

Can Maimonides claim to be regarded as the originator
of a new system? This is a question which has exercised
various authors; but we may leave it to those who attach
importance to names. We may give Maimonides that
title or not: but two facts are beyond dispute. On the

[1] [Allusion to well-known speeches at Zionist Congresses. —*Tr.*]

one hand, the fundamental assumptions on which he
built up his system were not his own, but were borrowed
by him almost in their entirety from the philosophy of
Aristotle as presented at second hand by the Arabs,
who introduced into it a good deal of neo-Platonic
doctrine. But, on the other hand, it is indisputable that
Maimonides carried to their logical conclusion the
ethical consequences of those assumptions, as the Greeks
and the Arabs, with whom the assumptions originated,
did not ; and in this way he did say something that was
new and hitherto unsaid, though it was logically implied
in the fundamental principles which he took from other
thinkers.

If, then, we would understand the ethical system of
Maimonides, we must set clearly before our minds the
metaphysical assumptions on which it was built. Those
assumptions are so far removed from the philosophical
and scientific conceptions of our own time that the
modern man can scarcely grasp them. But in those
days even the greatest thinkers believed these airy
abstractions to be the solid truths of philosophy, rock-
based on incontestable evidences. Hence it is not surprising that Maimonides, like the rest, was convinced
beyond doubt that this " scientific " teaching was the
uttermost limit of human understanding, and could never
be changed or modified. So absolute, indeed, was his
conviction that he went so far as to put this teaching in
a dogmatic form, as though it had been a revelation
from above.[1]

The following is an outline of his dogmas, so far as is
necessary for our purpose :

" All bodies beneath the firmament are compounded

[1] *Mishneh Torah, Foundations of the Law*, chaps. i.-iv.

of matter and form."[1] But " form " here is not "form as vulgarly understood, which is *the picture and image of the thing* "; it is "the natural form," that is to say, the reality of the thing, " that by virtue of which it is what it is," as distinct from other things which are not of its kind.[2]

" Matter is never *perceived* without form, nor form without matter; it is man who divides existing bodies in his consciousness, and *knows* that they are compounded of matter and form."[3] For since the form is the reality, by virtue of which the thing is what it is, it follows that matter without form would be a thing without a real existence of its own : in other words, a mere intellectual abstraction. And it is superfluous to add that form without matter does not exist in the sublunar world, which consists wholly of " bodies."[4]

" The nature of matter is that form cannot *persist* in it, but it continually divests itself of one form and takes on another." It is because of this property of matter that things come into being and cease to be, whereas form by its nature does not desire change, and ceases to be only " on account of its connection with matter." Hence "*generic* forms are all *constant,*" though they exist in *individuals which change,* which come and go ; but *individual* forms necessarily perish, since their existence is possible only in combination with finite matter.[5]

---

[1] *Ibid.,* chap. iv. 1.

[2] *Guide,* Part I., chap. i. [In rendering quotations from the *Moreh Nebuchim (Guide for the Perplexed)* the translator has used Dr. Friedländer's English version so far as possible. —*Tr.*]

[3] *Foundations of the Law, ibid.,* 7.

[4] In the upper world Aristotle's philosophy postulates the existence of forms divorced from matter : they are the " separate Intelligences," which emanate one from another and are eternal (see *Foundations of the Law, ibid.,* and *Guide,* Part II., chap. iv.).

[5] *Guide,* Part III., chap. viii.

" The soul of all flesh is its form," and the body is the matter in which this form clothes itself. " When, therefore, the body, which is compounded of the elements, is dissolved, the soul perishes, because it exists only with the body" and has no permanent existence except *generically,* like other forms.[1]

" The soul is one, but it has many different faculties," and therefore philosophers speak of parts of the soul. " By this they do not mean that it is divisible as bodies are ; they merely enumerate its different *faculties.*" The parts of the soul, in this sense, are five : the nutritive, the sensitive, the imaginative, the emotional, and the rational. The first four parts are common to man and to other animals, though " each kind of animal has a particular soul " special to itself, which functions in it in a particular way, so that, for instance, the emotion of a man is not like the emotion of an ass. But the essential superiority of the soul of man lies in its possession of the additional fifth part—the rational : this is " that power in man by which he thinks and acquires knowledge and distinguishes between wrong actions and right."[2]

Thus the soul of man differs from the souls of other living things only in the greater variety and higher quality of its functions. In essence it is, like " the soul of all flesh," simply a form associated with matter, having no existence apart from the body. When the body is resolved into its elements the soul also perishes with all its parts, *including the rational.*

This extreme conclusion had already been deduced from the teaching of Aristotle by some of his early com-

[1] *Foundations of the Law, ibid.,* 8 and 9.
[2] *Eight Chapters,* chap. i.

mentators (such as Alexander Aphrodisius). There were, indeed, other commentators who, unable to abandon belief in the survival of the soul, tried to explain Aristotle's words in conformity with that belief by excluding the rational part from the " natural form " and attributing to it a separate and eternal existence.[1] But Maimonides was too logical not to see the inconsistency involved in that interpretation ; and so he sided with the extremists, though their view was absolutely opposed to that belief in personal immortality which in his day had come to be generally accepted by Jews. Had he been content with that view alone, he would inevitably have gone back to the conception of primitive Judaism, as we find it in the Pentateuch : that immortality belongs not to the individual, but to the nation ; that the national form persists for ever, like the generic form in living things, and the changing individuals are its matter.   In that case his whole ethical system would have been very different from what it is. But Maimonides supplemented the teaching of Aristotle by another idea, which he took from the Arabs ; and this idea, amplified and completed, he made the basis of his ethical system, which thereby acquired a new and original character, distinguished by its fusion of the social and the individual elements.

The idea is in substance this : that while reason, which is present in a human being from birth, is only one of the faculties of the soul, which is a unity of all its parts and ceases wholly to exist when the body ceases, yet this faculty is no more than a " potential faculty," by virtue of which its possessor is able to apprehend ideas ; and therefore its cessation is inevit-

[1] See Munk, *Le Guide des Egarés*, I., pp. 304-8 (note)

able only if it remains throughout its existence in its original condition—in the condition, that is, of ε "potential faculty" whose potentiality has not been realised. But if a human being makes use of this faculty and attains to the actual apprehension of Ideas, then his intellect has proceeded from the stage of potentiality to that of actuality : it has achieved real existence, which is permanent and indestructible, like the existence of those Ideas which it has absorbed into itself and with which it has become one. Thus we are to distinguish between the " potential intellect," which is given to a human being when he comes into the world, and is merely a function of the body, and the " acquired intellect," which a human being wins for himself by apprehending the Ideas. This acquired intellect " is not a function of the body and is really separate from the body." Hence it does not cease to exist with the cessation of the body ; it persists for ever, like the other " separate Intelligences."[1]

Now since the form of every existing thing is that individual essence by virtue of which it is what it is and is distinguished from all other existing things, it is clear that the acquired intellect, which gives its possessor immortality, is the essence of the human being who has been privileged to acquire it : in other words, his true form, by which he is distinguished from the rest of mankind. In other men the form is the transient soul given to them at birth ; but in him who has the acquired intellect even the soul itself is only a kind of matter. His essential form is " the higher knowledge," " *the form*

[1] *Guide,* Part I., chaps lxx. and lxxii. and *passim.* For details see Munk (*ibid.*), and Dr. Scheyer's monograph, *Das Psychologische System des Maimonides,* Frankfort a/M, 1845.

of the soul," which he has won for himself by assimilating " Ideas which are separate from matter."[1]

Thus mankind is divided into two species, the difference between which is greater than that between mankind as a whole and other kinds of animals. For man is distinguished from the rest of animate nature only by having a distinctive form : in quality his form is like the forms of other living things, seeing that in his case as in theirs the individual form perishes. But the distinctive form of the man who has the acquired intellect is distinct in *quality;* for it persists for ever even after its separation from matter. Its affinity is not with the other forms in the lower world, but with those "separate forms " in the world above.[2]

Thus far Maimonides followed the Arabs. But here the Arab philosophers stopped : they did not probe this idea further, did not carry it to its logical conclusions. Maimonides, on the contrary, refused to stop half-way ; he did not shrink from the extremest consequences of the idea.

First of all, he defined the content and the method of the intellectual process by which man attains to "acquired intellect." If we say that the intellect becomes actual and eternal by comprehending the Ideas and becoming one with them,[3] it follows that the content of the Ideas themselves must be actual and eternal. For how could

---

[1] *Foundations of the Law,* chap. iv., 8, 9.

[2] There is some ground for thinking that Maimonides thought of the eternal existence after death of the possessors of " acquired intellect " not as personal, but as a common existence in which they are all united as a single separate being. See *Guide,* III., chap. xxvii., and *Foundations, ibid.,* and chap. ii., 5-6. This has been pointed out by Dr.Joel in *Die Religionsphilosophie des Mose ben Maimon,* Breslau, 1876 (p. 25, note).

[3] *Guide,* I., chap. lxviii.

something real and eternal be created by the acquisition of something itself unreal or not eternal? Thus we exclude from the category of Ideas by the apprehension of which the acquired intellect is obtained : (1) those sciences which contain only abstract laws and not the explanation of real things, such as mathematics and logic ; (2) those sciences which teach not what actually exists, but what ought to be done for the achievement of certain objects, such as ethics and æsthetics; (3) the knowledge of individual forms, which have only a temporary existence in combination with matter, such as the histories of famous men and the like. All knowledge of this kind, though it is useful and in some cases even necessary as preparation, is not in itself capable of making the intellect actual. What, then, are the Ideas by the apprehension of which the intellect does become actual? They are those whose content is true and eternal Being. This Being includes (going from lower to higher) : (1) the generic forms of all things in the lower world, which are, as we know, constant ; (2) the heavenly bodies, which, though compounded of matter and form, are eternal ; (3) the forms which are free of matter (God and the separate Intelligences).[1] All this relates to the *content* of the intellectual process ; but there is also a very important definition of its *method*— a definition which is implied in the conception itself. The result must be achieved *by the intellect's own activity* : that is to say, man must apprehend the truth of Being by rational proofs, and must not simply accept truth from others by an act of faith. For apprehension by this latter method is purely external ; reason has had

[1] According to the division of the sciences current in those days, all this knowledge of true Being is contained in Physics and Metaphysics.

no active part in it, and therefore that union of the intellect with its object, which is what makes the intellect actual, is lacking.[1]

And now let us see what are the ethical consequences of this idea.

The question of the *ultimate* purpose of the universe is for Maimonides an idle question, because it is not within our power to find a satisfactory answer. For whatever purpose we find, it is always possible to ask : What is the purpose of that purpose? And in the end we are bound to say : " God willed it so," or, "His wisdom decided so." But at the same time Maimonides agrees with Aristotle and his school that the *proximate* purpose of all that exists in this world of ours is man. For in that " course of genesis and destruction" which goes on in all the genera of existing things we see a kind of striving on the part of matter to attain to the most perfect form possible (" to produce the most perfect being that can be produced ") ; and since "man is the most perfect being formed of matter," it follows that " in this respect it can truly be said that all earthly things exist for man."[2]

Now if man is the proximate purpose of all things on earth, " we are compelled to inquire further, why man exists and what was the purpose of his creation."

---

[1] All this teaching is scattered up and down Maimonides' works, partly in explicit statements and partly in hints (see, *e.g., Guide,* III., chap. li.). Dr. Scheyer was the first to work out these definitions in detail (*ibid.,* chap. iii.). In general it must be remembered that Maimonides nowhere explains his whole system in logical order, and we are therefore compelled, if we would understand his system as it was conceived in his mind, to make use of scattered utterances, hints, and half-sentences written by the way, to explain obscure statements by others more precise, and to resort freely to inference.

[2] *Guide,* III., chap. xiii., and Introduction to *Commentary on the Mishnah,* section *Zera'im.*

Maimonides' view of the human soul being what it is, there is, of course, a ready answer to this question. The purpose of man's existence, like that of all material existence, is " to produce the most perfect being that can be produced " : and what is the most perfect being if not the possessor of the " acquired intellect," who has attained the most perfect form possible to man? The purpose of man's life, then, is "to picture the Ideas in his soul." For " only wisdom can add to his inner strength and raise him from low to high estate ; for he was a man potentially, and has now become a man actually, and man before he thinks and acquires knowledge is esteemed an animal."[1]

But if this is so, can we still ask what is the highest moral duty and what is the most perfect moral good? Obviously, there is no higher moral duty than this : that man strive to fulfil that purpose for which he was created ; and there is no more perfect moral good than the fulfilment of that purpose. All other human activities are only " to preserve man's existence, to the end that that one activity may be fulfilled."[2]

Here, then, we reach a new moral criterion and a complete " transvaluation of values " as regards human actions in their moral aspect. Every action has a moral value, whether positive or negative, only in so far as it helps or hinders man in his effort to fulfil the purpose of his being—the actualisation of his intellect. " Good" in the moral sense is all that helps to this end ; " evil " is all that hinders. If we determine according to this view the positions of good actions in the ethical scale, we shall find that higher and lower have changed places.

[1] Introduction cited in last note.
[2] *Ibid.*

At the very top, of course, will stand that one activity which leads direct to the goal—the apprehension of eternal Being by rational proof : that is to say, the study of physics and metaphysics. Below this the scale bifurcates into the two main lines of study and action. In the sphere of study, mathematics and logic have special moral importance, because knowledge of these sciences is a necessary preliminary to the understanding of Being by rational proof. Below them come subjects which have a practical object (ethics, etc.) : for the actions with which these subjects deal are themselves only means to the attainment of the supreme end, and therefore the study of these subjects is but a means to a means.[1] In the sphere of action, again, there are different degrees. Those human actions which have as their object the satisfaction of bodily needs have positive moral value only in a limited sense : in so far as they effectively keep off physical pain and mental distraction, and thus allow a man to give himself untroubled to the pursuit of the Ideas.[2] Above these are actions which are connected with " perfection of character," because that perfection is necessary for the attainment of true wisdom. " For while man pursues after his lusts, and makes feeling master over intellect, and enslaves his reason to his passions, the divine power—that is, Reason—cannot become his."[3] Hence even perfection of character has no absolute moral value, any more than

---

[1] *Guide,* III., chap. li. Maimonides does not there emphasise the difference between practical studies on the one hand and mathematics and logic on the other, because this is not germane to his purpose at the moment. But the distinction is necessarily implied.

[2] *Guide,* III., chaps. xxvii. and liv. ; *Hilchoth De'oth,* chaps. iii. and iv.

[3] Introduction to *Zera'im.*

other things which appertain to practical life.   The
moral value of everything is determined by its relation
to the fulfilment of the intellectual purpose, and by that
alone.[1]

Starting from this standpoint, Maimonides lays down
the principle that virtue is " the mean which is equidistant from both extremes."[2] This principle is taken,
of course, from Aristotle's doctrine of virtue.   But
Aristotle did not set up a higher moral criterion by
reference to which the mean point could be determined
in every case.   For him all virtue was really but a code
of good manners to which the polite Greek should conform, being enabled by his own good taste to fasten
instinctively on the point equidistant from the ugliness
of the two extremes.   Not so Maimonides, the Jew.
He made this principle the basis of morality in the true
sense, because he coupled with it a formulation of the
supreme moral end.   This moral end, for which the
virtues are a preparation,[3] compels us and enables us
to distinguish between the extremes and the mean. For
the extremes, being apt to impair physical health or
mental peace, prevent a man from fulfilling his intellectual function ; the mean is that which helps him on
his road.[4]

But with all this we have not yet a complete answer

[1] Maimonides' attitude to perfection of character is most clearly
revealed by the fact that he calls it " bodily perfection," in contrast
to " perfection of the soul," which is *intellectual* perfection (*Guide*,
III., chap. xxvii.).

[2] See *Hilchoth De'oth*, chap. i. ; *Eight Chapters*, chap. iv.

[3] *Guide*, III., chap. liv.

[4] See *Eight Chapters*, end of chap. iv. and beginning of chap. v.
Lazarus (*Ethik des Judentums*, I., chap. xiv.) fails to notice this
difference between Aristotle and Maimonides, and therefore finds it
strange that Maimonides introduces Aristotle's doctrine of the mean
into Jewish ethics.

to our question about the purpose of the existence of
the human race as a whole.   We know that the human
race really consists of two different species : "potential
man " and "actual man."   The second species, indeed,
does not come into existence from the start as an independent species, but is produced by development out of
the first.   But this development is a very long one, and
depends on many conditions which are difficult of fulfilment, so that only a few men—sometimes only " one
in a generation "—are privileged to complete it, while
the great majority of mankind remains always at the
stage of " potential man."   Thus the question remains :
What is the purpose of the existence of the great mass
of men   " who cannot picture the Idea in their souls " ?
For when we say that all material things exist for the
sake of the existence of man, we do not mean that all
other things are but a " necessary evil," an evil
incidental to the production of the desired end—in other
words, merely Nature's unsuccessful experiments in her
struggle towards " the production of the most perfect
being that can be produced," like the many imperfect
specimens of his art that the inexpert artificer turns out
before he succeeds in creating one that is perfect.   We
cannot so regard them in the face of the evidence that
we have of the wonderful wisdom of creative nature,
which proves that the Artificer can do his work in the
way best fitted to achieve his object.   We must therefore assume that " things do not exist for nothing " ;
that Nature, in her progress towards the production of
the most perfect being, has formed all other things for
the benefit of that most perfect being, whether for food
or " for his advantage otherwise than by way of food,"
in such a way that the sum-total of things in the inferior

world is not merely a ladder by which to ascend to the production of man, but also a means to secure the permanence of man when once he has been produced.   It follows, therefore, that all the millions of men " who cannot picture the Idea in their souls " cannot be void of purpose, like the spoilt creations of the artist, which, not being suited to their object, are left lying about until they perish of themselves. There must of necessity be some advantage in their existence, as in that of the other kinds of created things.   What, then, is this advantage?   The answer is implied in the question. " Potential man," like other earthly things, exists without doubt for the benefit of the " perfect being," of " actual man."   In conformity with this view Maimonides lays it down that " these men exist for two reasons. First, to serve the one man (the ' perfect ') : for man has many wants, and Methuselah's life were not long enough to learn all the crafts whereof a man has absolute need for his living : and when should he find leisure to learn and to acquire wisdom?   The rest of mankind, therefore, exists to set right those things that are necessary to them in the commonwealth, to the end that the Wise Man may find his needs provided for and that wisdom may spread.   And secondly, the man without wisdom exists because the Wise are very few, and therefore the masses were created to make a society for the Wise, that they be not lonely." [1]

Thus the existence of the majority of mankind has a purpose of its own, which is different from that of the existence of the chosen minority.   This minority is an end in itself—it is the embodiment of the most perfect form in the inferior world ; whereas the purpose of the

[1] Introduction to *Zera'im*.

majority lies not in its own existence, but in the fact that it creates the conditions necessary to the existence of the minority : it creates, that is, human society with all its cultural possessions (in the material sense), without which it is impossible that wisdom should spread.

Thus we have introduced into ethics a new element—the social element.

For if each man could attain the degree of " actual man " without dependence on the help of human society for the provision of his needs, the moral criterion would be purely individual. Each man would be free to apply for himself the formula at which we arrived above :— all that helps me to fulfil my intellectual function is for me morally good; all that hinders me is for me morally evil. But if the attainment of the supreme end is possible only for the few, and is possible for them only through the existence of the society of the many, which has for its function the creation of the conditions most favourable to the production of the perfect being : then we are confronted with a new moral criterion, social in character. All that helps towards the perfection of society in the manner required for the fulfilment of its function is morally good ; all that retards this development is morally evil. This moral criterion is binding for the minority and the majority alike. The majority, whose existence has no purpose beyond their participation in the work of society, can obviously have no other moral criterion than the social. But even the minority, though they are capable of attaining the supreme end, and have therefore an individualistic moral criterion, are none the less bound to subordinate themselves to the social criterion where the two are in conflict. For as society becomes more perfect, and the material basis

is provided with less expenditure of effort, so much the
greater will be the possibility of producing the perfect
being with more regularity and frequency.   Hence from
the point of view of the supreme end of the whole human
race—and that is the source of moral duty—the well-
being of society is more important than that of an
individual man, even though he belong to the perfect
few.[1]

From this point of view all branches of man's work
which further the perfection of society and the lighten-
ing of the burden of life's needs have a moral value,
because they help more or less to create that environment which is necessary for the realisation of the most
perfect form in the chosen few.   Hence, to take one
instance, Maimonides reckons the fine arts among the
things that further the attainment of mankind's end
(though naturally beauty has in his system no independent value) : " for the soul grows weary and the
mind is confused by the constant contemplation of ugly
things, just as the body grows weary in doing heavy
work, until it rest and be refreshed, and then it returns
to its normal condition : so does the soul also need to
take thought for the repose of the senses by contemplat-
ing pleasant things until its weariness is dispelled."
Thus "the making of sculptures and pictures in build-
ings, vessels, and garments " is not " wasted work."[2]

To sum up : society stands between the two species
of men and links them together.   For the " actual
man " society is a means to the attainment of his end ;

<hr>

[1] See *Guide,* III., chaps. xxvii., xxxiv.   Maimonides is not explicit
on the relation of the minority to social morality ; but his view on this
question is evident from what he says in the chapters quoted, and
passim.

[2] *Eight Chapters,* chap. v.

for the "potential man" it is the purpose of his own being. The "potential man," then, being in himself but a transient thing, which comes into being and ceases to be, like all other living things, must content himself with the comforting knowledge that his fleeting existence is after all not wasted, because he is a limb of the social body which gives birth to the immortal perfect beings, and his work, in whatever sphere, helps to produce these perfect beings.

Thus Maimonides gets back to the view of early Judaism, which made the life of society the purpose of the life of the individual, although at first he seemed to diverge widely from it in setting up the one "perfect man," the possessor of "acquired intellect," as the sole end of the life of humanity at large.

It is possible, indeed, at first sight to find a certain resemblance between Maimonides' ethics and another doctrine which has recently gained such wide currency —the doctrine of Nietzsche. Both conceive the purpose of human existence to lie in the creation of the most perfect human type ; and both make the majority a tool of that minority in which the supreme type is realised. But in fact the two doctrines are essentially different, and the resemblance is only external. In the first place, Nietzsche's Superman is quite unlike Maimonides' Superman in character. Nietzsche, Hellenic in spirit, finds the highest perfection in a perfect harmony of all bodily and spiritual excellences. But Maimonides, true to the spirit of Judaism, concentrates on one central point, and gives pre-eminence to a spiritual element— that of intellect. And secondly, the relation of his "actual man" to society is different from that of Nietzsche's Superman. The Superman seeks an outlet for his powers in the world outside him; he strives to embody his will in action, and tolerates no obstacle in his path. He is therefore eternally at war with human society; for society puts a limit to his will and sets obstacles on his path by means of its moral laws, which have been framed not to suit his individual needs, but to suit the needs of the majority. Maimonides' " actual man," on the contrary, aims not at embodying his will in the external world, but at perfecting his form in his inner world. He demands nothing of society except that it satisfy his elementary wants, and so leave him at peace to pursue his inner perfection. He does not therefore regard society as his enemy. On the contrary, he sees in society an ally, without whose aid he cannot attain his end, and whose well-being will secure his own.

II

So far I have purposely refrained from bringing the religious element into the ethics of Maimonides, with the object of showing that he really based his view of human life on philosophy alone, and did not give way a single inch in order to effect a compromise between his philosophy and the religious ideas which were accepted by Jews in his time. None the less, there is no doubt that Maimonides was a religious man, and believed in the divinity of the Law of Moses: only his idea of the nature of religion, its function and its value, was a new one, and differed entirely from the accepted idea, because here also, in the sphere of religion itself, he remained faithful to those fundamental axioms on which he based his moral system.

Does philosophy leave any room for a belief in the

existence of a revealed religion—that is to say, in a Law given to men by God through a supernatural revelation of himself to one or to many individuals? This question turns on another : Is the existence of the world independent of time and external cause, or is it the result of a creative act of God, as the Pentateuch teaches? According to the first view, " everything in the Universe is the result of fixed laws, Nature does not change, and there is nothing supernatural." There is therefore no room for revelation, which upsets the order of nature, and " the whole teaching of Scripture would be rejected." But if the world is the result of a creative act, and nature is consequently nothing but a revelation of the divine will, made in such time and place as God's wisdom decreed, then it is no longer impossible that the divine will should one day reveal itself a second time in a supernatural manner. Hence, "accepting the Creation, we find that . . . revelation is possible, and that every difficulty in this question is removed." For if we ask : "Why has God inspired a certain person and not another? Why has he revealed his Law to one particular nation, and at one particular time? " and so forth—" We answer to all these questions : He willed it so ; or, His wisdom decided so. Just as he created the world according to his will, at a certain time, in a certain form, and as we do not understand why his will or his wisdom decided upon that peculiar form, and upon that peculiar time, so we do not know why his will or his wisdom determined any of the things mentioned in the preceding questions."[1]

Maimonides gave much thought to the question of the creation of the world, and examined it from every side.

[1] *Guide,* II., chap. xxv.

He tried to ascertain whether there was anything conclusive in the evidences adduced by his predecessors in favour of the eternity of the world or of its creation ; and he did not scruple to avow that if he had found a convincing proof of the eternity of the world he would not have rejected it out of respect for the *Torah*. But purely philosophic investigation led him to the conclusion that there was really no convincing proof one way or the other. Seeing then, he says, that " the eternity of the universe has not been demonstrated, there is no need to reject Scripture," and we may believe in the creation theory, which has " the authority of Prophecy," without any sin against our reason.[1]

But when once we have adopted the creation theory, revelation becomes possible, and there is nothing to prevent our holding the belief which our nation has accepted throughout its history : that at a definite point in time the Law was given to our people from heaven through the instrumentality of the chief of the Prophets, who received a unique inspiration from the divine source, and was taught what to tell his people in the name of God.[2]   It is not relevant (as we have seen above) to ask why this Law was given to us and not to others, at that

---

[1] *Guide*, II., chaps xxv. and xvi.

[2] Maimonides explains his views on the methods of divine revelation and the nature of prophecy in general, and of the prophecy of Moses in particular, in several places : especially in *Guide*, II., chaps. xxxii.-xlviii., and in *Mishneh Torah*, section *Foundations of the Law*, chap. vii.   But for our present purpose we need not enter into these speculations.   It suffices to say that here also he was true to his own system.   The Prophet is for him the most perfect " actual man " ; and the divine inspiration reaches the Prophet through that separate Intelligence (" active intellect ") which is, according to the philosophical system adopted by Maimonides, charged with the guidance of the world and with the raising of all forms (including the form of the soul) from potentiality to actuality.

particular time and at no other. But it is relevant to
ask what is the purpose of this Law and what benefit it
was meant to produce. For it can scarcely be supposed
that God would interfere with the order of nature for
no advantage or object ; and if we cannot understand
the working of the divine wisdom in every detail, we
must and we can form for ourselves some general conception of the object for which the divine teaching was
given to us and the way in which it can help men to
attain their end.[1]

Now it is clear that the divine teaching, whether on
its theoretical or on its practical side, cannot lead a
man straight to his supreme goal—the raising of his
intellect from potentiality to actuality. For this goal,
as we know, is to be attained not by good actions, and
not even by the *received* knowledge of truth, but only
by the activity of the intellect itself, which must arrive
at truth by the long road of scientific proof. And if
religion cannot raise its followers to the stage of "actual
man " in a direct way, we must conclude that its whole
purpose is to prepare the instrument which is necessary
for the attainment of that end : to wit, human society,
which creates the environment of the "actual man."
The aim of religion, then, is " to regulate the soul and
the body " of society at large, so as to make it capable
of producing the greatest possible number of " actual
men."   To this end religion must necessarily be
popular : its teachings and prescriptions must be aimed
not at the chosen few, who strive after ultimate perfection, but at the great mass of society. To this mass
it must give, in the first place, true opinions in a form
suited to the intelligence of the many ; secondly, a code

[1] See *Guide,* III., xxvi.

of morals, individual and social, which makes for the health of society and the prosperity of its members; and thirdly, a code of religious observances intended to educate the many by keeping these true opinions and moral duties constantly before their minds.[1]   In these three ways—the third of which is merely ancillary to the other two—religion aims at raising the cultural level of society, so as to make a clear road for the perfect individual : to provide him from the beginning of his life with an environment of correct opinions and good morals, and save him from the necessity of frittering away his strength in a twofold battle—against the evil conditions of a corrupt society, and against false opinions implanted in himself by that society.   Religion is there to save him from this battle against corruption without and falsehood within : to secure that as soon as he shows the ability and the will to attain perfection he shall find favourable conditions prepared for him, and proceed towards his goal without let or hindrance.

This was how Maimonides conceived the function of the divine religion; this was how he was bound to conceive it, his philosophy being what it was.   But as he was also persuaded by various reasoned proofs that the Law of Moses was the divine religion,[2] he could obviously have no doubt that this Law must contain on its theoretical side the "true opinions" (that is, those philosophical opinions which he considered true), albeit in popular form, and on its practical side a moral doctrine for the individual and for society which was adapted to the end desiderated by his philosophy, together with the form of religious observance best calculated to

---

[1] *Ibid.*, chaps. xxiii. and xxviii. ; see also II., chaps. xxxiv. and xl.
[2] See *Guide*, II., chaps. xxxix. and xl. ; and especially the *Iggereth Teman.*

educate society in the right opinions and the right morality.

It is at this point that Maimonides' task becomes difficult. Armed with this *a priori* judgment, he comes to close quarters with the *Torah* : and he finds that in many matters, both of theory and of practice, it is, if taken at its face value, diametrically opposed to what his pre-conceived ideas would lead him to expect. The beliefs embodied in the *Torah* seem to be directly opposed to the most fundamental philosophical truths of Maimonides' system ; the actions prescribed in the *Torah* contain much that it is difficult to reconcile with the social purpose of the divine religion as conceived by that system. What course, then, was open to Maimonides ? To compromise between philosophical and religious truth, as many had done before, was for him impossible. For every compromise means simply that both sides give way ; and how could Maimonides, with his conviction that the attainment of truth by means of proof is the end of human existence and the only way to eternal happiness, give up one jot of this truth for the sake of another truth, of inferior value inasmuch as it has come to us only through tradition ? Thus he has but one possible course. Necessity compels him to subdue religion absolutely to the demands of philosophy : in other words, to explain the words of the *Torah* throughout in conformity with the truth of philosophy, and to make the *Torah* fulfil in every part the function which philosophy imposes on it.

This necessity worked wonders. By dint of enormous labour Maimonides discovered various extraordinary ways of interpreting the *Torah* ; with wonderful skill he found support for his interpretations in words and phrases scattered about the Scriptures and the Talmud ; until at last he succeeded in making religion what it had to be according to his belief.

This is not the place to explain Maimonides' methods of exegesis in detail. For us to-day they are but a sort of monument to the weakness of the written word in the face of a living psychological force which demands that " yes " shall become " no " and "no " be turned into "yes." This psychological force led Maimonides to turn the " living God " of the *Torah* into an abstract philosophical conception, empty of all content except a collection of negations ; to make the " Righteous Man" of Judaism a philosopher blessed with " acquired intellect " ; to transform the " future world " of the Talmud into the union of the acquired intellect with the " active intellect " ; to metamorphose the Biblical penalty of "cutting off" into the disappearance of the form when the matter is resolved : and so forth. All this he did in conformity with his " philosophic truth," of which he refused to change one atom.[1]

So, too, with the practical side of religion. Only in a very roundabout way could practical religion be brought under the general principles which Maimonides deduced from his philosophy. The difficulty was especially great in the case of the laws of religious worship, many of which have no apparent educative value as a means of confirming true opinions and morality. But here also necessity did its work, and Maimonides managed to find educational " reasons " for all the religious laws, not excepting those which seem on the face of them actually to confirm false

[1] All this is explained in many passages throughout Maimonides' books, which are too numerous to be particularised.

opinions and to arouse inclinations opposed to morality —such as, for instance, sacrifices and the accompanying rites.[1] None the less, he was compelled after all his hard labour to lay down this strange axiom : that there is a reason for the commandments in a general way, but not for their details, these having been ordained only because there can be no universal without particulars of some kind or other.[2]

Maimonides had an easier task in bringing the moral laws of the *Torah* within his system. In themselves these laws demanded as a rule no heroic exegesis to show their utility for the social order : indeed, the *Torah* often emphasises this utility, which in any case is self-evident in most commandments of this class. But in arranging these commandments in order of moral value Maimonides was compelled to coerce religion by his characteristic methods into conformity with his system, according to which good actions—whether moral or religious—are of an inferior order, having no value except that of a necessary preparation of the individual and of society for the attainment of the supreme moral good, the perfection of intellect. This attitude of Maimonides towards moral actions, which we have met already as a philosophical postulate, is just as strongly maintained after such actions have been invested with a

---

[1] For the " reasons of the commandments " see *Guide,* III., chaps. xxvi.-xlix.

[2] For instance : there is a reason for sacrifices in general. " But we cannot say why one offering should be a lamb, whilst another is a ram ; and why a fixed number of them should be brought. . . . . You ask why must a lamb be sacrificed and not a ram? but the same question would be asked, why a ram had been commanded instead of a lamb, so long as one particular kind is required. The same is to be said as to the question why were seven lambs sacrificed and not eight ; the same question might have been asked if there were eight." *Guide,* III., chap. xxvi.

religious sanctity. Hence religion affects Maimonides' philosophical ethics only to this extent, that it makes all the observances of religious worship a moral duty, equal in value to the other moral duties, because religious worship is one way of leading mankind to the attainment of the supreme moral good in the chosen individuals.

What, then, is the " divine religion "—that is to say, the teaching of Judaism—according to the system of Maimonides?

On its theoretical side it is popular metaphysics, and on its practical side social ethics and pædagogics.   It cannot bring man to his ultimate perfection ; its whole function is to regulate society—that is, the masses—in accordance with the requirements of the perfect man. Hence religion is not above reason, but below it : just as the masses, for whom religion was made, are below the perfect man. Reason is the supreme judge ; religion is absolutely subordinate to reason, and cannot abrogate one jot of its decisions. For God, who implanted the reasoning faculty in man, that by it he might attain truth and win eternal Being, could not at the same time demand of man that he believe in something opposed to that very truth which is attained by reason, and is the goal of his existence and the summit of his happiness. Even if a Prophet works miracles in heaven and earth, and requires us therefore to believe that there has been prophetically revealed to him some " divine" truth which is opposed to reason, we must not believe him nor " regard his signs." " For reason, which declares his testimony false, is more to be trusted than the eye which sees his signs."[1]

[1] Introduction to *Zera'im.*

But all this does not detract from the general and eternal duty of observing in practice all the commandments of the divine religion. Religion, like nature, is a creation of God, in which the divine will is embodied in the form of immutable laws. And just as the laws of nature are eternal and universally valid, admitting of no exception, though their usefulness is only general, and " in some individual cases they cause injury as well," so also " the divine guidance contained in the *Torah* must be absolute and general," and does not suffer change or modification "according to the different conditions of persons and times." For the divine creation is "that which has the absolute perfection possible to its species " ; and that which is absolutely perfect cannot be perfected by change or modification, but only made less perfect.[1] Religion, it is true, was given through a Prophet, who received the divine inspiration ; but when once it had been given it was placed outside the scope of creation, and became, like Nature after its creation, something independent, with laws which can be investigated and understood by the function of reason, but cannot be changed or abrogated by the function of prophecy. It may happen, indeed, that in accordance with the divine will, which was made an element in the nature of things when nature was created, the Prophet can change the order of the universe in some particular detail for a moment, so as to give a sign of the truth of his prophecy ;[2] and similarly the Prophet can sometimes abrogate temporarily some point of the Law, to meet some special need of the time. But just as the Prophet cannot modify or change completely any law of nature,

---

[1] *Guide,* II., chap. xxxix., and III., chap. xxxiv.
[2] See *Guide*, II., chap. xxix. ; *Eight Chapters*, chap. viii.

so he cannot modify or change completely any law of the *Torah*. Nor can he, by his function of prophecy, decide between opposing views on a matter which is capable of different interpretations, because his opinion on a question of this kind is important by virtue of his being a wise man, and not by virtue of his being a Prophet, and it is therefore no more decisive than that of another wise man who is not a Prophet. And " if a thousand Prophets, all equal to Elijah and Elisha, held one view, and a thousand and one wise men held the opposite view, we should have to follow the majority and decide according to the thousand and one wise men and not according to the thousand venerable Prophets." For " God has not permitted us to learn from Prophets, but from wise men of reasoning power and knowledge."[1]

What I have said so far, in this section and the preceding one, is sufficient, I think, to give a clear idea of the fundamental beliefs of Maimonides as to the function of man and his moral and religious duties. But before we pass on to consider how Maimonides tried to make these ideas the common property of his people, and what mark his system has left on the development of Judaism, it is worth while to mention here that Maimonides himself has given us the essence of his system in a perfectly unmistakable form, by dividing men into various classes according to their position on the scale of perfection. He compares the striving of man after the perfection of his form to the striving of a king's subjects " to be with the king in his palace" ; and using this simile he finds in mankind six successive stages, as follows :—

[1] Introduction to *Zera'im* ; see also *Foundations of the Law,* chaps. ix. and x.

1. Men who are outside the country altogether—
that is, savages "who have no religion, neither one
based on speculation, nor one received by tradition."
They are considered " as speechless animals."

2. Men "who are in the country," but "have their
backs turned towards the king's palace, and their faces
in another direction." These are "those who possess
religion, belief and thought, but happen to hold false
doctrines, which they either adopted in consequence of
great mistakes made in their own speculations, or
received from others who misled them. Because of
these doctrines they recede more and more from the
royal palace the more they seem to proceed. These are
worse than the first class, and under certain circumstances it may become necessary to slay them, and to
extirpate their doctrines, in order that others should not
be misled."

3. "Those who desire to arrive at the palace, and
to enter it, but have never yet seen it." These are
" the mass of religious people ; the multitude that
observe the divine commandments, but are ignorant."

4. "Those who reach the palace, and go round
about in search of the entrance gate." These are
"those who believe traditionally in true principles of
faith, and learn the practical worship of God, but are
not trained in philosophical treatment of the principles
of the *Torah*." On the same level with them are those
who " are engaged in studying the Mathematical
Sciences and Logic."

5. Those who "have come into the ante-chamber"—
that is, " those who undertake to investigate the principles of religion," or those who have " learnt to understand Physics."

6. Those who have reached the highest stage, that of being " with the king in the same palace." These are they " who have mastered Metaphysics—who have succeeded in finding a proof for everything that can be proved—who have a true knowledge of God, so far as true knowledge can be attained, and are near to the truth wherever only an approach to the truth is possible."[1]

In this classification Maimonides sets forth his ethical system in plain terms, with perfect coldness and calm, as though there were nothing startling about it. We of the present day feel our moral sense particularly outraged by his cruel treatment of the second class—"those who happen to hold false doctrines "—though we can understand that a logical thinker like Maimonides, who always went the whole length of his convictions, was bound to draw this conclusion from his philosophical system. For that system regards " true opinions " as something much more than " opinions " : it attributes to them the wonderful power of turning the reasoning faculty into a separate and eternal being, and sees therefore in the opposite opinions a danger to life in the most real sense. But in Maimonides' day the persecution of men for holding false opinions was a common thing (though it was done in the name of religion, not of philosophy) ; and even this piece of philosophic ruthlessness created no stir and aroused no contemporary protest. What did stir contemporary feeling to its depths was another conclusion involved in his classification : namely, " that philosophers who occupy themselves with physics and metaphysics are on a higher plane than men who occupy themselves with the

[1] *Guide,* III., chap. li.

Torah.''[1] Whoever knows in what esteem our ancestors
of that period held the study of the *Torah* will not be
surprised that " many wise men and Rabbis" were
driven to the conclusion that "this chapter was not
written by the Master, or if it was, it should be suppressed, or, best of all, burnt.''[2]

Poor, simple men! They did not see that this
chapter could not be either suppressed or burnt except
in company with all the other chapters of Maimonides'
system, which led him inevitably to this extreme conclusion. But there were other men in Israel who saw
more clearly, and actually condemned all the chapters
to the fire. To them we shall return later.

III

The supremacy of Reason! Can we to-day, after the
eighteenth and nineteenth centuries, conceive how tre-
mendous, how fundamental a revolution the phrase
implied in the time of Maimonides?

We all know that the outstanding characteristic of the
human mind in the Middle Ages was its negative attitude
to human reason, its lack of faith in the power of reason
to direct man's life and bring him to the goal of real
happiness. Reason was almost hated and despised as
a dangerous tempter and seducer : it led men away from
the pursuit of truth and goodness, and was to be
eschewed by all who cared for their souls. Fundamental
questions about life and the universe had to receive
super-rational answers. The simpler and more reasonable the answer, the more suspect and the less satis-

[1] Sec R. Shem-Tob's Commentary on the *Guide, loc. cit.*
[2] *Ibid.*

factory it was; the stranger the answer, the more violently opposed to sane reason, the more cordial was its welcome and the more ready its acceptance. The famous *Credo quia absurdum* of one of the Church fathers was the cardinal rule of thought for all cultured nations, Christian and Mohammedan alike. Nor had Judaism escaped the sway of this principle. Not only the mass of the people, but the leaders and teachers, generally speaking, believed in the literal sense of the Scriptures and the Talmud, even where it was plainly contrary to reason. The coarsest and crudest ideas about the nature of the divine power and its relation to men, and about the soul of man and its future in " the world to come "—ideas which reason cannot tolerate for a moment—were almost universally held; and even those learned in the Law staunchly maintained these ideas, because so they had found it written in Bible or Talmud, and that which was written was above reason, and no attention should be paid to that impudent scoffer. It followed naturally from this fundamental point of view that the important things in the sphere of morals were to know and to perform all that was written. The function of reason was not to understand life and the universe, but to understand what was written about life and the universe. The thing best worth doing for a Jew was to ponder on the written word and to work out its details, theoretically and practically, to infinity.[1]

No doubt some Jewish teachers before Maimonides had tried to introduce into Judaism more rational principles, which they had derived from Arabic philosophy. But these attempts only affected details; the cardinal

---

[1] Maimonides himself describes the contemporary state of culture among his people in several places. See, for instance, the *Treatise on Resurrection*.

principle remained untouched. Reason remained sub-ordinate to the written word ; its truths were still dis-carded for the higher truth of religion. The Gaon Saadiah, the greatest of the earlier Jewish religious philosophers, explains the relation of reason to religion by the following simile : '' A man weighs his money, and finds that he has a thousand pieces.'' He gives different sums to a number of people, and then, ''wish-ing to show them quickly how much he has left, he says that he has five hundred pieces, and offers to prove it by weighing his money. When he weighs the money—which takes little time—and finds that it amounts to five hundred pieces they are bound to believe what he told them.'' But there may be among them a par-ticularly cautious man, who wants to find the amount left over by the method of calculation—that is, by add-ing together the various amounts distributed and sub-tracting their sum from the original amount.[1] Religion, of course, is the weighing process, which gives us the truth at once, by a method which is direct and cannot be questioned. Reason corresponds to calculation : a cautious man with plenty of time may use it to establish a truth which has already been proved to him by the short and certain method of weighing. But obviously calculation cannot change the result which weighing has already given ; and if there is any difference in the results, the weighed money will neither be increased nor diminished, and the mistake must be in the calculation. This way of regarding reason and its relation to religion was common to all the Jewish thinkers who laboured, before Maimonides, to reconcile religion and philosophy. They regarded their labour only as a necessary evil.

[1] *Emunoth v' Deoth*, Preface.

They shouldered the burden because they saw that it had to be done; but in their heart of hearts they were wholly on the side of religion, and it never occurred to them to give reason precedence.[1] In this respect they were like the Arabic religious philosophers; and like them they chose the philosophical views which confirmed their religious faith rather than those which were confirmed by reason. "They did not investigate," writes Maimonides, jeering at "philosophers" of this kind, "the real properties of things; first of all they considered what must be the properties of the things which should yield proof for or against a certain creed." They forgot "that the properties of things cannot adapt themselves to our opinions, but our opinions must be adapted to the existing properties."[2]

If we remember that this was the general attitude of mind, we cannot help asking how it could happen that in such a period and in such an atmosphere Maimonides arrived at the doctrine of the supremacy of reason in its most uncompromising form. No doubt, if we care to be satisfied with any answer that comes to hand, we may say that Maimonides, starting out with a predisposition in favour of the Arabic version of the Aristotelian philosophy, and a sternly logical mind, could not stop half-way, or fail to see the logical consequences of Aristotelianism. But when we observe how, with a devotion far greater than that of his non-Jewish teachers, he set himself to develop and extend the idea of the

[1] R. Jehudah Halevi, despite his profound knowledge of contemporary philsosophy, says categorically: "He who accepts this [the Law] completely, without scrutiny or argument, is better off than he who investigates and analyses" (*Cuzri*, II., xxvi. [Dr. Hirschfeld's translation]).

[2] *Guide*, I., chap. lxxi.

supremacy of reason till it became a complete, all-embracing theory of life ; and when we remember also his love for the teachings of Judaism, which ought to have induced in him a disposition not to extend the empire of reason, but to restrict it : we are forced to confess that logic alone could never have produced this phenomenon. There must have been some psychological force, some inner motive power, to make Maimonides so extreme and uncompromising a champion of reason.

We shall discover what this motive power was, I think, if we take account of the political position of the Jews at that time.

It was a time when religious fanaticism was rife among the Moslems. In many countries to profess another religion meant death, and large numbers of Jews, who could with difficulty change their place of abode, accepted Mohammedanism, though but outwardly. One of these countries was Southern Spain, the birthplace of Maimonides, who was a boy of thirteen when religious persecution broke out in that country. It may or may not be true, as recent historians maintain, that he and his father and the whole family changed their religion under compulsion : the question has not yet been definitely settled. But there is no doubt that even if he was saved by some means from an open change of faith, he was at any rate forced to conceal his Judaism, for fear of oppression, so long as he lived in Spain and in Fez (where religious persecution first started, and fanaticism had its stronghold). It was only in Egypt that his troubles ceased, and when he reached Egypt he was already about thirty years of age. This, then, was the terrible position in which Maimonides spent his years of development. He was surrounded by lying and religious hypocrisy ; Judaism had to hide from the light of day ; its adherents had to wear a mask whenever they came out of their homes into the open. And why? Because Mohammed had called himself a prophet, had performed miracles, according to his followers, to win their faith, and by virtue of his prophetic power had promulgated a new Law and revealed new truths, which all men were bound to believe, although they were contrary to reason. This state of things was bound to make a profound impression on a young man like Maimonides, with his fine nature and his devotion to truth. He could not but feel every moment the tragedy of such a life ; and therefore he could not but become violently opposed to the source of religious fanaticism— to that blind faith in the truth of prophecy which relies on supernatural " evidence," and despises the evidence of reason. It was this blind faith that led the Moslems to force the Jews into accepting the teaching of the new prophet ; and it was this that led many of these very Jews, after they had gradually become accustomed to their new situation, to doubt of their Judaism and ask themselves why they should not be able to believe in Mohammed's prophecy, just as they believed in that of Moses. If Moses had performed miracles, then surely Mohammed might have done the same ; and how could they decide between the one teaching and the other with such certainty as to pronounce one true and the other false ?[1]

These impressions, which were constantly influencing Maimonides' development in his childhood and youth,

---

[1] As to the state of mind of the forced converts at that time see what Maimonides says in the *Treatise of the Sanctification of the Name* and the *Iggereth Teman.*

were bound to swing him violently over to the other side, to the side of reason. Ultimately he was led to subject man—and God too, if one may say so—to that supreme ruler : because Judaism could trust reason never to allow any new prophet with his new teaching to work it harm. When once Judaism had accepted the supremacy of reason and handed over to reason the seal of truth, it would never again be difficult to show by rational proof that the first divine religion was also the only divine religion, never to be displaced or altered till the end of time; and then, even if ten thousand prophets like Mohammed came and performed miracles beyond telling, we should never believe in their new teaching, because one proof of reason is stronger than all the proofs of prophecy.[1]

Perhaps, too, Maimonides' rationalism is traceable to yet another cause, which lies like the first in the situation of the forced converts of that period. These men were no doubt able to observe the Jewish law within their own homes ; the Moslems did not, like the Christians later, invent an Inquisition to pry into every hole and corner. None the less, Maimonides himself makes it clear that the Jews were often compelled to break the commandments of their Law, when they could not observe them without arousing suspicion in the minds of the authorities. This naturally caused the unfortunate Jews great distress, and drove some of them to despair. What, they asked themselves, was the use of

[1] See Section II. above. Note especially what Maimonides says about prophecy in the Introduction to his *Commentary on the Mishnah* (written at the time when he lived among the forced converts). Some of this is quoted in Section II. He writes there with such incisive force as to make it clear that he has left the realm of pure speculation and theory, and has a practical object connected with actual circumstances which had stirred him deeply at the time.

remaining true to their ancestral faith at heart, if they could not in practice keep clear of transgressions both great and small, and must in any case merit the pains of hell?[1] It is reasonable, therefore, to suppose that this painful feeling also helped to lead Maimonides—though unconsciously—towards the doctrine of the supremacy of reason, which teaches that man's "ultimate perfection does not include any action or good conduct, but only knowledge "[2]—thus implying that man may win salvation by attaining to true opinions, though he is sometimes forced in practice to transgress the commands of religion.

However that may be, whether for these reasons or for others, we do find that Maimonides had his system perfected and arranged in all its details even in his early days, when he first came out of his study into public life, and that he made scarcely any change in it from that time till the day of his death.[3] All his efforts went to the propagation of his teaching among his people, and to the endeavour to repair by its means all the shortcomings which he found in contemporary Judaism.

These shortcomings were great indeed. Judaism, as Maimonides found it, was by no means fulfilling its function as "the divine religion." It was not "true opinions" that the people derived from Judaism : on the contrary, they had come, through a literal acceptance of all that it taught, to hold false ideas about God and man, and had therefore by its means been removed

---

[1] All this is clearly hinted in Maimonides' *Treatise of the Sanctification of the Name.*

[2] *Guide,* III., chap. xxvii.

[3] We find all the principles of his system in the Introduction to his first book (the *Commentary on the Mishnah*), and again at the end of his last book (*Guide,* III., chap. li.).

still further from perfection. Even the practical duties
of morality and religion could not easily be learnt by the
people generally from their religious writings. For in
order to deduce practice from theory it was necessary
to navigate the great ocean of the Talmud, and to spend
years on minute and tangled controversies—a task for
the few only, not for the masses. Here, then, was an
odd state of things. The whole purpose of religion was
to improve society at large, to speak to the masses in a
language which they understood ; but if the masses could
not understand the language of religion, and could learn
from it neither true opinions nor practical duties, then
religion was not fulfilling its function in society, and
its existence was useless.

This state of affairs produced in Maimonides, while
he was still young, an ardent desire to stand in the
breach and make Judaism fit to fulfil the double function
—theoretical and practical—which it had as the only
" divine religion."   For this purpose it was necessary
on the one hand to show the whole people, in a form
suited to its comprehension, the " true opinions " contained in the Torah, and on the other hand to rescue
the practical commandments from the ocean of Talmudic
disputation and to teach them in a short and simple
manner, so that they should be easily remembered and
become familiar to the people.

But in those early days Maimonides had not the
courage to strike out a new line and to present the whole
content of religion in an entirely fresh manner in conformity with his philosophical system. Hence he chose
a line which was already familiar, and decided to supply
the need of his own age by the help of a book which in
its time had been intended to fulfil a somewhat similar

purpose—the Mishnah. Thus it was in the form of a Commentary on the Mishnah that he tried to give his contemporaries what they lacked : to wit, clear doctrine and a plain rule of practice. Wherever the Mishnah leaves a point in doubt, he gives the decision laid down in the Talmud ; and wherever the Mishnah hints at some theoretical opinion, he takes advantage of the opportunity to explain the " true opinions."[1] This latter process was, of course, especially important to him ; and he sometimes expatiates on the subject at much greater length than is usual in a Commentary of the ordinary kind.[2] Thus he was able to introduce into his Commentary, besides a mass of scattered notes, complete essays on questions of faith and philosophy in the form of Introductions to different sections of the Mishnah.[3]

Maimonides gave a great deal of work to this Commentary, which he began and finished in his years of trouble and wandering. In the result he produced a masterpiece, which remains to this day superior to all later Commentaries on the Mishnah. But he did not achieve the principal object for which he took so much trouble : he did not make religion effective. His Commentary did not become widely known, and made no great impression ; still less did it bring about a revolution in popular opinion, as its author hoped that it would. And it failed of its object on the practical as

---

[1] See Introduction to *Commentary on the Mishnah.*

[2] " This is not the place to treat of this matter ; but it is my intention, wherever a matter of belief is mentioned, to explain it briefly. For I love to teach nothing so much as one of the principles of religion " (end of *Berachoth*).

[3] Especially important in this connection are the Introductions to *Zera'im,* to chapter *Chelek* (where he brings in all the principles of religion), and to *Aboth (Eight Chapters).*

well as on the theoretical side.   Many of the later laws,
which have no basis in the Mishnah, could not be
included in it ; and those that were included were scattered about in no proper order, because the Mishnah
itself has no strict order.

But as Maimonides grew older and reached middle
life, years brought him wider knowledge and greater
confidence in himself.   This self-confidence gave him
courage and decided him to approach his goal by another
road.   He would produce a work of striking originality,
such as no Jew had ever produced before.

So he set to work on his *Mishneh Torah*.   Instead
of   a   Commentary on the Mishnah of R. Jehudah,
Maimonides now produced a Mishnah of his own, new
in content as in arrangement.[1]   Here he sets forth all
the practical laws of religion and morality and all the
" true opinions " in the form best adapted to the understanding of ordinary men, in beautiful and clear language
and in perfect logical order.   Everything is put in its
right place ; decisions are given without hair-splitting
arguments ; opinions are set out untrammelled by
arguments or proofs.   In a word, the book presents all
that the divine religion ought to give in order to fulfil
its function, and presents it in precisely the right
manner.[2]

[1] His Preface makes it clear that he regarded his book as a sort
of Mishnah in a new form ; and it seems (though he does not say it
in so many words) that he intended to hint at this idea by the title
of the book—*Mishneh Torah*.

[2] There were many writers who suspected that Maimonides' idea
was to do away altogether with the study of the Talmud.   But this
suspicion could arise only from failure to understand clearly the real
purpose of the book.   Even theories are presented here in dogmatic
form ; but could it possibly be imagined that Maimonides wanted to
do away with the study of philosophy by the long method of argument and proof—that study which he regarded as the purpose of the

This time Maimonides was justified in supposing that he had fulfilled his duty to his people and his religion, and had attained the end which he had set before himself. Within a short time this great book spread through the length and breadth of Jewry, and helped considerably not only to make the practical commandments more widely known, but also to purify and transform popular religious notions. Views distinguished by their freedom and their antagonism to current religious ideas appeared here in the innocent guise of canonical dicta; and as they were couched in the language of the Mishnah and in the familiar terminology of the old religious literature, people did not realise how far they were being carried, but swallowed the new ideas almost without resistance. If the dose was accepted not as pure philosophy, but as religious dogma, that was precisely what Maimonides intended : for according to his system religion was to teach philosophical truth to the masses in the guise of "divine" truth which needed no proof.

But Maimonides' work was not yet completed. In the *Misnheh Torah* he had reformed religion so far as its social function was concerned : that is to say, so far as the needs of the common people demanded. He had still to reform it from the point of view of the function of society itself : that is to say, to meet the needs of the chosen few. For the common people it was necessary to clothe philosophical truth in religious garb ; for the

human race ? The truth is that he had in view the social function of religion, and for this reason he set forth both theories and practical commands in brief and in a manner suited to the comprehension of ordinary men. He left it to the chosen few to study the principles of both the theoretical and the practical law, and to obtain from the original sources a knowledge of the reasons for both.

few it was necessary to do just the reverse—to discover
and expose the philosophical truth that lay beneath the
religious garb., For this minority, consisting of those
whom " human reason had attracted to abide within its
sphere "—who had learnt and understood the prevailing
philosophy of the time with all its preambles and its
proofs—could not help seeing the deep gulf between
philosophy and Judaism in its literal acceptation.   It
was impossible to hide the inner contradiction from
such men by means of a superficial gloss, or to harmonise
discrepancies of detail by a generalisation.   What then
should one of these men do if he were not only a
philosopher, but also "a religious man who has been
trained to believe in the truth of our Law " ?   He must
always be in a state of " perplexity and anxiety."   " If
he be guided solely by reason . . . he would consider
that he had rejected the fundamental principles of the
Law ; . . . and if, instead of following his reason, he
abandon its guidance altogether, it would still appear
that his religious convictions had caused him loss and
injury.   For he would then be left with those errors
[i.e., those derived from a literal interpretation of
Scripture], and would be a prey to fear and anxiety,
constant grief and great perplexity."[1]

If we remember Maimonides' conception of the
" actualisation " of intellect, and how it obtains independent existence through understanding the Ideas, we
shall see that he was bound to regard this perplexity of
the " perfect individuals " as being in itself not merely
something undesirable, but a grave danger from the
point of view of the supreme end of mankind.   For how
could these perplexed men attain to the summit of per-

[1] *Guide*, Introduction.

fection, to "acquired intellect," if they doubted the truth of reason because it did not square with the truths of religion, with the result that subject and object could not be united in them and become a single, indivisible whole? If the divine teaching itself brings "loss and injury" to the chosen few, the harm that it does more than outweighs the good that it has done in improving the multitude and thus removing social obstacles from the path of the few.

This grave evil required a remedy; the "perplexed" had to be satisfied that they could devote themselves peacefully to the acquisition of the Ideas, without being disturbed by the thought that in so doing they were rejecting the fundamental principles of the Law. This was the task which Maimonides set himself in his last book, the *Guide for the Perplexed*. The book is in a way his own confession of faith; it shows his perplexed pupils the method by which he has succeeded in escaping from his own perplexity. After what has been said above, we need not here deal with this book at length. The "true opinions" which it contains have already been explained in outline; the method by which these opinions are discovered in the *Torah* has been broadly indicated, and the details are not essential to our present purpose. It does not matter to us *how* Maimonides subordinated religion to reason; the important thing is that he did subordinate it. From this point of view we may put the whole teaching of the *Guide* in a single sentence. "Follow reason and reason only," he tells the "perplexed," "and explain religion in conformity with reason: for reason is the goal of mankind, and religion is only a means to the end."

Had Maimonides written the *Guide* before he wrote

the *Mishneh Torah,* he would certainly have been pronounced a heretic, and his book would have made no
deep impression either in the orthodox camp or in that
of the doubters. The orthodox would have turned their
backs on it and have striven to blot out its memory, as
they did with so many other books which they thought
dangerous to their faith ; and the doubters would not
have accepted its views as a perfect doctrine, but would
have regarded it as merely an attempt on the part of
one of their fellow-doubters to escape from his perplexity, and an attempt which in many details had failed
and could not give entire satisfaction.

But in fact the *Guide* was written after the *Mishneh
Torah,* when Maimonides was already considered the
greatest exponent of the Law, and enjoyed an unequalled
reputation throughout the Diaspora. Hence even the
Guide could not dethrone him from his eminence. Wil-
lingly or unwillingly, his contemporaries accepted this
further gift at his hands. The believers stormed and
raged among themselves, but did not dare to attack
Maimonides openly so long as he lived. The doubters
welcomed the book with open arms ; they did not stop
to test or criticise, but drank eagerly of the comforting
draught for which their souls had been thirsting. It was
not some sophist, but the greatest sage in Israel, the
light of the Exile, who went before them like a pillar of
fire to illumine their path. How could they but be
satisfied with such a guide ?

But things changed when Maimonides' death freed
the zealots from the restraint of fear. A fierce conflict
broke out about him, and raged for a hundred years.
The religious leaders, long accustomed to ban every
book that did not suit their views, could not possess their

souls in silence when they saw, for the first time in Jewish history, that revolutionary books like the *Guide* and the *Book of Science* were spread abroad without let or hindrance, and were more popular and more esteemed by the people at large than almost any of the other books which the teachers and sages of Israel had placed in the treasury of Judaism.[1] The details of this conflict are familiar to scholars, and it is not my intention here to write the history of that period.   But it is worth pointing out that most of Maimonides' opponents at that time did not recognise clearly the fundamental change which he had introduced into Judaism. No doubt they all felt that his teaching meant a complete revolution in the national outlook ; but they did not all understand what was the pivotal issue of the revolution. For the most part they merely pointed to certain details in which they found heresy, such as the denial of resurrection, of hell and paradise, and so forth.   Only a few of them understood that Maimonides' teaching was revolutionary not because of his attitude on this or that particular question, but because he dethroned religion altogether from the supreme judgment-seat, and put reason in its place : because he made it his basic principle that " whenever a Scripture is contradicted by proof we do not accept the Scripture," but *explain* it in accordance with reason.[2]

This emancipation of reason from its subordination to an external authority is the great and eternal achieve-

[1] After the publication of the *Guide* many people discovered that its opinions were already contained in the innocent-looking dicta of the *Mishneh Torah,* especially in its first part (*The Book of Science*), and from that time onward they regarded that book also as heretical, and waged war on it as well as on the *Guide.*

[2] See the letter of R. Jehudah Alfachar to Kimchi : *Collected Responses of Maimonides* (ed. Leipsic), Part III., p. 1, *et seq.*

ment which has so endeared Maimonides to all those of
our people who have striven after knowledge and the
light.   The theoretical system at which Maimonides
worked so hard from his youth to the end of his life has
long been swept away, together with the Arabic metaphysics on which it was based.   But the practical consequence of that system—the emancipation of reason—
remains, and has left its mark on the history of Jewish
thought up to the present day.   Every Jew who has left
the old school and traversed the hard and bitter road
that leads from blind faith to free reason must have met
with Maimonides at the beginning of his journey, and
must have found in him a source of strength and support
for his first steps, which are the hardest and the most
dangerous.   This road was traversed not only by Men-
delssohn, but also by Spinoza,[1] and before and after them
by countless thinkers, many of whom won golden repu-
tations within Judaism or outside it.

S. D. Luzzatto's criticism of Maimonides, on the
ground that his views on the nature of the soul led to
the degradation of reason in Jewish thought, is superficial.   Maimonides, according to him, " laid down
what we must believe and what we must not believe,"
whereas before his time there was no rigid dogma, "and
there was no ban on opinions to prevent each thinker
from believing what he thought true."[2]   Now this is
not the place to show how far Luzzatto was from
historical accuracy when he credited pre-Maimonidean
Judaism with freedom of thought.   To understand the
true nature of that freedom we need only remember how

[1] See Dr. Joel's monograph, *Spinoza's Theologisch-Politischer
Traktat auf seine Quellen geprüft*, Breslau, 1870.

[2] See *Kerem Chemed*, III., pp. 67-70.

Maimonides' opponents—who were certainly faithful to the older Judaism—spoke and acted in the period of conflict. But as regards Maimonides himself, Luzzatto overlooks the fact that, while his psychological theory no doubt led him to regard certain opinions as obligatory, he placed the source of the obligation no longer in any external authority, but precisely in human reason. That being so, the obligation could not involve a ban on opinions. For as soon as other thinkers are persuaded that human reason does not make these particular opinions obligatory, they are bound, *in conformity with Maimonides' own system,* to believe each what he thinks true, and not what Maimonides erroneously thought true. In other words : if we wish to judge Maimonides' system from the point of view of its effects on Judaism, we must look not at the Thirteen Articles which he laid down as obligatory principles in accordance with that system, but at the one principle which underlies all others—that of the supremacy of reason. A philosopher who frees reason from authority in general must at the same time free it from his own authority ; he cannot regard any view as obligatory except so long as it is made obligatory by reason. Imagine a man put in prison and given the key : can he be said to have lost his liberty ?[1]

---

[1] I may remark in passing that Luzzatto (*ibid.*) accuses Maimonides of yet another disservice to Judaism. By making opinions the essential element of perfection Maimonides, according to him, abolished the difference between the righteous man and the wicked. " The philosopher," he says, " may commit theft, murder, and adultery, and yet attain eternal life : salvation does not depend on merit." This charge was already brought against Maimonides by his medieval opponents, but it is quite mistaken. Maimonides insists, over and over again, that until a man has moral perfection it is impossible for him to reach intellectual perfection to the degree necessary for the attainment of acquired intellect. See, for instance, the passage from the introduction to *Zera'im* quoted above (p. 174).

IV

Here ends what I wished to say about the supremacy of reason in Maimonides' system ; and here I might conclude this Essay. But I should like to add some remarks on another supremacy—on that of the national sentiment. In these days we cannot discuss the thought of one of our great men, even if there are seven hundred years between him and us, without wanting to know whether and to what extent his thought reveals traces of that sentiment which we now regard as the most vital element in the life of Judaism.

But this question really contains two different questions, which have to be answered differently so far as Maimonides is concerned. The first question is : Did Maimonides recognise the supremacy of the national sentiment in the spiritual life of his people, and allow it consciously and of set purpose an important place in the teaching of Judaism ? The second is : Do we find traces of the supremacy of the national sentiment—as an unconscious and spontaneous instinct—in the mentality of Maimonides himself ?[1]

The first question cannot be answered in the affirmative : the evidence is rather on the negative side. Had

[1] Though the conception of " nationalism " in its current sense is modern, the national sentiment itself has existed in our people at all times ; and its existence and value have been realised in our literature in every period, from the Bible and the Talmud to the literature of Chassidism, though it used to be called by other names (" the love of Israel," etc.). But the sentiment and its expression do not appear to the same extent or in the same form in all ages and in all individuals, and it is therefore legitimate to ask what was the attitude of any particular age or any particular thinker to the national sentiment. An interesting book might be written on the history of the national sentiment and consciousness in Israel, dealing with their different manifestations in different ages, their growth and decline, and their expression in the life of the nation and the thought of its great men in each period.

Maimonides recognised clearly the strength of the national sentiment as a force in Jewish life, and its importance as a factor in the development of Judaism, he would undoubtedly have used it, as Jehudah Halevi did, to explain the numerous features of Judaism which have their origin in the national sentiment. At any rate, he would not have endeavoured to invest those features with a universalistic character. For instance, in seeking reasons for the commandments he could easily have found that many of them have no purpose but to strengthen the feeling of national unity; and he would not have said of the Festivals that they "promote the good feeling that men should have to each other in their social and political relations."[1]   Nor would he have said, in dealing with the future redemption, that " the wise men and the prophets only longed for the days of the Messiah in order that they might be free to study the *Torah* and its wisdom, without any oppression or interference, and so might win eternal life."[2]   No doubt we do sometimes find in his Letters, and especially in those that were written to encourage his people in times of national trouble, feeling references to the fortunes and the mission of the Jewish people.[3]   But despite these isolated and casual references, only one conclusion can be drawn from the general tenor of Maimonides' teaching : that he did not recognise the value of the national element in Jewish life, and did not allow that element due weight in his exposition of

---

[1] *Guide,* III., chap. xliii. Similarly in chap. xlviii.

[2] End of *Mishneh Torah.*

[3] See the *Iggereth Teman* and the *Treatise of the Sanctification of the Name.*

Judaism.[1] On the other hand, various indications show
that in Maimonides himself the national sentiment was,
without his knowledge, a powerful force : so much so,
that it sometimes actually drove him from the straight
road of logic and reason, and entangled him—of all
men—in contradictions which had no ground or justification in his theory. We shall always find in the
psychology of even the most logical thinker, despite his
efforts to give to reason the undivided empire of his
thought, some remote corner to which its sway cannot
extend ; and we shall always find a rebel band of ideas,
which reason cannot control, breaking out from that
point of vantage to disturb the order of its realm. Of
this truth Maimonides may serve as an example. It is
particularly evident in regard to the dogmas of Judaism
which he laid down, accompanied by a declaration that
"if any man rejects one of these fundamental beliefs,
he severs himself from the community and denies a
principle of Judaism : he is called a heretic and an
unbeliever, and it is right to hate him and to destroy
him."[2] As we have already seen, it is an inevitable
consequence of Maimonides' teaching that the dogmas
of religion must be formulated clearly and made
obligatory on the whole people. But in strict accordance with his system Maimonides ought to have included
among the dogmas only those " true opinions " without
which religion could not have been maintained or have

---

[1] A German Jewish scholar, Dr. D. Rosin, in his monograph on
the ethics of Maimonides (*Die Ethik des Maimonides,* Breslau, 1876),
finds under the heading of " Nationalism " (p. 148) only two laws in
the whole *Mishneh Torah* which allude to the duties of the Jew to
his people. But in fact the two laws which he quotes (*Hilchoth
T'shubah,* chap. iii. 11, and *Hilchoth Matnath 'Aniim,* chap. x. 2)
emphasise rather the unity of the members of one faith.

[2] Introduction to chapter *Chelek.*

fulfilled its function. And in fact all his dogmas are of that character, except only the two last—those which assert the coming of the Messiah and the resurrection. How, then, did he come to include these two?

This question was raised soon after Maimonides' own time (especially in regard to the belief in the Messiah); and his critics rightly pointed out that before laying down dogmas one must define exactly what is meant by a dogma, so that we may know how to distinguish between what may and what may not be properly so called.[1] It is indeed strange that Maimonides forgot so elementary a rule of logic, and still more strange when we remember that elsewhere, in enumerating the six hundred and thirteen commandments of the Law, he was fully alive to the necessity of explaining first of all "the principles which it is proper to take as a criterion," in order to select from the multitude of ordinances in the *Torah* those capital commandments from which the rest are derived. For this reason he fell foul of the earlier enumerations, which he regarded as ignorantly made and full of mistakes; and for his own part he first laid down fourteen "principles," and then proceeded to enumerate the commandments according to those principles.[2] But if this procedure was necessary in dealing with the practical commandments, surely it was even more necessary in the case of the dogmas of faith. How, then, did it happen that Maimonides embarked on so important a task as the enumeration of dogmas without first laying down some principle by which to guide himself?

It seems to me that we have to do here not with a casual mistake, but with one of those facts which

[1] See Albo, *Ikkarim*, Part I, chap. 1.
[2] See his Introduction to the *Sepher Hammitzvoth*.

indicate that the national sentiment was strong enough
in Maimonides to conquer even logic.   If Maimonides
had set out to define the term "dogma" in its purely
religious sense, he could not have found the slightest
justification for regarding the national belief in a future
redemption as a dogma.   But he felt that a national
hope was necessary to the existence of the nation ; and
without the existence of the nation the continuance of
its religion is unthinkable. It was this feeling that made
him for once oblivious of logic, and prevented him from
clearing up in his own mind the nature of religious
dogmas in general, so that he might be able to include
among them that national belief on which the nation
depends for its existence, although it has no direct
relation to the maintenance of religion as such.[1]

So also with the belief in resurrection, by which our
people has always set great store in its exile.   Every
individual Jew has suffered the pain of exile not merely
in his own person, but as a member of his people ; his
indignation and grief have been excited not by his
private trouble only, but by the national trouble.   He
could find personal consolation in the hope of eternity
in paradise ; but this did not blunt the edge of the
national trouble, which demanded its consolation in the
prospect of a bright future for the nation.   In those
days the individual Jew was no longer, as in ancient
times, keenly conscious that successive generations were
made one by the organic life of the nation ; and he could
not therefore find consolation in the happiness which
awaited his people at the end of time, but which he himself would not share.   Hence he clung to the belief in

---

[1] I remarked on this point years ago in " Past and Future." [See
Selected Essays by Ahad Ha'am, p. 87. —*Tr.*]

resurrection, which offered what he required—a reward to himself for his individual share of the national grief. Just as every Jew had participated, during his own lifetime, in the national sorrow, so would every Jew be privileged in the future to see with his own eyes the national consolation and redemption.[1] Thus the belief in resurrection was complementary to the belief in the Messiah. United, they gave the people heart and strength to bear the yoke of exile and to battle successfully against a sea of troubles, confident that sooner or later the haven would be reached. When, therefore, Maimonides found it written in the Mishnah (beginning of chapter *Chelek*) that he who denies resurrection forfeits eternal life, he did not feel any need to explain this statement in a sense opposed to its literal meaning, as he usually did when his system so demanded, but took it just as he found it, and made it a dogma. He satisfied his heart at the expense of his head.

Strangely enough, Maimonides himself was perplexed over the question of resurrection, and could not explain why he clung to a belief which it was not easy to combine with his own theory of the soul and the future life. When he formulates the dogmas in his Commentary on the Mishnah, he passes hurriedly over this one, and dismisses it in a few words, as though he were afraid that if he lingered at this point logic would catch him up and ask awkward questions. In the *Mishneh Torah*, again, he does not explain this dogma at all, either at the beginning of the book, where he deals with the Foundations of the Law, or at the end, where he discusses the Messianic Age. This omission led some of his critics to suspect that he did not really believe in a literal resur-

[1] Cf. *supra*, p. 10.

rection of the body, but explained it in the sense of the
rebirth of the soul hereafter (on which he enlarges
very often). This suspicion made him very indignant,
and he wrote a whole treatise to prove that he had never
intended to take resurrection in any but its literal sense.
On the contrary, he maintained that the belief must be
accepted literally, and that it was in no way inconsistent
with what he had written or with his general view.[1]
But the arguments in this treatise are all very weak,
and the general impression which it leaves is that he did
not clearly understand his own mind. He felt instinctively that he could not give up this belief, though it
was foreign to his system ; but it was only with great
difficulty that he could explain why he allowed it such
importance. It was, of course, impossible for a man
like Maimonides to admit to himself that he was following feeling rather than reason. He tried therefore to
justify his standpoint on rational grounds, but without
success.[2]

We find the same struggle between philosophical
system and national sentiment in Maimonides' attitude
to the Hebrew language. From the point of view of
his system he naturally saw no difference between one
language and another : what matters is the idea, not its
external dress. Hence he lays it down that speech "is

[1] See the *Treatise on Resurrection.*

[2] Luzzatto (*ubi supra*) seems to suspect that Maimonides' whole
treatment of resurrection was insincere, and that he was deliberately
throwing dust in the reader's eyes, in order to conceal his heresy.
But this suspicion is absurd : Maimonides was a man who was not
afraid openly to reject even the immortality of the soul, and to recast
all the fundamental beliefs of Judaism. Any unbiassed reader of the
treatise must realise that Maimonides defends resurrection with
perfect sincerity, but that he is unable to find the real grounds of his
own conviction, because he looks for them in his reason and not in
his feelings.

not to be forbidden or allowed, loved or despised,
according to the language, but according to the subject.
That which is lofty may be said in whatever language ;
that which is mean may not be said in any language.''[1]
Practising what he preached, he wrote most of his books
not in Hebrew, but in Arabic, because he thought that
by being written in the ordinary language of his age and
his surroundings they would be of greater use from the
point of view of their subject-matter. The only book
that he wrote in Hebrew was the *Mishneh Torah* ; and
here also he was guided by practical considerations. He
chose the language of the Mishnah because he wanted
his people to regard the book with respect as a kind of
second Mishnah. The beautiful Mishnaic language
would carry off the " true opinions," which needed the
help of a sacred language to make them holy and bring
them under the ægis of religion. Thus far Maimonides
the philosopher. But in his letters we find clear indications that after he had finished his work his national
sentiment proved stronger than his philosophy, and he
regretted that he had not written his other works in
Hebrew as well. Not only that, but he actually thought
of translating them into the national language himself,
so as " to separate that which is precious from that
which is defiled, and to restore stolen goods to their
rightful owner." But the decline of his powers in old
age did not permit him to carry out this intention, and
the Hebrew translation had to wait for other hands.
Some of it was done in his lifetime ; and his letter to the
translator of the *Guide* shows how pleased he was.[2]

[1] *Commentary on the Mishnah, Aboth,* chap. i. 17.
[2] See his letters to Joseph ben Gabar, to the community of Lunel,
and to R. Samuel Ibn Tibbon (*Collected Responses of Maimonides*
(Leipsic), Part II., pp. 16, 27, 44).

But there is really no need to look for the influence of the national sentiment in particular parts of Maimonides' work. His work as a whole cannot be fully understood unless we allow for this sentiment. Of course, as we have seen, Maimonides' efforts to improve religion were the result of his philosophy, which taught him that religion must be made fit to fulfil its function in the spheres of theory and practice ; and for his own part he certainly believed that he was actuated solely by this conviction, and was doing, as needs he must, what reason demanded of him. But we, who look at things in the light of modern psychology, which tells us that intellectual conviction is not sufficient to produce sustained effort unless it is accompanied by a strong emotion, whereby the will is roused to conquer all obstacles—we cannot conceive the possibility of arduous work without a compelling emotion. And when we look for the emotion which is most likely to furnish an explanation in this particular case, we shall find none except the national sentiment.

For we know, on the one hand, that religious laws were for Maimonides nothing but an instrument of education—a means of confirming people in true beliefs and good habits of life. Moreover, he regarded many of them (sacrifices and the ceremonial associated with sacrifices) as merely a necessary evil, designed to restrict a bad practice which had taken root in the national life at an early period, and could not be abolished entirely ; and even this justification applied only to the laws as a whole, while their details, as we saw above, were in his opinion wholly without meaning or significance. And yet, holding such views, he worked day and night for ten years to collect all these laws and arrange them, with meticulous exactness, down to their smallest details. Whoever realises the enormous labour that it required to get together the mass of legal prescriptions, scattered over an extensive literature, must admit that no man can be qualified for the work (even if he recognises its usefulness from a certain point of view) unless the work itself has a strong attachment for him. To see the usefulness of the work is not enough ; it must be a real labour of love. What then can have kept Maimonides to his task if not the national sentiment, which made him love his people's Law and ancient customs even where his philosophy did not attach to them any particular importance ?

And on the other side, Maimonides could not have laboured to turn Judaism into a pure philosophy without the help of the national sentiment. We can understand the religious philosopher who tries to effect a compromise between religion and philosophy. The impelling force is his religious feeling : anxious to save religion from the danger threatened by rationalism, he adopts the familiar expedient of dressing religion in the trappings of philosophy, so as to safeguard its essential meaning. But when a philosopher starts, as Maimonides did, with the conviction that there is no room for compromise, but that religion is compelled, willy-nilly, to teach only what reason approves and when he labours indefatigably to purify religious belief of all superrational elements, and to turn its essential content into a pure philosophical system, and all this by long and devious methods, which reason cannot always approve : then we are bound to ask what emotion it was that gave him the strength and the will-power required for so difficult a task. Religious emotion certainly gained nothing from a process by which religion was driven from its own throne and deprived of its letters patent as a guide to eternal happiness along a private road of its own. Philosophical emotion—if the term may be used—might have gained more if Maimonides had accepted and prescribed the method adopted by free-thinkers before and after him—that of leaving faith to the believing masses and being satisfied for his own part with reason alone. But the national sentiment did gain a great deal by the transformation of the Jewish religion —the only national inheritance which had survived to unite our scattered people in exile—into philosophical truth, firmly based on rational and (as Maimonides sincerely believed) irrefragable proofs, and consequently secure for all time against assault.

So we come finally to the conclusion that Maimonides, too, like the other Jewish thinkers, had as the ultimate aim of his great work (though perhaps he did not realise it clearly) the shaping of the content and form of Judaism into a fortress on which the nation could depend for its continuance in exile. There is only this difference : that whereas his predecessors held Judaism secure because it was *above* reason, Maimonides came and said : " No ! Judaism is secure because it *is* reason."

JUDAISM AND THE GOSPELS

(1910)

English Jewry is at ease. There are no doubt traces here and there of anti-Semitism, nor are there wanting in the inner life of the community indications of what may be called "servitude in freedom." But when all allowances are made, the Jews enjoy a firmer and a more secure position here than in other countries, and anxiety for the future, with all that it involves, plays a smaller part in their mental life. Hence their internal develop-ment is more "normal" than elsewhere ; it is less at the mercy of external and accidental influences ; it is rather determined by the spiritual and cultural resources of the community itself, and corresponds at any given time to the extent of those resources. To this circum-stance is due the comparatively late appearance of the Reform movement in Anglo-Jewry. True, in the hey-day of the German Reform movement a few people in England attempted to follow the German example ; but their small experiment never grew to considerable dimensions, or showed any capacity for development. The reason is that whereas in Germany there was an external, political impulse towards Reform—the desire to combat anti-Jewish feeling, and thus to facilitate the attainment of civil and political rights—in England this motive was less felt. For though certain political restrictions were still in force, the position of the Jews was much better, and their relations with non-Jews were much more satisfactory, than in Germany.

But in more recent years education and the circumstances of life have brought about a change in the internal, spiritual condition of the Anglo-Jewish community : a new generation has arisen, which is very far removed from the *spirit* of Judaism. It is this internal change in the Jews which has called into being the Reform movement which we now see developing before our eyes. To the difference in origin corresponds a difference in character. In Germany the Reform movement, practical in its motives, took a practical shape. Geiger and other Reformers endeavoured, on the one side, to alter the religious practices, and to bring them into conformity with what they conceived to be the needs of the time; but on the other side they laid stress on the grandeur of the religious and moral principles on which Judaism peculiarly was based, and tried to emphasise the *difference* between Judaism and Christianity. But in England the Reform movement springs from a spiritual cause—from a conviction on the part of many Jews that they are spiritually *akin* to their Christian environment. It is not merely the external observances of traditional Judaism that fail any longer to appeal to them ; its innermost spirit, the fundamental ideas by which it is distinguished from Christianity, have lost their hold. Hence the movement here aims right at the heart ; it wants to change the *spirit* of Judaism, and to overthrow its historical foundations, so as to reduce its distinctive features to a small compass, and to bring it as closely as possible into accord with the Christian ideas of the non-Jewish community. Thirteen years ago this movement was begun in England by a body of

young men, who thus straightforwardly and clearly
expressed their aim :

". . . Our triumphant emancipation is now working
out its natural result upon us. Constant intercourse with
non-Jews and extensive secular education must materially
affect our opinions. We, who are young and earnest
lovers of our religion, are struggling with new ideas
which we hardly dare to formulate, because they are
contrary to all accepted traditions. Such are the notions
that our separateness seems now merely external and
artificial, our racial distinctiveness often scarcely perceptible, and our religious ideas almost identical with
those of Theists and true Unitarians."[1]

But as it was difficult for them, in spite of everything,
to abandon Judaism altogether, and to join the "Theists
and true Unitarians," they conceived the idea of attaining their object in the reverse way. They would transform Judaism itself, until it should contain nothing but
the fundamental ideas of the " Theists and true Unitarians," and then—so they fondly imagined—these
latter would come and find shelter in Judaism, and so
the " external and artificial " distinction would be comfortably and pleasantly removed ! This movement did
not take definite shape at the time, and after a while
it disappeared and was no longer heard of. But the
causes which had given it birth did not cease to work
silently beneath the surface ; and quite recently it has
come forth again into the light of day, to play its part
in the visible life of Anglo-Jewry. This time it appears
in a more concrete form and with a clearer consciousness of the goal for which it is making. Its promoters
have come to see, after all, that even if their Judaism is

[1] *Jewish Quarterly Review*, January, 1897, p. 187.

to teach the very doctrine of the "liberal" Christian
sects, there will still be an "external and artificial"
distinction between themselves and the non-Jew, so long
as they do not accept the *source* of that doctrine—so
long as they do not admit, with the "liberal" Christians,
that the New Testament is the last word in religious
and moral development, and Jesus the most perfect
embodiment of the religious and moral ideal.   For in
matters of religion men value not alone the abstract
beliefs in themselves, but also—and perhaps more
highly—the historical and psychological roots from
which those beliefs have grown up in their hearts.   It
was well said many years ago by Steinthal that if ever a
new religion, a philosophical religion, suited to modern
times, should unite Jews and Christians, they would
still be divided on the question whether the Old Testament or the Gospels had contributed in greater measure
to the birth of the new religion.

Our English Reformers, therefore, have decided to
remove even this stumbling-block from the path which
leads to unity, and have decreed that the New Testament (or at least the Gospels) must be considered a
part—and the most important part—of Judaism, and
that Jesus must be regarded as a prophet—and the
greatest of the prophets—in Israel.   This pronounce-
ment is certainly a step forward along a certain line of
development, of which we are not yet at the end.   We
need not therefore be surprised if these Reformers do
not realise the strangeness of their attitude, with its
combination of contradictory and mutually destructive
postulates.   Whereas revolution overthrows the old at
a single stroke, and puts the new in its place, evolution
destroys and builds in sections, so that, until its work

is complete, it is full of contradictions and inconsistencies—the old and the new jostling one another in confusion, and creating by their unnatural juxtaposition the impression of a caricature, which is obvious to the onlooker, but not to those who are engaged in the work. So this Reformed Judaism, which wants to be two opposites—Jewish and Evangelist—at once, has its place as a rung in the middle of the ladder, a step on the road of evolution to its final goal. At this stage of the journey our Reformers still think that it is possible to put the Gospels *beside* the Old Testament and the Talmud. But when they reach the next stage they will recognise that the two cannot exist side by side, but only one above the other, and that when one stands the other falls. The early Christians went through the same process : they regarded their " message " at first simply as a part of Judaism ; but when they had travelled the full length of their development, they saw that the Gospels meant the overthrow of the very foundations of Judaism, and then they left it altogether.

If anybody is doubtful about the true character and tendency of this movement, let him read the commentary on the Synoptic Gospels recently published by the leader of the movement, Mr. C. G. Montefiore. The author makes no secret of the fact that the book has been written for Jewish readers, with the object of convincing them that the New Testament ought to occupy an important position in Judaism at the present time, albeit from a Jewish point of view. The claims of the " Jewish point of view " he thinks to satisfy by his frequent efforts to show that the Law of the Rabbis was not so bad as it is painted by the authors of the New Testament and its commentators, and that in many respects the old Judaism rose to the level of the Gospels, nay, had in certain details actually more of truth.[1] But the general atmosphere of the book is so utterly alien from the essential character of Judaism as to make one fact clear beyond a shadow of doubt to any Jew in whom Judaism is still alive—that the Gospels can be received only into a Judaism which has lost its own true spirit, and remains a mere corpse.

The author is doubtless correct in saying that a Jewish commentary on the New Testament is needed at the present time.[2] Living in a Christian environment, we imbibe a culture in which many Christian ideas and sentiments are inwoven, and it is therefore necessary for us to know their source, so as to be able to distinguish between them and the universal elements of culture. But this Jewish commentary must be far removed from any polemical propagandist intention on one side or the other. Its sole object must be to *understand* thoroughly the teaching of the Gospels, to define with *scientific* accuracy its character, the foundations on which it rests, and the differences which distinguish it from Judaism. What is needed is not the " scientific accuracy " of the Christian commentators (that spring from which Mr. Montefiore drinks with such avidity), who set out with the preconceived idea that the teaching of the Gospels is superior to that of Judaism, and use their "science " merely to find details in support of this general belief. When a writer claims to be " scientific," he must recog-

---

[1] Notes of this kind are found right through the book (see e.g. pp. 498—503, 691—3, and many other places); and it is unfair of some Jewish critics to have passed over this fact in silence, and to have described the book as though it were throughout simply an attack on Judaism.

[2] Introduction, pp. xvii. xviii. ci.

nise above all that in the field of religion and morality
it is impossible to set up a universal scientific criterion,
by which to measure the different teachings, and to pronounce one superior to another. In this sphere everything is relative, and the judge brings to his task a subjective standard of his own, determined by his tempera-
ment, his education and his environment. We Jews,
being everywhere a minority, are always subject to
various influences, which counteract and weaken each
other; and we, therefore, are possibly better able than
others to understand objectively ideas which are not our
own. Hence it was indeed right that there should be a
Jewish commentary (not a Jewish panegyric) on the
New Testament. Such a commentary might perhaps
have enabled Jews of our author's stamp to recognise
that it is possible to treat with seriousness and justice
a religion which is strange to us, without shutting our
eyes to the gulf which separates it from ourselves.

I should like to dwell for a brief space on the nature
of this " gulf." So large a subject needs a whole book
for its full treatment; but something, it seems to me,
ought to be said just at this moment—and perhaps the
need is not confined to England.

If the heathen of the old story, who wished to learn
the whole *Torah* standing on one leg,[1] had come to me,
I should have told him : " ' Thou shalt not make unto
thee any graven image or any likeness '—that is the
whole *Torah*, and the rest is commentary." The essential characteristic of Judaism, which distinguishes it
from other religions, is its absolute determination to

[1] [The story is that a heathen made this demand of Hillel, whose
reply was : " What is hateful to thyself do not unto thy neighbour—
that is the whole *Torah*, and the rest is commentary : go thou and
fulfil it." —*Tr.*]

make the religious and moral consciousness independent
of any definite human form, and to attach it *immediately*
to an *abstract* ideal which has " no likeness." We
cannot conceive Christianity without Jesus, or even
Islam without Mohammed. Christianity made a god of
Jesus, but that is not the important fact. Even if Jesus
had remained the " son of man," had been only a
prophet, as Mohammed is to the Mussulmans, that
would not have affected the thing that really matters—
the attachment of the religious and moral consciousness
to the figure of a particular man, who is regarded as the
ideal of absolute perfection, and the goal of men's
vision ; to believe in whom is an essential part of a
religion inconceivable without him. Judaism, and
Judaism alone, depends on no such human "likeness."
God is the only idea of absolute perfection, and He only
must be kept always before the eye of man's inner consciousness, in order that many may " cleave to his attributes." The best of men is not free from shortcomings
and sins, and cannot serve as an ideal for the religious
sentiment, which strives after union with the source of
perfection. Moses died in his sin, like any other man.
He was simply God's messenger, charged with the giving
of His Law ; his image was not worked into the very
fabric of the religion, as an essential part of it. Thus
the Jewish teachers of a later period found nothing to
shock them in the words of one who said in all simplicity : " Ezra was worthy to be the bearer of the Law
to Israel, had not Moses come before him " (*Sanhedrin,*
21*a*). Could it enter a Christian mind, let us say, to
conceive the idea that Paul was worthy to be the bearer
of the " message," had not Jesus come before him ?
And it need scarcely be said that the individual figures

of the other Prophets are not an essential part of the
fabric of Judaism. Of the greatest of them—Hosea,
Amos, Isaiah, and others—we do not even know who or
what they were ; their personalities have vanished like a
shadow, and only their words have been preserved and
handed down from generation to generation, because
they were not *their* words, but " the word of the Lord
that came unto them."

This applies equally to the Messiah, who is awaited
in the future. His importance lies not in himself, but
in his being *the messenger of God* for the bringing of
redemption to Israel and the world. Jewish teachers
pay much more attention to " the days of the Messiah"
than to the Messiah himself. One of them even dis-
believed altogether in a personal Messiah, and looked
forward to a redemption effected by God Himself without an intermediary ; and he was not therefore regarded
as a heretic.

This characteristic of Judaism was perhaps the principal obstacle to its wider acceptance. It is difficult
for men in general to find satisfaction in an abstract
ideal which offers no hold to the senses ; a human figure
much more readily inspires enthusiasm. Before the
triumph of Christianity the Greeks and the Romans used
to accuse the Jews of having no God, because a divinity
without " any likeness " had for them no meaning ; and
when the time came for the God of Israel to become
also the God of the nations, they still could not accept
His sway without associating with Him a divine ideal
in human form, so as to satisfy their need for a more
concrete and nearer ideal.

This is not the place to discuss the origin of this distinctive preference on the part of Israel for an *abstract*

religious and moral ideal. Be the reason what it may, the fact remains true, and has been true these thousands of years ; and so long as Israel undergoes no fundamental change, and does not become something different, it cannot be influenced on the religious side by a book like the Gospels, which finds the object of religious devotion and moral emulation not in the abstract Godhead alone, but first and foremost in a man born of woman. It matters not whether he be called " Son of God," " Messiah," or " Prophet " : Israel cannot accept with religious enthusiasm, as the word of God, the utterances of a man who speaks in his own name—not " thus saith the Lord," but " *I* say unto you." This " I " is in itself sufficient to drive Judaism away from the Gospels for ever. And when our author speaks in glowing terms of the religious and moral exaltation which spring from attachment to Jesus as the ideal of holiness and per- fection, meaning, as is evident from his tone, to intro- duce this attachment into Judaism (pp. cvii, 210, 527), he is simply proving that he and those who think with him are already estranged from the essential nature of Judaism, which does not recognise ideal holiness and perfection in man. " Ye shall be holy, for I the Lord your God am holy "—that is Judaism. " Ye shall be holy, because the Messiah (or the Prophet) is holy "— that is an ideal better calculated, no doubt, to inspire enthusiasm and exaltation among the peoples ; but it will never kindle the religious fire in Israel unless the very last drop of true Judaism be dried up. It was not for nothing that our ancient teachers called God " *the holy one,* blessed be He " : for Judaism absolute holiness exists only in the one God. We have had no doubt, at various periods, our mystic sects, which, influenced con-

sciously or unconsciously by foreign ideas, have here
turned aside more or less from the Jewish road.   But
the sect is only a temporary and partial phenomenon,
pointing to some internal disease which affects the
national life in a given period.   Our history shows that
the end of these sects is to die out, or to leave Judaism.
Sects come and sects go, but Judaism remains for ever.

This fundamental tendency of Israel to rise clear of
" any likeness " in its religious and moral life is evident
not only in relation to the religious and moral *ideal*, but
also in relation to the religious and moral *goal*.   There
is no need to dilate on the well-worn truth that the Law
of Judaism sees its goal not in the " salvation" of the
individual man, but in the prosperity and perfection of
the general body ; that is to say, of the nation, and, in
" the latter end of days," of the whole human race—a
collective idea which has no defined concrete form.   In
the most fruitful period of Judaism, the period of the
Prophets and "the giving of the Law," it had no clear
idea on the subject of the survival of the soul and reward
and punishment after death.   All the enthusiasm of the
Prophets and their disciples was derived not from this
source, but from the conviction of their being children
of " the chosen people," which was entrusted by God
(as they believed) with the mission of embodying
religion and morality, in their highest form, in its
national life.   Even in later times, when the Babylonian
exile had destroyed the nation's freedom, and the desire
for individual salvation had consequently come to play
a part in the religious consciousness, the *highest* good
of Judaism still remained collective. Scholars will need
no proof of this fact.   For those who are not scholars
it will be sufficient to examine the daily and festival

prayer-books, in order to realise that only a small part
of the prayers turns on the particular needs of the
individual, while most deal with the concerns of the
nation and the human race in general.

Which of these two goals is " superior " ? This question has already been endlessly debated ; and the truth
is that we cannot here establish a scale of values.   A
man may attain to the highest eminence in his religious
and moral life, whether he pursues this goal or that.
But individual salvation is certainly nearer to the hearts
of most men, and is better suited to kindle their imagination and to inspire them with the desire for moral and
religious perfection.   If Judaism, as distinguished from
other religions, prefers the collective goal, this only
means that here also there makes itself felt that tendency to abstraction and to the repudiation of the
human image which is peculiar to Israel.   So long as
this tendency remains—so long, that is, as our people
does not lose its essential character—no true Jew will
be able to feel any great fondness for the doctrine of the
Gospels—a doctrine which rests (despite our author's
endeavours to present the matter in a more favourable
light, cf. pp. 211, 918) wholly and solely on the pursuit
of individual salvation.

The tendency of Judaism which I have mentioned
shows itself in yet one other matter, and this perhaps
the most important—in the basis of morality.   It is an
oft-repeated formula that Jewish morality is based on
justice, and the morality of the Gospels on *love*.   But
it seems to me that not all those who draw this distinction fully appreciate its meaning.   It is usual to regard
the difference only as one of degree, the moral scale and
its basis being the same in either case.   Both doctrines,

it is supposed, are directed against egoism; but the Christians hold that their religion has reached a higher stage, while the Jews refuse to admit their claim. Thus the Christian commentators point proudly to the *positive* principle of the Gospels: " Whatsoever ye would that men should do to you, do ye even so unto them " (Matt. vii. 12; Luke vi. 31), and thereby disparage Judaism, which has only the *negative* principle of Hillel: " What is hateful to thyself do not unto thy neighbour." Mr. Montefiore debates the matter, and cannot make up his mind whether the positive principle really embraces *more* in its intention than the negative, or whether Hillel and Jesus meant the same thing. But of this at least he is certain, that if Hillel's saying were suddenly discovered somewhere in a positive form, the Jews would be "rather pleased," and the Christians would be " rather sorry " (p. 550).

But if we look deeper, we shall find that the difference between the two doctrines on this point is not one of less or more, but that there is a fundamental difference between their views as to the basis of morality. It was not by accident that Hillel put his principle in negative form; the truth is that the moral basis of Judaism will not bear the positive principle. If the positive saying were to be found somewhere attributed to Hillel, we should not be able to rejoice; we should have to impugn the genuineness of a "discovery" which put into Hillel's mouth a saying opposed to the spirit of Judaism.

The root of the distinction lies here also, as I have said, in the love of Judaism for *abstract* principles. The moral law of the Gospels beholds man in his individual shape, with his natural attitude towards himself and

others, and asks him to reverse this attitude, to substitute the " other " for the " self " in his individual
life, to abandon plain egoism for inverted egoism. For
in truth the altruism of the Gospels is neither more nor
less than inverted egoism. Altruism and egoism alike
deny the individual *as such* all *objective* moral value,
and make him merely a *means* to a subjective end ; but
egoism makes the " other " a means to the advantage
of the " self," while altruism does just the reverse.
Now Judaism removed this subjective attitude from the
moral law, and based it on an abstract, objective foundation, on *absolute justice,* which regards the individual
as such as having a moral value, and makes no distinction between the " self " and the " other." According to this view, it is the sense of justice in the human
heart that is the supreme judge of a man's own actions
and of those of other men. This sense must be made
independent of individual relations, as though it were
some separate abstract being ; and before it all men,
including the self, must be equal. All men, including
the self, must develop their lives and their faculties to
the utmost possible extent, and at the same time each
must help his neighbour to attain that goal, so far as he
is able. Just as I have no right to ruin another man's
life for the sake of my own, so I have no right to ruin
my own life for the sake of another's. Both of us are
men, and both our lives have the same value before
the throne of justice.

I know no better illustration of this point of view than
the following well-known *B'raitha :* " Imagine two men
journeying through the desert, only one of whom has a
bottle of water. If both of them drink, they must both
die ; if one of them only drinks, he will reach safety.

Ben P'tura held that it was better that both should drink and die, than that one should witness the death of his comrade. But Akiba refuted this view by citing the scriptural verse, ' and thy brother shall live with thee.' *With thee*—that is to say, thine own life comes before thy neighbour's " (*Baba M'zia, 62a*).

We do not know who Ben P'tura was, but we do know R. Akiba, and we may be sure that through him the spirit of Judaism speaks. Ben P'tura, the altruist, does not value human life for its own sake; for him it is better that two lives should perish, where death demands but one as his toll, so long as the altruistic sentiment prevails. But Jewish morality regards the question from an objective standpoint. Every action that leads to loss of life is evil, even though it springs from the purest feelings of love and mercy, and even if the sufferer is himself the agent. In the case before us, where it is possible to save one of the two souls, it is a moral duty to overcome the feeling of mercy, and to save. But to save whom? Justice answers—let him who can save himself. Every man's life is entrusted to his keeping, and to preserve your own charge is a nearer duty than to preserve your neighbour's.

But when one came to Raba, and asked him what he should do when one in authority threatened to kill him unless he would kill another man, Raba answered him : " Be killed, and kill not. Who hath told thee that thy blood is redder than his? Perhaps his blood is redder" (*P'sachim, 25b*). And Rashi, whose "sense of Judaism" generally reveals to him the hidden depths of meaning, correctly understands the meaning here also, and explains thus : " The question only arises because thou knowest that *no religious law is binding in the face of danger to life,* and thinkest that in this case also the prohibition of murder ceases to be binding *because thine own life is in danger.* But this transgression is unlike others. *For do what thou wilt, there must here be a life lost.* . . . Who can tell thee that thy life is more precious in the sight of God than his? Perhaps his is more precious."

If a man brought a question like this to a Christian priest, the priest would certainly begin to expatiate in glowing terms on the duty of a man to sacrifice his life for another, to " bear his cross " in the footsteps of his " Messiah," so that he might win the kingdom of heaven—and so forth. But the Jewish teacher weighs the question in the scales of objective justice : " Seeing that in either case a life must be lost, and there is none to say which of the two lives is more precious in God's sight, therefore your own danger does not entitle you to break the sixth commandment. Be killed ; kill you must not ! " But suppose the case reversed ; suppose the question to be " Another is going to be killed, and I can save him by giving my life instead of his, what shall I do ? " Then Raba would have replied : "Let such a one be killed, and do not destroy thyself. For do what thou wilt there must here be a life lost ; and who hath told thee that his blood is redder than thine? Perhaps thine own is redder." From the standpoint of Judaism every man's blood is as red as any other's, every soul is " precious in the sight of God," be it mine or another's, therefore no man is at liberty to treat his life as his own property ; no man has a right to say : " I am endangering myself; what right have others to complain of that ? " (Maimonides' Code, *Laws of Murder,* XI. 5). The history of Judaism can tell, indeed, of many acts of self-sacrifice, the memory of which will remain precious and holy for all time.   But these are not cases of one life given for the preservation of another similar life, they are sacrifices of human life for " the sanctification of the Name" (the religious ideal) or for " the good of the community " (the religious goal).

And justice demands that we rise above sentiment not only in deciding as between the self and another, but also in deciding as between two other persons.   Forty years ago Abraham Geiger—the man in whom our latter-day " Reformers " see their spiritual father—pointed out that the Jewish commandment " Neither shalt thou countenance a poor man in his cause" reveals a morality of unparalleled loftiness.[1]   All other moral codes warn us only against favouring the persons of the rich and the powerful ; and the Gospels, as is well known, favour the persons of the poor, and have much to say of their merits and their future greatness.   All this is very well from the point of view of the heart ; but a morality based on justice rises above sentiment, and teaches that it is our duty to help the poor man if we are able, but that mercy must not induce us so far to sin against justice as to favour the poor man in his suit.

Herbert Spencer anticipates, as the highest possible development of morality, the transformation of the altruistic sentiment into a natural instinct, so that at last men will be able to find no greater pleasure than in working for the good of others.   Similarly Judaism, in conformity with its own way of thought, anticipates the development of morality to a point at which *justice* will become an instinct with good men, so that they will not need long reflection to enable them to decide between different courses of action according to the standard of

[1] *Das Judentum und seine Geschichte* (2nd edition), p. 26.

absolute justice, but will *feel* as in a flash, and with the certainty of instinct, even the slightest deviation from the straight line. Human relations and social grades will not affect them in the least, because the "true judge" within them will pronounce justly on each deed, swayed by no human relation to the doer or the sufferer, considering not whether this one or that is the self or another, is rich or poor. And since Judaism associated its moral aspirations with the "coming of the Messiah," it attributed to the Messiah this perfection of morality, and said that "he will smell and judge" (*Sanhedrin,* 93*b*), on the basis of the scriptural verse: "And shall make him of quick understanding [Heb. "smell"] in the fear of the Lord; and he shall not judge after the sight of his eyes." "Because the smell is a very delicate sense, he gives the name of *smell* to the most delicate feeling . . . that is to say, the Messiah *with little attention will feel which men are good, and which evil*" (Isa. xi. 3, with Kimchi's commentary).

But this development lies far ahead in the hidden future. At present the human race still lacks the instinctive "sense of justice," and even the best men are apt to be blinded by self-love or prejudice, so as to be unable to distinguish between good and evil. At present, therefore, we all need some touchstone, some fundamental principle, to help each of us to avoid weighting the· scales of justice to suit his own ends or satisfy his personal inclinations. Such a principle Hillel gave us: "What is hateful to thyself do not unto thy neighbour." Altruism teaches: "What thou desirest that others should do unto thee, that do thou unto them." In other words: take the circle of egoism, and put in its *centre,* instead of the "self," the "other"; then you will know your whole duty.   But Judaism cannot find satisfaction in this substitution, because it demands that *justice* shall be placed at the centre of the circle—justice, which makes no distinction between " self " and " other."   Now in the circle of egoism there is no place for justice except in a negative form.   What egoism does *not* wish for itself—that, certainly it will be just *not* to do to another.   But what egoism *does* wish for itself is something which has no limits; and if you oblige a man to *do* this to others, you are inclining the scales of justice to the side of the " other " as against the " self."

Even that " great principle in the Law" (as R. Akiba called it), " thou shalt love thy neighbour as thyself," though in form it appears to be positive, is in reality, if rightly understood, negative.   If the Torah had meant that a man must love his neighbour to the extent of sacrificing his life for him, it would have said : " Thou shalt love thy neighbour *more than* thyself."   But when you love your neighbour *as* yourself, neither more nor less, then your feelings are in a state of perfect equilibrium, with no leaning either to your side or to your neighbour's.   And this is, in fact, the true meaning of the verse.   " Self-love must not be allowed to incline the scale on the side of your own advantage ; love your neighbour as yourself, and then inevitably *justice* will be the deciding factor, and you will do nothing to your neighbour that you would consider a wrong if it were done to yourself."   For proof that this is the real meaning we have only to look further in the same passage of Leviticus, where we find : " And if a stranger sojourn with thee in your land, ye shall not vex him.   But the stranger that dwelleth with you shall be unto you as one

born among you, and thou shalt love him as thyself''
(Lev. xix. 33, 34).   Here it is evident that to love the
stranger '' as thyself'' means to carry out the negative
precept '' ye shall not vex him '' ; and if the stranger is
expressly placed on the same footing as the native, this
shows that in relation to the native also the intention is
only that self-love must not prove a stronger motive
than justice.

But in the Gospels the commandment '' Thou shalt
love thy neighbour as thyself'' receives an altruistic
sense : it means that your own life is less important
than your neighbour's. Hence it is possible to find some
small justification for the habit which Christians have of
attributing this verse to the Gospels, as though it
appeared there, and not in the Mosaic Law, for the first
time.   It is true that *the meaning which they put on the
verse* belongs not to our Law, but to the Gospels.[1]

But it must be remembered that in addition to the
relation of individual to individual, there is another and
more important moral relation—that of nation to nation.
Here also some '' great principle '' is needed to keep
within bounds that *national* egoism which is fraught,
perhaps, with even greater danger to the collective progress of humanity than individual egoism.   If we look
at the difference between Judaism and Christianity, in
regard to the basis of morality, from this point of view,

---

[1] John Stuart Mill writes : '' In justice to the great Hebrew lawgiver, it should always be remembered that the precept to love thy
neighbour as thyself already existed in the Pentateuch ; and very
surprising it is to find it there'' (*Three Essays on Religion,* 2nd
edition, p. 98). Had Mill understood the precept in its original sense,
he would certainly not have been surprised to find it in the Mosaic
Law. But even so logical a thinker could not free himself from the
influences of his education and his environment, and he did not see
that a meaning had been read into this verse which was opposed to
its literal sense.

we shall see at once that the altruism of the Gospels is in no way suited to serve as a basis for international relations.   A nation can never believe that its moral duty lies in self-abasement, and in the renunciation of its rights for the benefit of other nations.   On the contrary, every nation feels and knows that its moral duty is to keep its position and use its powers as a means of creating for itself satisfactory conditions of life, in which it can develop its potentialities to the utmost.   Since, then, Christian nations could not base their relations one with another on the moral basis of their religion, national egoism inevitably remained the sole determining force in international politics, and " patriotism," in the Bismarckian sense, attained the dignity of the ultimate moral basis.

But the Jewish law of justice is not confined within the narrow sphere of individual relations.   In its Jewish sense the precept, " Thou shalt love thy neighbour as thyself," can be carried out by a whole nation in its dealings with other nations.   For this precept does not oblige a nation to sacrifice, for the benefit of other nations, its life or its position.   It is, on the contrary, the duty of every nation, as of the individual human being, to live and to develop to the utmost extent of its powers ; but at the same time it must recognise the right of other nations to fulfil the like duty without let or hindrance, and " patriotism "—that is, national egoism —must not induce it to disregard justice, and to fulfil itself through the destruction of other nations.[1]   Hence

[1] The Russian philosopher Vladimir Solovioff was the first, if I am not mistaken, to attempt to find a moral basis for international relations in the precept " Thou shalt love thy neighbour as thyself," taken in the sense mentioned above. This philosopher was an untiring student of Judaism, for which he had an appreciation unusual among Christians—a fact not without its significance.

Judaism was able thousands of years ago to rise to the lofty ideal expressed in the words, " Nation shall not lift up sword against nation." This ideal is, in fact, only an inevitable logical consequence of the idea of absolute justice, which lies at the foundation of Judaism.

Many pages might be filled with the further development of these general ideas ; and as many more might without difficulty be given to an exposition of the differences between the two doctrines in points of detail, in such a way as to show that the detailed differences are but the outcome of the broad and fundamental difference between Judaism and Christianity, and that all the compromises and concessions whereby Mr. Montefiore tries to make peace between the two creeds have no real value, either theoretical or practical. But it is not my purpose here to write a book, and I will content myself, so far as general principles are concerned, with the brief hints above set forth. As for details, I will touch here on only one point, to which our author himself attaches more than ordinary importance, and will leave the reader to draw his own conclusions as to the rest.

The Gospels, unlike Judaism, forbid divorce, either absolutely, as in the version of Mark (x. 2-12), or with an exception in the case of unfaithfulness, as in the version of Matthew (xix. 3-12). At the present time, when all Christian nations are struggling with the prohibition of divorce, which came to them from the Gospels, and are trying to annul it or restrict its operation within narrow limits, it may be taken as fairly evident that the recognition of divorce, even on other grounds than unfaithfulness, is demanded by the conscience of society. Nor is it surprising that Judaism, with its essentially social aim, has been true to its general spirit in its attitude on this question, and has decided, with the school of Hillel, that divorce is permissible not alone on the ground of unfaithfulness, but also when there is from other causes a rupture of the bond of sympathy between man and wife. The important thing here is not the cause, but the effect—the rupture within the home, which must lower the moral tone of the life of the family, and interfere with the proper upbringing of the children. Long experience has taught Judaism that there is no reason to go back on this decision. Even the enemies of Israel cannot deny that Jewish family life has reached a high level of morality; and a result like this does not come about by a miracle, in the teeth of the national code of law, least of all in the case of the Jews, whose life has always been so profoundly influenced by the prescriptions of the *Torah*.[1] It must indeed be admitted that at first only the husband had the right of divorce, and no wife could divorce her husband. In conformity with the primitive view (a view still widely accepted all over the world) that man alone is important, and woman is but "an help meet for him," it was demanded above all things of the husband that his position in the home should correspond to his moral obligations as the father of the family, and that he should not be compelled by law to live with a woman who was distasteful to him, and to become the father of " children of a hated wife." But when once it came

---

[1] Mr. Montefiore, indeed, does not admit this. In his opinion the morality of Jewish family life is a fact not because of the laws, but in spite of them. If you ask how such a thing is possible, he replies somewhat as follows: It has already been remarked that Judaism does not obey the laws of cause and effect, and we sometimes see a certain tendency in Jewish life which ought logically to have certain effects, but has in practice just the opposite results (p. 335). Truly an easy and comfortable " philosophy of history "!

to be recognised that married life cannot tolerate constraint, this recognition, limited at first to the side of
the husband, was bound to be gradually extended to the
wife.   Hence arose the provisions under which a man
may be compelled to divorce his wife (*K'thuboth,* ch.
vii).   These provisions enabled the wife to obtain a
divorce against the husband's will, by decree of the
courts, on many and various grounds.   Thus it is impossible to assert that Judaism does not allow a woman to
divorce her husband.   In the cases just mentioned it is,
in fact, the wife who divorces, though the bill of divorce-
ment is technically given by the husband. What matters
is not who performs the legal action, but whose wish it
is that brings about the divorce.   This tendency to
emancipate the wife reached its highest development in
the dictum of Maimonides, that if a woman says " My
husband is distasteful to me, and I cannot live with
him," although she gives no specific reason for her dislike, the husband is yet compelled to divorce her,
"because she is not like a captive woman, that she
should consort with a man whom she hates" (*Laws of
Marriage,* xiv. 8).   Here we see the Jewish attitude to
marriage in its full development. Marriage is a social and
moral cord, the two ends of which are in the hearts of
husband and wife ; and if the cord is broken at either
end—whether in the husband's heart or in the wife's—
the marriage has lost its value, and it is best that it should
be annulled.   It is true that the jurists who came after
Maimonides could not rise to the conception of so
perfect an equality of the sexes, and did not wholly
accept his dictum.   But the mere fact that the greatest
authority deduced this decision *from the Talmud* (and
the Talmud, in fact, affords ground for his view—see

Maggid Mishnah ad loc.) is proof conclusive as to the real tendency of the Jewish law of divorce, and shows whither it leads in the straight line of development.

But the New Testament view of marriage and divorce reveals a very different tendency (Matthew and Mark, *locc. citt.* ; Paul, First Epistle to the Corinthians, vii.). As in all the teaching of the Gospels, so here the important thing is *individual* salvation. For the sake of his individual salvation it is better that a man should not marry at all, but should " suffer," and be " a eunuch for the kingdom of heaven's sake." But he who has not strength to suffer may enter into the covenant of marriage with a woman ; only this covenant, too, is an *individual* matter, based on *religious mysteries,* not a social and moral act, and therefore it can never be annulled, even if it results in injury to the life of society. " He which made them at the beginning made them male and female and said . . . they twain shall be one flesh. Wherefore they are no more twain, but one flesh. *What therefore God hath joined together, let not man put asunder."* From this standpoint it is immaterial whether there is love or hatred between the couple, whether their union is or is not a good thing for the life of the family and of society. All this does not affect the real point : God has united them, and how shall man dare to separate them ?[1]

The Catholic Church, correctly understanding the Gospel teaching, has built countless houses of refuge

[1] Even Matthew, who permits divorce on the ground of unfaithfulness, makes this exception (as some Christian commentators have pointed out) only because the sanctity of the marriage is profaned by the sin, and the divine union is annulled *of itself.* The point of view is essentially the same in both versions.

for celibates of both sexes, and has forbidden divorce
absolutely, without regard to all the evil results of this
prohibition in the embitterment of the life of families
and the moral corruption of thousands of men and
women.   Other Christian Churches have stopped short
of this extreme, but have still been unable to free themselves from the Gospel standpoint, so that until recently
they have tried to restrict and render ineffective the
recognition of divorce.   But now at last all Christian
nations are beginning to see that this standpoint is not
productive of good to the world, and are approaching
nearer to the Jewish view.[1]

But Christian theologians, in commenting on the
Gospels, cannot give up that great principle of theirs,
that the Gospel teaching is always based on a higher
morality than that of Judaism.   And in this case, too,
they have found a way—rather far-fetched, it is true—
of establishing the truth of their principle.   In forbid-
ding divorce, they say, Jesus only meant to protest
against the injustice of Judaism to the wife, who could
be divorced but could not divorce.   He therefore took
the right of divorce away from the husband, so that he
should have no advantage over the wife.   Here, then,
is moral '' progress,'' a battle on woman's behalf
against the oriental barbarism of the Jews, and so forth.
We might perhaps point out that there was a more
sensible way of bestowing equality on the wife, if that
was Jesus' object—to wit, by giving the wife also the
right of divorce.   And we might ask, further, how it is

[1] In England the question has become so acute that the Government has appointed a Commission to find means of making divorce
easier.   Men of knowledge and experience, in evidence before the
Commission, have expressed the opinion that the restriction of the
possibility of divorce has very evil results.

that Matthew, who allows the husband to divorce his wife for *her* unfaithfulness, never hints at any right on the part of the wife to demand a divorce from the husband on the ground of *his* unfaithfulness.[1] Where, in fact, is the vaunted assertion of the wife's rights? The commentators vouchsafe no answer to these plain and simple questions. But, indeed, there is no need of much questioning. It must be perfectly clear to all who read these passages in the Gospels without preconceived ideas that Jesus, in prohibiting divorce, had not the remotest notion of fighting the wife's battle. The plea is from beginning to end a theological invention, designed to bolster up the theory.

Let us now see what our *Jewish* commentator has to say on this subject (pp. 235-42, 508-10, 688-92). Whoever has not the leisure or the inclination to read the whole eleven hundred pages of Mr. Montefiore's book will find it sufficient to read the pages given to this question, in order to obtain an adequate idea of the real spirit which prevails among our author's following. As he repeatedly pours out the vials of his wrath in harsh and crude denunciations of the Jewish law of divorce, his tone is that of a monk just emerging, Gospel in hand, from his retreat, who has no desire to know anything whatever as to the views which prevail at the present day in the world around him. It is " to his eternal dishonour" that Hillel allowed divorce on other grounds than that of unchastity; it is " most unfortunate " for the Rabbinic law that it endorsed his decision. But "the unerring ethical instinct of Jesus led him to put

---

[1] In England the law to-day is still in the spirit of Matthew; the wife's unfaithfulness is sufficient ground of divorce for the husband, but the reverse does not hold good.

his finger upon the weak spots and sore places of the established religion," and "of all such weak spots and sore places this was the weakest and the sorest." Hence " in no other point was the opposition of Jesus to the Rabbinic law of profounder significance " (p. 235). In this strain our author continues, with a varied selection of choice phrases. Nor does he forget to adopt from the Christian commentators the theory that the Gospels were fighting the wife's battle; he repeats it several times, here also in a tone of harsh condemnation of Judaism and grateful praise of Jesus (p. 240 and elsewhere). It does not occur to him that the Christian commentators were driven to invent this theory because they saw that from the standpoint of our own age the prohibition of divorce is not in itself a sign of moral progress. But if the recognition of divorce on other grounds than that of unfaithfulness is " an eternal dishonour," then of course there is no need to invent this plea of a battle for the wife's rights, the mere prohibition being sufficient proof of "progress." Nay, there seems to be more lost than gained by this "battle," for if that was really the intention of the prohibition of divorce, then the prohibition must of necessity be absolute (to the exclusion even of the ground of unfaithfulness), since otherwise we are at a loss to understand why the wife, too, was not permitted to obtain a divorce on that ground. But our author himself admits that the prohibition of divorce in case of unfaithfulness had very evil results (p. 242). Where, then, is the "unerring ethical instinct"? There are other similar difficulties, and even plain inconsistencies, to be found in our author's treatment of this subject. But we have already dwelt on it at sufficient length.

Whoever reads all the related passages in the book will
be satisfied that there is here neither logic nor
"science," nor true, unbiassed judgment, but such
partiality to Jesus and the Gospels as the most pious
Christian might envy.

It may be worth while, by way of completing the
picture, to add just one further point. When our author
reaches the end of the passage in Matthew, where the
" eunuchs for the kingdom of heaven's sake " are
extolled, he finds himself in some perplexity (pp. 690,
691). Clearly, his moral sense is revolted. But how
gentle is his language ! You will find nothing here
about " eternal dishonour " or the like. He lowers his
voice in submissive reverence, and tries to find excuses
for the Gospel, so that you cannot recognise in him that
" higher tribunal" which condemned without mercy
what he thought the " weak spot" in *the law of his
ancestors.* True, this fact demands no comment ; but
I am reminded of the author's anticipation (Introduction, p. xix) that Christian critics would find him
too Jewish, and Jewish critics too Christian, and I
merely wish to remark that this difference of attitude
will stamp him, even in the eyes of Jewish critics, as,
in one respect at least, *too much of a Jew.*

After what has been said above, it may perhaps
appear to many that it was not worth while to give so
much attention to such a book, and possibly from the
point of view of scholarship and literature they are right.
But, as I have already hinted, the book deserves special
attention as a revelation of the psychology of a certain
section of Jews. It shows us a new kind of Jew, hitherto
unknown to history, who has lost every trace of the
mighty sorrow which his ancestors felt for the exile of

the nation and the exile of the *Shechinah,*[1] and who yet
has a sorrow of his own—the sorrow of a meaningless
isolation.   He sees that the world has gone its own
way, leaving the Jews alone with their *Torah*.   This
isolation is not unbearable so long as the Jew understands or feels that it is necessary to the preservation
of his sacred ideals ; but the real need for it can certainly
not be felt by those Jews who think that the difference
between themselves and their neighbours is " external
and artificial," and for whom Judaism is nothing but a
dear inheritance, which must be preserved out of respect
for their fathers.   Hence they seek in various ways to
escape from their isolation.   Thirteen years ago they
believed that they could attain their object by basing
Judaism on certain universal beliefs of the Theists. Now
they recognise that this is not enough ; they go a step
further, and tack on Jesus and the Gospels.   This
development appears clearly from many passages in the
book under notice, of which I will quote here one of the
most explicit :

" Dogmatic Christianity in the course of centuries
may disappear ; Trinitarianism may be succeeded by
Unitarianism ; but the words of Jesus will still continue
to move and cheer the heart of man.   If Judaism does
not, as it were, come to terms with the Gospels, it must
always be, I am inclined to think, a creed in a corner,
of little influence and with no expansive power. Orthodox Jews would, I suppose, say that they want no more.
Liberal Jews should be less easily satisfied " (p. 906).

We can certainly understand the state of mind of
these Jews ; but they themselves ought also to understand it aright.   They would then see that their state

[1] [Divine Presence.   See p. 97.]

of mind has no relation to the question of "orthodox" and "liberal" Judaism in the usual sense of the words. A Jew may be a liberal of liberals, without forgetting that Judaism was born "in a corner" and has always lived "in a corner," apart from the great world, which has never understood it, and therefore hates it. Such was the lot of Judaism before the rise of Christianity, and such it has remained since. History has not yet satisfactorily explained how it came about that a tiny nation in a corner of Asia produced a unique religious and moral point of view, which has had so profound an influence on the rest of the world, and has yet remained so foreign to the rest of the world, unable to this day either to conquer it or to surrender to it. This is a historical phenomenon to which, despite a multitude of attempted answers, we must still attach a note of inter-rogation. But every true Jew, be he "orthodox" or "liberal," feels deep down in his being that there is something in the spirit of our people—though we know not what it is—that kept it from the high-road taken by other nations, and impelled it to build up Judaism on those foundations for the sake of which the people remains to this day confined "in a corner" with its religion, being incapable of renouncing them. Let them who still have this feeling remain within the fold; let them who have lost it go elsewhere. *There is no room here for compromise.*